HIRE ME, HOLLYWOOD!

Your Behind-the-Scenes Guide to the
Most Exciting—and Unexpected—
Jobs in Show Business

MARK SCHERZER and KEITH FENIMORE

Aadamsmedia
Avon, Massachusetts

Copyright © 2011 by Mark Scherzer and Keith Fenimore
All rights reserved.
This book, or parts thereof, may not be reproduced in any
form without permission from the publisher; exceptions are
made for brief excerpts used in published reviews.

Published by
Adams Media, a division of F+W Media, Inc.
57 Littlefield Street, Avon, MA 02322. U.S.A.
www.adamsmedia.com

ISBN 10: 1-4405-1212-4
ISBN 13: 978-1-4405-1212-4
eISBN 10: 1-4405-1228-0
eISBN 13: 978-1-4405-1228-5

Printed in the United States of America.

10 9 8 7 6 5 4 3 2 1

Library of Congress Cataloging-in-Publication Data
is available from the publisher.

This book is available at quantity discounts for bulk purchases.
For information, please call 1-800-289-0963.

DEDICATION

To my parents Harold and Marilyn, who mean the world to me.

—Mark

To my precious little boy Kase, I promise that there will never be a "no" in life that you are unable to get over . . . but for those things you believe in, keep at it until you get a "yes!" My love, Da-da.

—Keith

CONTENTS

ACKNOWLEDGMENTS

Although our names appear on the front cover, we would like to acknowledge the contributions of others in bringing these pages to life. We'd like to begin by thanking all thirty participants. Without your success this book would not be possible, so thanks for being so gracious and letting us ride your coattails. To our editors at Adams Media, Brendan O'Neill and Meredith O'Hayre, thanks for your enthusiasm and for making this such a wonderful experience from page 1 through page 384.

Mark

David, thanks for encouraging me during this entire process and making life one great adventure. I can't wait to see what's next. To Linda, Mitch, and Maureen, you're each very special to me. I'm so glad we're all (finally) on the same coast! Keith, I can't think of anyone better to have in the trenches with me. You're a great friend and writing partner and you made this fun. Finally, my deep gratitude goes to the late Linda Mancuso who gave me my first job writing in television and sent my life in a whole new direction.

Keith

To my wife Kristina who's an utterly amazing woman and whose support, wisdom, love, and encouragement motivates me every day to be the best husband and Da-da I can be. I'd be lost without you. Mom and Dad, your endless love and support has fueled me all thirty-nine years of my life. Kathy, things are just that much better knowing I have you in my corner. Finally, to my writing partner in crime, not that anything we did here was illegal, we're living proof that two friends can successfully work together in a creative capacity and come out even better friends in the end. (Mark, if you have any issue with what I wrote above, please contact my attorney.)

INTRODUCTION

Hollywood. The undisputed entertainment capital of the world. It's a force of nature, a magnet that pulls people from all four corners of the globe, seduced by the idea of a career in front of, or behind, the camera. Ever since the first motion picture studios broke ground, people have been flocking to this town like prospectors to gold to stake their claim. But what does it take to make it here? How do you get that big break? Is there a path to success . . . and if so, where is it? This is *Hire Me, Hollywood!*

The film and television industry is made up of a multitude of diverse jobs, and there are many different ways of landing them (casting couch excluded). We've both worked in this industry for many years and have discovered that no two people in Hollywood have the same story, nor have they taken the same path. There's really no blueprint for success in this business. With that in mind, we compiled thirty fascinating success stories to make navigating the industry a little bit easier. Even if you don't aspire to break into the business, you're sure to be inspired by the stories and the opportunity to get a look at the inner workings of Hollywood.

Hire Me, Hollywood! is not a "how to" as much as it is a "how did." It's a candid look at thirty people from across the entertainment industry who are at the top of their game as producers, actors, editors, and the like. You'll discover how they broke into the business, what their path has been, and what advice they have for getting a job in their chosen field. Each chapter will have takeaways that you can apply to your own life or career path . . . unless of course you want to fly planes or become a surgeon!

There are literally hundreds of jobs in the entertainment industry, and most of them are legal. While we couldn't possibly feature them all in this book, we did our best to cover a cross-section. Here are a few people you'll hear from:

- Conan O'Brien's **head talent booker**
- Abigail Breslin's **on-set tutor** for *Little Miss Sunshine*
- *True Blood* **star**, Sam Trammell
- The **cohost** of *Entertainment Tonight*, Mark Steines
- Shane Hurlbut, the **director of photography** on *Terminator Salvation*
- The **creator/voice/puppeteer** of Elmo, Kevin Clash
- The **superhero guru**, Stan Lee
- **Executive producer** of *Live! with Regis and Kelly*, Michael Gelman
- The **stage manager** for *American Idol*, Debbie Williams
- Jackie Burch, **casting director** for *Sixteen Candles* and *The Breakfast Club*

It was a privilege to interview such inspiring, passionate, and successful people. We thank them for allowing us to share their stories with the world, and wish them continued success . . . not like they'll need it.

Enjoy the read! In three, two . . .

STAN LEE
Comic Book Legend

Photo provided courtesy of POW! Entertainment

We discovered this young guy from New York named Stan Lee. Nobody has ever heard of him, but he's got some great ideas. It's our hope that putting him in this book will catapult his career. Maybe, just maybe, someone in Hollywood will read this chapter and give this kid his big break.

That first paragraph would have made sense if this book was published in 1938. But this is present day, and that young kid from New York with the big ideas is an eighty-eight-year-old living legend with a resume that's as impressive as it is implausible. We're sure one day it will become known that Stan Lee took part in a top-secret experiment in the 1940s and cloned himself; at least that would explain his superhuman success.

1

Stan was president of Marvel Comics, where, years earlier, he created some of the most memorable superheroes of our time: Spider-Man, Incredible Hulk, Fantastic Four, X-Men, Thor, Avengers, Iron Man, and Daredevil. Back in the day, his comics resonated with kids and adults alike. Now, some fifty years later, they're being made into blockbuster after blockbuster and are wowing audiences worldwide. Stan realized early on that creating magnificent stories with amazing characters wasn't enough to make his comics universally appealing. He had the keen foresight to give his characters human flaws, making them vulnerable and more relatable. He mixed that with a comic undertone, and the result . . . unparalleled timeless creations. Oh, and he's a nice guy to boot! We're sitting with Stan in the headquarters of his new company POW! Entertainment in Beverly Hills, California. Ladies and Gentlemen, it is our pleasure to introduce, Stan "The Man" Lee!

ART DEPARTMENT: The department at a magazine or ad company or book company made up of illustrators.

DIALOGUE BALLOONS: A device created for comics where the writer tells a story with dialogue by placing text in balloon-like bubbles above the character's head.

ILLUSTRATOR: An artist who draws, sketches, or paints. The aim of an illustration is to provide textual information to a story.

PULP MAGAZINE: A very inexpensive or cheaply made fiction-based magazine popular from the 1890s through the 1950s.

Please state your name and explain what you do for a living.
Well, my name is Stan Lee, and I'm kind of a hustler. (Laughs.) I do whatever I can to make a buck. I recently formed a new company called *POW! (Purveyors of Wonder) Entertainment* and we attempt to make movies and television shows.

Let's dive in with a little bit of background. When did the light bulb go off where you realized you wanted to pursue a job in entertainment?
Well, I don't ever think that a light bulb went off where I said, "Entertainment is for me." I wanted to be a lot of things. When I was young I did well in school at composition, so I figured, "Gee, maybe I ought to become a writer." I remember when I was twelve years old I was the biggest phony in the world because I would walk around with a little briefcase hoping it would make me look like a writer. I also thought I'd like to be an actor. I was a big fan of Errol Flynn, and I thought, "Gee, it must be great to play all those roles." Then I wanted to be an advertising man as I got a little older because I loved ads. I would read a magazine and spend more time reading the ads than reading what the actual magazine was about.

So you wanted to be a writer, actor, and ad man? That's it?
No, I also wanted to be a marine because I'd seen a movie where John Wayne was a marine and I thought, "Wow, that must be great!" I wanted to be a lawyer and make great speeches in front of a jury. You know, I wasn't very bright; I thought everything was glamorous and everything sounded good to me when I was young.

So how did Timely Comics come about?

Actually, it was more of an accident than anything else. My family never had very much money growing up so I had part-time jobs when I was in high school to help out. I was an usher at a big Broadway theater. I was a delivery boy at a drug store. I brought sandwiches up to offices in Radio City. I was an office boy at the second-largest trouser manufacturer in the world. Whatever job I could get.

Then, I found out the husband of a cousin of mine, whom I hardly knew, owned a publishing company and they were looking for an assistant, and I figured, "*Oh boy, publishing!*" I was about seventeen years old and I applied for the job. I guess nobody else applied because they gave me the job, and that is how I got into the business. Fate is an amazing thing. I mean if the job had been at the office of an architect or the office of a construction guy, I would have been in that business.

I could not see Spider-Man in a hard hat. What was it like starting out in publishing as an assistant?

The publishing company produced regular magazines, *pulp magazines*, movie magazines, and comic books. They needed help in the comic book department, so that's where I ended up. I assisted two very talented guys, Joe Simon and Jack Kirby. They were the entire *art department* at the company. They were the fellas who created Captain America. I was doing really important jobs for them like getting them sandwiches, filling the ink wells, making sure they had enough drawing paper, and running errands, you name it. I actually loved every minute of it!

Some months later, they were both let go and I became the whole department. The publisher asked me to look after things until he could hire an adult. Well, when you're seventeen, what do you know? So I told him I could handle it. The publisher never hired that adult, so I became the writer, the editor, and the art director. Eventually

I hired other writers and artists and before I knew it, I was in the comic book business. I've sort of stayed in it my whole life. Even now, seventy years later, I'm in it peripherally.

As much as you loved comics, there was a time during your career when you were not sure if you wanted to continue in the business, right?

Yes, I had come to a crossroads. I had been with the same company for twenty years and I realized, I'm not getting anywhere. I mean, I was making a good living, but there were always ups and downs in the business. I remember saying to my wife, "If something goes wrong and they go out of business, where do I go? What do I do?"

At that time comic books had no respect. I couldn't have gone to the *Saturday Evening Post* or to *Time* magazine or even Hollywood. I was a comic book writer, nobody cared about a comic book writer. So I said to myself, even though I've spent twenty years in the business and I was thirty-seven years old, I think I ought to quit while I am still young enough to do something else. To make matters worse, I was at creative odds with the publisher. My publisher wanted me to write things with a lot of action and didn't want me to concentrate on characterization or to use big words. He felt the comics were only read by very young children or illiterate adults, and at the time he was partly right.

So Joanie, my wife, says to me, "Why don't you do one (comic) book the way you would like to do it? The worst that'll happen is he'll fire you, but you want to quit anyway, so what do you have to lose?" So I took her advice and I did this book called *The Fantastic Four*, and I violated a lot of rules. I didn't give the characters superhero costumes, I gave them personal problems, all the things that superheroes hadn't had before.

So you broke all the rules. What happened?

You know what? The book sold well, and before I knew it, my publisher, Martin, asked me to do some more. So we did *The X-Men* and then *The Incredible Hulk* and *Iron Man* and all the others. It was a reinvention, it was like a whole new career for me, and suddenly people were reading these magazines.

Can you talk about the creative process of putting a comic book together with your collaborators?

In the beginning I was writing most of the stories, and it was hard to keep up. All of our artists/illustrators were freelancers, so if they weren't drawing something, they wouldn't get paid. I wanted them to get paid, so I had to get creative.

I'd be writing a story for, say, Steve Ditko, and Jack Kirby would be finishing the story he was working on. Jack would have to wait for his next story, but I hadn't finished Steve Ditko's story yet. So instead of writing the entire script I would tell the *illustrator* the plot and let them draw the action, and I would come in later and fill in the *dialogue balloons*. I was doing about twenty books a month that way and also promoting Marvel. I was lecturing and running around and I had less and less time to do all the writing. Those were crazy times!

What was it like when you saw your iconic character Spider-Man on paper for the first time?

Oh, it was great. Wait. Actually, it wasn't great. (Laughs) I gave it to Jack Kirby to draw and I told Jack I didn't want him to do this character like he had done a lot of his other characters. Jack drew things kind of heroic. I told him I wanted Spider-Man/Peter Parker to be like a nerd or a nebbish. He's just a kid, he's shy, not that popular and not that good looking. Jack did the first couple of pages and made the guy look like Captain America. So I scrapped it and brought in

Steve Ditko, and Steve drew the character perfectly, just the way I wanted him to look.

People always say write what you know, but you can't really know a completely fictional character, and you definitely can't know a superhero. So what was your secret?

I'll tell you the secret, but it's got to remain with the three of us because I don't need more competition.

We promise not to put this in the book. Please tell us!

~~The secret is, write what you would want to read. See I am my biggest fan. I love everything I write. If it isn't something that I would want to read personally, I wouldn't bother with it. I don't feel you can ever know what other people want to read or want to see, but you know what you like. If I write something that I like there will be a lot of people that like it as well. That is all I have ever done. Whether it is writing or making a speech or whatever I do, I just try to please myself.~~

There's a comic edge or slant to most everything you write. Do you purposely infuse the comedy?

Well, it's nothing I think about consciously, but I do love comedy. In fact if I had my druthers I would write funny stories, but people expect superhero stories from me so that's what I give them. Whenever I can inject a little bit of humor in a story then I do. I feel there is always humor to be found in everything. I have a feeling if I were kidnapped by somebody I would probably still find the funny in it. I mean there's something funny about two grown men who are probably smarter than I am asking me all these questions. (Laughs)

Thanks for referring to us as men . . . and grown. Who are some of your mentors?

Maybe the word *mentor* isn't right for me. Maybe *idol* would be a better word. There were so many people who I admired and idolized, people like Mark Twain, Charles Dickens, H. G. Wells. I'm a guy who always wanted to be like other people that I admired, I tried to figure out why I like them so much, and I tried to put those elements I learned into whatever I did.

Is there a time or two in your career where you can look back and say this was absolutely a pivotal moment?

This interview is a pivotal moment in my career. (Laughs)

Pivotal for us and our careers as well!

Let's see, well, I think when I wrote *The Fantastic Four* that changed everything. Suddenly it brought a whole new audience into comics. The books that followed and the months and the years that followed made comics a little more respectable. But *The Fantastic Four* was a pivotal moment, though I didn't know it at the time. When I became publisher, that was a pivotal moment. I stopped writing and spent my time traveling around the world and realizing what a fantastically wonderful lecturer I was. I don't know, my whole life has been a series of pivotal moments in a way, because great things just keep happening.

You are a passionate man with an amazing drive. Is passion at the core of what you do?

Well, I haven't thought of it that way, but it's a good point. I think whatever you do in life, it should be something you enjoy and have a passion for. It's the only way you can succeed. I enjoy writing. Wait, no, that isn't true. I really don't like *writing*; I like the result when I'm *finished* writing.

It's so hard when I have to write something, I'll wait until the last minute. I talk to my wife, watch television, shine my shoes . . . anything to keep me from having to get started. I think I like it because I'm conceited and I just like admiring myself as I'm doing it. I think, "Jesus that is good. You're doing it Stan, you thought of that, you're the best." (Laughs)

So for someone reading this who's starting out you need to ask yourself, "What am I passionate about?" and get into that field by hook or by crook. Then you don't feel like you are working. I feel I'm playing every time I come to the office.

When is Stan Lee going to downshift and retire?
This will surprise you because I am so young, but people will say, "Why don't you retire?" and I say, "Retire and do what?"

Leave us with one thing you have never said in an interview.
Gee, I hated this interview! ('Cause I really enjoy them.)

A DAY IN THE LIFE OF STAN LEE

6:00 A.M.: Wake up. Feed the four dogs and try not to wake my wife. Shave and shower.

7:00 A.M.: Breakfast at home while reading newspaper.

8:00 A.M.: Take fifteen-minute drive to office.

10:00 A.M.: Read *Variety* between returning phone calls and answering e-mails.

10:30 A.M.: Write copy for promo piece regarding upcoming N.Y.C. Comic Con.

11:00 A.M.: Meet with my partner Gill (not a typo; he spells it with two Ls) to discuss upcoming pitch at Lionsgate for new superhero movie concept I have written.

11:30 A.M.: Spend the next hour doing four fifteen-minute phone interviews; two concerning POW! Entertainment for business publications and two about new comic book titles I'm doing with Boom Comics.

12:30 P.M.: Phone screenwriter Jim Hart to tell him what a great first draft he delivered on the tent-pole-type movie he and Jake have been writing for us.

12:45 P.M.: Interview replacement for one of our secretary/assistants.

1:00 P.M.: Off to lunch with Gill and Yoshiki (Japanese rock idol, leader of X Japan) to discuss major new musical project for POW! Entertainment.

2:30 P.M.: Drive to Burbank to perform my voice-over role as The Mayor in Marvel's *Superhero City* animated show.

4:45 P.M.: Return to office in time to edit next two weeks of *Spider-Man* newspaper strip which just arrived via e-mail.

5:15 P.M.: Quickly add a more dramatic ending to concept for proposed new sci-fi TV series which I want to send to CAA before going home.

6:00 P.M.: Discuss tomorrow's schedule with Gill. We'll be going to our offices at the Walt Disney Company and want to be sure all our meetings there are correctly set up.

6:20 P.M.: Leave for home.

7:00 P.M.: Best part of the day. Drink and dinner with my wife, Joanie.

8:30 P.M.: Into my workroom to write my tweets for the day.

8:45 P.M.: Work on the various outlines and treatments I have to write in order to keep POW! Entertainment always ahead of the curve.

11:00 P.M.: Watch the TV news.

11:30 P.M.: Bedtime at last.

SAM TRAMMELL
TV/Film/Stage Actor

Photo courtesy of Jeff Vespa

Sam Trammell was born in New Orleans, Louisiana, and is a graduate of Brown University. He's best known for his role as Sam Merlotte on the hit HBO series *True Blood*. If you have yet to see *True Blood*, grab your bookmark, place it on this page, and go watch. We'll wait.

Would you believe, in addition to playing the coolest shape shifter on TV, Sam also has a Tony nomination to his credit for his work on Broadway in *Ah, Wilderness!* Throughout his career he has appeared with such notables as Kiefer Sutherland, Richard Gere, Winona Ryder, Faye Dunaway, Christian Slater, and Academy Award–winner Anna Paquin. Now more recognizable than ever, Sam continues to bounce between TV and film.

If you talk to most successful actors, they'll tell you they always knew they wanted to act and that their dream was to one day work in film and TV. Not Sam. Sam's dream was to become a physicist. In fact, he didn't even attempt to act until his senior year at college, but once he did, he was hooked. Pretty soon the TV offers started rolling in, only problem . . . Sam wasn't interested in TV. Well, Sam, we're interested in you.

FINAL CUT: A term that describes the director's power to have the final say on how a film or TV show is creatively edited and released.

HEAD SHOTS: A photograph taken of an actor that's usually a close-up, but can be a full-length as well. It serves as the actor's calling card when submitting for roles.

MEISNER TECHNIQUE: A style of acting in which the actor uses personal emotion from his own memories to feed the acting process. One of the ways this is achieved is through exercises called "repetitions." The technique was developed by Sanford Meisner.

METHOD: A form or technique of acting that allows an actor to embody the character they are playing and to create a certain level of realism by relying on previous experiences and raw emotion. This style was first taught in 1930 in Russia by Konstantin Stanislavski.

MONOLOGUE: A speech an actor makes in a play. It's often used in the audition process. The actor prepares a monologue that allows him or her to portray a wide range of emotions.

PILOT SEASON: The period in Hollywood between January and April when the premiere episode of a potential new series is cast and filmed. A network will decide if they want to pick up a full season of a series based on the pilot episode.

SCREEN TEST: A filmed audition that enables producers and directors to see how an actor comes across on camera. It can be used when the actor being tested is not in the same location as the producers.
TEST: The final audition where an actor goes before the heads of the network.

Before we dive into your past, tell us about *True Blood*. How did that come about?

I heard about this vampire show and I talked to my agents and told them that I wanted to audition for the lead vampire. They told me they were looking for someone European for the vampire Bill role, but there was this other part that I might be right for. I got the script, which was written by Alan Ball, who I am a huge fan of and who wrote and created *Six Feet Under*. At the time, it was kind of *the* script. This was the one to get. So I read it and went in to audition for the part of Sam with the casting director.

Can we assume you nailed that audition?

Well, a few days later I got a call from the casting director saying that Alan saw my audition tape, liked it, and he wanted to *test* me. I couldn't believe it happened so fast. He wanted to meet me and read the scenes together, so I went in, we read a scene, and he gave me some notes. Then I went for the test and there were three other guys up for the same part. So in no way was I sure this part was mine. It was the same situation I was always in. You test for so many pilots in your career and only actually get a few of them. So I auditioned and I thought I did okay. I didn't feel like I nailed it. I left. Three, four hours had passed. I was driving down Abbott Kinney in Los Angeles and it was raining. And I got the call that I'd gotten the part and I literally started screaming in my car like a little girl, I was so excited.

Most of the time when you make it this far into auditioning for a part in a pilot you don't hear anything for days. And you know that means you didn't book the job. It's a testament to Alan that I was called immediately. He knows what he wants, and he told me later, "I wanted you for the part."

Man, that must've been exciting. Okay, let's back up a bit. Pre–*True Blood*, pre-commercial success, pre-acting altogether.
Yeah, I never wanted to be an actor. As a kid my family moved around a lot, and we eventually ended up in West Virginia. My dad was a general surgeon. I knew that I didn't want to be a doctor because I just can't deal with blood and pus. I figured I was going to be some kind of scientist because I was always better at math than English. Outside of studies, my passions were sports and music. I played piano a little when I was a kid. I could play by ear; it came naturally to me. Then I started playing guitar when I was about thirteen years old. Playing guitar landed me in a bunch of bands when I was in my teens. I also played the cello and was in a chamber group.

Wow, so all that music and performing, and you never acted in high school?
No, the closest I came to the craft was living next door to Nick Nolte. He married a West Virginia girl and they got a place next to my parents. During my summer breaks from college, I would hang out with him and play golf and it was kind of cool to see his lifestyle, how he carried himself, the unkempt long hair. He's a *method* actor, and I would watch him transform into these characters. Seeing him did make me think that being a professional actor was a pretty cool job. But I was very conservative. I was like, you follow a path. You go to graduate school and you get on a career path.

So you said goodbye to your cool, unkempt famous friend and went back to college. What did you study?
Well, I had gotten into Brown University and began studying semiotics, the theory of signs and sign systems.

Which means?
Pure semiotics is a lot like linguistic theory and codes. Figuring out how something represents something else.

Uhhhhhh . . .
Yeah, I know, heavy stuff. I studied deconstructionism and read French philosophers. I was very into these thinkers. So I thought, alright, I'm going to major in semiotics. That was my sophomore year. I also decided to study in France because all the rock stars of semiotics were teaching in Paris, like Jacques Derrida. It would be like taking acting classes with Al Pacino.

I'm sure Pacino gets compared to Jacques Derrida all the time.
(Laughs) I had taken four years of high school French, but in order to enroll in this program, I had to take an additional year to have the bare minimum. It was intense.

Was your pilgrimage to France all you had hoped for?

What it did was totally burn me out. It was the hardest thing I'd ever done, taking those classes and writing papers in French. After that year I came back to the States and went to summer school at Brown and took a sculpting class.

So at this point you're a piano-, guitar-, and cello-playing science major who speaks French and is friends with Nick Nolte. Sounds like a typical actor's resume so far . . .

Actually, I was introduced to the Brown summer theater program the summer before my senior year because my roommate was cast in it. I started to see some plays and I noticed there were a lot of pretty women involved in the whole scene. One day I was coaxed by my friend to audition for this New Plays Festival at school and I thought, yeah, you know, that sounds insane, I'll do it.

But you had no experience. What did you do?

I prepared for the audition by learning the lines and trying to figure out how I would approach the character. I was very intimidated. The acting scene was very cliquey and all the students had put so much into the program and their training. I was among great actors, and there I was, my last semester of college, all of a sudden getting involved and trying it for the first time. I got the part. I can still remember being on stage. It was the most exciting thing I'd ever done. I was able to pretend, to become another person, do a different accent, and carry myself a different way. And literally, I did that play and it was a calling, a vocation. It was a massive epiphany. I thought, "This is it!"

So that was it. Where did IT take you?
After school, I ended up getting a free bus ticket to New York without telling anybody I was coming. I was twenty-two. I found a place in the East Village, and I was literally living on a mattress in a room on the floor for the first month. It was skanky, but I was in the city and I was going to act.

Then what?
I had some *head shots* made. I didn't realize you could reproduce them so I found this photographer who made a hundred real prints of me. I was trying to figure out what I needed and figured I needed to get an agent in order to get sent out to casting sessions. There were these books for actors that would tell you where the agencies were in the city. In the book they said "no walk-ins," but of course, that's exactly what I did. I showed up at this agency, which today is Paradigm, and I just walked in to the lobby with my headshot and resume and there was an agent who just happened to be in the lobby at the same time and saw me. He took my resume. A couple days later they called me in and had me do a *monologue*. I guess they liked it because they sent me out on an audition for *Scent of a Woman*. I was going for the part opposite Al Pacino.

Oh, your Jacques Derrida experience comes full circle, so what happened?
It was amazing, I went through six auditions all the way up to doing an actual *screen test* with Al Pacino. It came down to three of us, me, Ethan Hawke, Chris O'Donnell. It was a long and tedious process. All three of us had to sign contracts before we actually got to read with Pacino. When the day finally came to audition with him it was really interesting. Because he was playing a blind guy, he never really even looked at me. He never broke character. But he was really cool,

we met and read practically the whole movie, and I obviously didn't get it in the end, but I got really close.

Where do you go after your first audition is with Al Pacino?
It's funny because that first thing was the biggest thing ever. The agency was really behind me and they sent me out time and time again, but I didn't book anything for like nine months. That year I took acting classes and I started doing regional theater. And I ended up testing. I was flown out to Los Angeles three times, which was a big deal. The entire time in the back of my mind I was thinking about graduate school at Yale or Juilliard, but I was already being flown out to Los Angeles for *pilot season*, so I thought, you know what, I'm not going to pay $80,000 to go and learn how to act because it's already started happening. So I decided not to do it.

You may have just saved a reader 80k. What was the first thing you booked?
I got cast in a play called *Another Time*. It was one of the hardest things I ever had to do because in the first act my character had a South African accent, which is the most difficult accent to do. And in the second act, I played my character's father, who had an English accent. After regional theater I started to go for off-Broadway and then Broadway shows. At the same time I got my first lead in a feature film. The movie was low budget, but I still had the lead. It was called *The Hotel Manor Inn*. Hardly anyone saw it, but I got paid to practice in front of the camera and you can't beat that. I was an academic at heart, so I'd been reading these *Meisner* books and other books about acting in front of a camera and I was into the theories of acting and thinking about it a lot and watching movies. So I was very inspired.

So you come to New York and things really seem to fall into place for you.

They did. They did. But I wasn't really making any money. So I got a job at a video rental store. I actually had to take a test on movie knowledge to get the job, which I did not do well on. But the owner, who I'm still friends with after all these years, figured I was good with people and a working actor, so he hired me. I also ended up doing a little bit of window design work with my roommate at the time and I became a proofreader at a proofreading company. Whatever I had to do to survive and keep acting I did. I was basically in that world of doing regional theater and then doing a small movie. I struggled for a few years, but by the age of twenty-five I was able to make a living acting.

So when would you say you got your first break?

It was 1997, I got this play off-Broadway at Manhattan Theater club called *Dealer's Choice*, it was an English play about poker. Which led to another play called My *Night with Reg* and then I booked the lead in *Ah, Wilderness!* which was a huge hit on Broadway. It was a real turning point for me.

We actually read some of those reviews while prepping for this interview. We saw things like, "Star-making performance" and "You've never seen anything like it." Words an actor dreams of.

Yeah, they were just insane. Then to top it all off, I got a Tony nomination.

My success on stage got the attention of Rick Nicita and Kevin Huvane, two power agents from CAA, who I signed with, and I booked my first pilot. It was a John Wells show called *Trinity*. So I was performing in *Ah, Wilderness!* at night and shooting that pilot during the day. And that was no easy feat. I was in a three-act play that I had the lead in, and it was three hours long. And I was doing eight shows a week. It was a massive, massive production. Somehow I was able to do that at the same time.

Were you excited to cross over from theater to television?

Actually, I didn't want to do television. I was really pretentious and snobbish about it. To the New York acting community, TV had a sort of stigma attached to it. Everyone who was in my coterie of people felt the same way. We would go out for pilot season and hope to book the pilot to make the money, but we didn't want the show to get picked up. It was hilarious, but that's what we all wanted. I was getting a lot of TV offers, and I said, "No." My agents would try to persuade me to take a meeting and I would say no. I eventually gave in and went on a couple of meetings, and they would ask how it went. I would say, "Great, they liked me, but I don't want to do it." One of the upsides of not having done a lot of TV is I remained relatively unknown and therefore, I'd say, more castable in *True Blood*.

What's Alan Ball like to work with?

He very much has his hand on the tiller. He's involved with each script, the editing, and he gets *final cut*. He's very supportive and very much not Hollywood. He's not someone you have to joke around with or kiss their ass. You don't need to do that kind of thing. You just need to be good, which is refreshing. The first season felt like we were making a little movie in our backyard. Alan set the tone, the set was always very mellow. Luckily HBO gave us time to do things right, and we did not have to hurry. It never felt like other network shows where people were kind of stressed out. It's very chill. You want to do another take, you do another take. I think that really helped us become a success.

So are you happy that your career worked out the way it did and you didn't become famous too early on?
You know, I think I would've handled it differently. If all this happened earlier, I would never have appreciated it the way I do now. Because I'm a little older I am really able to enjoy it. I understand how great it is, I have respect for the business and how hard it is to achieve success doing what you love, being an actor.

Can you offer a word of advice to the people who are reading this book and aspire to do what you do?
I would encourage anybody to go for it. It's a cliché, but literally, follow your dreams. I would never discourage anyone, because somebody like me made it. I'm the most random person to make it. I didn't even start acting until my senior year in college. I just stuck with it. So just try it, give it a shot. The worst thing is to sit around and think, "What if?"

Thanks, Sam, for your time. We'd like to end your interview with a political question. Do you prefer butter or cream cheese on your bagel?
Cream cheese.

A DAY IN THE LIFE OF SAM TRAMMELL

5:00 A.M.: Wake up and drive to the studio.

5:45 A.M.: This is my call time and first up is a wardrobe fitting. Gotta try on a new pair of jeans.

6:00 A.M.: I go to the hair and makeup trailer. This is when I love not being a vampire. No white makeup for me. I'm in and out real quick.

7:00 A.M.: I start shooting a scene in Merlotte's with Sookie. We do about three takes each and finish ahead of schedule. I have a little down time before rehearsing the next scene just before lunch break.

12:00 noon: My agent comes to set and we discuss some upcoming interviews and appearances. I usually eat with everyone, but today was more of a business lunch. I have salmon and rice, if anyone cares.

5:00 P.M.: I do two more scenes during the afternoon and we finish a half hour earlier than scheduled. You have to love a great crew. Not to mention a group of actors who come to the set ultra prepared.

6:00 P.M.: I go surfing in Malibu. It helps me clear my mind and stay in halfway decent shape.

7:00 P.M.: Take the dog out for a walk.

7:30 P.M.: I look at the scenes for tomorrow and learn my lines.

8:30 P.M.: Meet some friends for dinner in Hollywood. Tomorrow I'll repeat. . . . Life is good!

RYAN RANDALL
Hairstylist/Makeup Artist

Photo courtesy of Marisa Leigh. www.marisaleightphoto.com

Before Ryan Randall became "Hairstylist to the Stars," he was hand-ing out peanuts at 35,000 feet and instructing passengers on what to do in the unlikely event of a water landing. Eventually he put down the PA mike, picked up a pair of scissors and his career took off in a completely different direction. It didn't take long for Ryan to enter that rarified airspace of celebrity-dom. Pretty soon, he found himself styling the likes of Jennifer Hudson, Kelly Osbourne, and Winona Ryder.

If you're hoping for good stories about any of his famous clients, he's not spilling. In fact, one gets the impression that if he has secrets, they're buried in a vault with ten-inch-thick steel walls, two miles underground. What he does open up about, however, is his exciting career path that includes an unexpected call to work on an *Oprah*-featured celebrity wedding and a stint on a little-known TV show called *American Idol*. He's also got some great advice for people who are looking to do what he does.

So without further ado, Ryan, if you can put down the hair product for a minute, we've got some questions for you.

> **AGENCY:** There are agents who represent hairstylists, makeup artists, photographers, and the like. The agent books work for the artist, maintains schedules, handles travel, etc.
> **EDITORIAL:** This refers to magazine work.
> **KEY HAIRSTYLIST:** The lead hairstylist on a TV show. In the film world, he or she is second to the department head.

Let's start with something pretty basic. How does one become a hairstylist?
To get licensed, you go to cosmetology school. It takes about eighteen months, part-time to get through it. I went to Paul Mitchell, but there are others like Tony and Guy and Vidal Sassoon. I had toured a few of those schools and ultimately Paul Mitchell was where I felt most at home.

What's the curriculum like?
The classroom work is pretty intensive to start, and then once you've done the book work there's a lot of the practical applications, like practicing techniques on mannequin heads. Then you have to test out to become a stylist on the floor, taking actual clients. Of course it's all done under great supervision and there's always an instructor there to help you should you need it.

Talk about your upbringing. Was hairstyling always something you wanted to do?

I grew up in Northern California. Pretty normal upbringing, my family is actually all still there. I went to junior college out of high school, did some course work at Sacramento State, and got a job at Wells Fargo Bank. In 2000, I got the travel bug, left Wells Fargo, and got a job with United Airlines. I was a flight attendant based in San Francisco and was transferred to London. I was living in London, loving my life when 9/11 happened. After 9/11, people were laid off and we were all fearful for our jobs. I took a leave of absence and it was a great time for me to get serious about what I really wanted to do. Hair had always been something that I thought about doing, and it was the perfect opportunity.

So you began studying at Paul Mitchell . . .

Yes. I worked during the day and went to school part-time at night. I worked almost every day for eighteen months. After ten months I got an internship on *American Idol* before I finished school. So Tuesdays and Wednesdays when *Idol* would tape I would go up to Los Angeles from Orange County, where I was living, to work on the show.

How did you go from cosmetology school to one of the biggest shows on TV?

Within the Paul Mitchell school, there are two programs. The normal program and a Phase II program. The Phase II is an honors program of sorts, and whether it was excelling early or just being lucky, I was accepted into the Phase II program in 2003. Back then, there was a show called *American Juniors*, a kid's version of *American Idol*, where the winners formed a band or group at the end of the show. The *key hairstylist* on both shows was Dean Banowetz.

Dean had called the Paul Mitchell school looking for some extra help with a music video for the group, and a lot of us were interested in doing that video. In the end, it was a scheduling conflict for me, so I didn't end up doing it. I sent Dean an e-mail following up, letting him know that I was interested in any other projects he had. At the time he was working with Ryan Seacrest, was key hairstylist on both shows, and fostering an endorsement deal. He was busy.

These events started a new thought process for me. I was intrigued by the idea of not being in the salon and saw great opportunity in doing something other than salon hair.

What happened next?

Shockingly, Dean e-mailed me back a day or two later and we set up a meeting for coffee in L.A. I had done a little research and knew what he was about, what he was working on, and what his background was. We talked about work, what his work life looked like, and how I could be involved. There weren't any offers made that day.

How did you finally get your big break?

A couple weeks after our coffee meeting, I got a phone call from Dean inquiring if I would be interested in assisting with a celebrity wedding. The two people getting married met on *Oprah* and she was going to have her team covering the wedding. Every weekly magazine and wedding magazine was going to be there and I jumped at the chance.

On the day of the wedding I was a nervous wreck. Dean had brought along another assistant, who ended up working on the bridesmaids and the family when she was supposed to be helping Dean with the bride. So I stepped in and helped him directly. I hadn't ever worked with him or in an environment like that. I remember thinking to myself, "Pay attention to the details and just go with your gut." Afterward, he told me he was impressed with my work, and that he would definitely reach out for help with projects in the future.

Afterwards, I went back to school like nothing happened. It was work, school, work, school. The next sort of leap was about six weeks later when Dean called, set up a lunch meeting, and told me he had a few things to discuss. It was during that lunch he shared his intentions of having an intern position created on *American Idol*, and offered me the position. A position he created for me. I was thrilled.

Paint a picture for us of that first day on the set of *American Idol*.

Basically I was just thrown into the mix. At the time, Ryan had his daytime talk show, *On-Air with Ryan Seacrest,* so Dean came later to the *Idol* set because he was shooting Ryan's show. I remember arriving and being nervous and a bit fearful, but full of adrenaline. The crew couldn't have been nicer. Minutes later, the room was full of fresh-faced talent and we were hard at work.

What do you remember about that fresh-faced talent?

The one thing I do remember about them was the vast range of personalities. Some loud and über funny, some shy and withdrawn, but ultimately all of them so talented and dealing with the stress of the show in their own ways. The next thing I knew we were heading to the stage for the show open. We would touch each of them up before they took to the stage. That two hours seemed like mere minutes, and before I knew it, we had wrapped. After a short debriefing about the day, I cleaned up and immediately started thinking about the next show. It was clear to me, at that moment, that I was a part of something special. I knew that the weeks ahead were going to be some of the greatest of my career.

Who were some of the people who sat in your chair your first season?

At one point or another, I basically worked on everyone. Fantasia . . . she was fantastic. There was Jennifer Hudson, LaToya London, Jon Peter Lewis. . . .

Was it exciting for you to see them at the beginning of their careers, say Jennifer Hudson, for instance?

Yeah. It was pretty amazing to watch them evolve, and it's our job, in part, to help them grow into the artist they want to become. A lot of people say there's no quicker way to attract press than to change your look. Hair, makeup, wardrobe, styling, anything like that and people are going to talk about your choices; they'll blog about it. We're sort of there just to be a guide to the contestants and to make suggestions. I think if you watch any season of the show you'll see there's a style evolution.

Did you work on any of the judges?

No, the judges had their own artists.

So no good Paula Abdul stories?

Not this time. Sorry.

You're taking all the good stuff to the grave, aren't you?

The thing is, the hair and makeup room is a very intimate space. There's a bond and a trust formed that's probably unlike any on set. You're not only in their personal space, i.e., touching their face and head, but you also spend a lot of time together. So you definitely build a relationship, and along with that comes an openness, if you will. So yeah, I've heard the good, the bad, and the ugly.

Let's delve a little bit into the job. How much time does it take to get someone camera-ready? Are you under tremendous pressure?

It depends on the job. *Idol*'s a little unique in that they tape the rehearsal. So we have to be done prior to the rehearsal. It's a live show so there's absolutely no stalling. They're going on whether they look fit to do so or not.

Has an extension ever fallen out onstage? Or any other hair malfunction?

Knock on wood, I haven't had any. Actually, that's not true. There's an actress who I work with fairly regularly and I have left clips in her hair, not that anybody saw. But we were taking her hair down at the end and . . . .

Oops. There it is!

Yeah. So live TV can be very stressful. Taped shows are a little easier. Depending on what you're doing, for women getting full hair and makeup, it can take about two hours. Locations can vary, too. Sometimes you're in a dark closet and you literally have only two feet of space and you're getting somebody ready; sometimes it's a glamorous hotel suite; sometimes it's the back of a car; sometimes you're in a limo—you do what has to be done.

Talk about some of the other shows you've worked on and the people you've worked with. This is your opportunity to show off.

After *Idol* I entered the freelance *agency* side of things. And there are jobs of all kinds there, anything and everything from music videos to catalog to advertising. Celebrity red carpet, runway, *editorial.* I've worked on shows like *America's Next Top Model, Ellen, The Biggest Loser, CNN Heroes, Teen Choice Awards.* I've worked on Carrie Underwood, Jon Heder, Kelly Clarkson, Andrew Garfield, Haylie Duff. . . . I've done print work like *Teen Vogue, Us Weekly, People, Entertainment Weekly.*

Okay, we're impressed. You mentioned print work. How does that differ from film and TV?

A lot of times with photo shoots you get to be a little more creative. You get to have a little fun. Oftentimes there are different looks, so the look you start out with in the morning will be built upon, whether that's more drastic hair, more stylized hair. Same with makeup—whether that's building the eye or bringing it down. So in the morning you're kind of allotted the first hour to get the first look set, and then you get to play.

For someone starting off, give us a range. What can someone expect to make in this line of work?

It varies so greatly. Editorial rates can be $150 for the day. So whether you're working with Angelina Jolie or you're working with . . . .

Carrot Top?

(Laughs) Right. It doesn't matter. You're doing it for the images. The higher-profile the clients, typically the higher the money. I would say a major A-lister today, working on an ad campaign or something that has a decent budget attached to it, $2,500 to $5,000 is a good solid rate. Obviously there are people working for a lot less, and some for more, but four figures is a good rate.

How can someone make it in your field?

Personality and relationships are two huge factors in determining one's success and longevity in this career. It's the little things that people don't think about. You have to have the X factor. There are lots of people trained to do amazing hair. There are millions of people who can do a roller set. But it's the added attention to detail, the story you tell while you're doing the set, or the bond you create with that client that makes them feel comfortable with you as opposed to somebody else.

Networking is also a huge part of it. Location is a huge part. I would say L.A., New York, Paris, and London. You have to be in a market that has working professionals in it. There are so many different avenues to get in, whether it's from a director or an actor himself or herself or you know someone who knows someone who's a personal assistant. You should also be familiar with everything that is hair related or makeup related. Within each field there's so much out there. Ultimately you should be as well versed as possible, and familiar with all the latest tips and tricks.

Final question. Any advice for Snooki on *Jersey Shore*?

I'm obsessed with Snooki because quite honestly she doesn't give a shit about what you or I think. And I love that about her. She is confident in the poof and she rocks it. It's fantastic.

A DAY IN THE LIFE OF RYAN RANDALL

Press junket for a music label exec and artist who shall remain nameless.

7:30 A.M.: In Vegas! Rise and shine. Day three of three.

7:35 A.M.: Check voice mail and any urgent e-mail.

8:30 A.M.: Car picks me up to go to the hotel where I will meet the label exec I'm grooming. He is running about twenty minutes behind, but that doesn't change the fact that we need to be ready to hop back in the car by 9:30.

9:05 A.M.: Finally, I have the man behind the music in my chair. Multitasking while getting his grooming done, he knows we're short on time and he hates to be late!

9:40 A.M.: A final check of the makeup in natural light, and we're good to go. Back out the door being escorted to the awaiting limo.

9:55 A.M.: We arrive and are greeted by label employees, hotel staff, and a bevy of security. We are whisked upstairs to the penthouse suite, where the day's press junket is scheduled to happen.

10:10 A.M.: Unpacked with touch-up kit in hand, I greet the artist when he arrives to make sure that he looks and feels great.

10:35 A.M.: Junket starts thirty-five minutes late. My job is to stand by and make sure both men look their best for the on-camera interviews that will be happening all afternoon. Standing by, I'm able to grab another coffee, check the e-mails I didn't get to in the morning, say hello to people that you only cross paths with every few months, and prepare my weekly blog for Conair.

This particular junket was scheduled so tightly, that there was no break until 3:00 P.M. when we were finished. Every ten minutes was another member of the press, asking questions and taking photos.

3:10 P.M.: The junket is finished and so is my blog. I e-mail that to the agency and pack up my things so I'm ready to escort the exec down to his waiting car. (Yes, it's more than just making pretty.) A quick good-bye and thank-you to the musical master and team, and we're out the door.

SHANE HURLBUT
Cinematographer/Director of Photography

Photo credit: Myles Hurlbut

Shane Hurlbut grew up on his family's farm in Aurora, a small farming community in upstate New York. A history buff with a radio announcer's voice, he got straight A's in college, and married his high school sweetheart. Shane was able to go from the top of a tractor to the top of his profession by working on films like the behemoth $200 million *Terminator Salvation*. How did he do it? The old-fashioned way—he worked hard.

Shane has televangelist-type passion for his craft. And when you combine his infectious personality and talent with that passion, he stands alone in his field. He's a behind-the-scenes guy, but his work can be seen in movies like *The Skulls, Drumline, Crazy/Beautiful, Mr. 3000, Semi-Pro, We Are Marshall, Swing Vote,* and the aforementioned

Terminator Salvation. He crossed mediums by working with legendary photographer Herb Ritts on countless *Vanity Fair* cover shoots and helped create the attitude and look for some of the most memorable music videos ever made for artists like Guns N' Roses, Michael Jackson, Smashing Pumpkins, and Nirvana.

Shane is a no-nonsense guy who believes in approaching every job with a clear vision and a collaborative spirit. He is a maestro with light and doesn't like to settle, so each shot that he brings to life is meticulously framed long before the cameras start rolling. His interview is chock full of good advice and amazing stories from someone who could have easily stayed on the farm, but who had his sights set on more ambitious undertakings.

ASC AWARD: The American Society of Cinematographers Award is the highest honor given to a professional Cinematographer who shows excellence in his or her field.

FLAG: A piece of equipment that's used by the grip department to shape light. The flag is placed in front of a light beam and blocks or redirects a portion of the light.

GRIPPING: A grip works with the gaffer and the DP to shape the lights on set. This can be done by holding flags, nets, and diffusion frames in front of or inside a lighting instrument.

HURRELL: Named after photographer George Hurrell, this term is used by DPs and photographers to express the look of something being lit in such a way that an object or person appears dramatically lit, almost angelic.

KEY GRIPPING: The person in charge of the grip department and who usually communicates directly with the DP.

RENTAL HOUSE: A company that owns various supplies for the film and TV industry that are rented to productions for the day or the week. A rental house can stock lights, cameras, expendables, props, and wardrobe.

SLINGING CABLE: The act of dragging miles of cable from one area to another on set.

WALKIED: A term used to mean someone who's summoned to the set via the use of a two-way walkie-talkie, which is the primary form of communication on set.

Start at the beginning. Where are you from and where did you grow up?

I grew up in a very small farming community in upstate New York in a town called Aurora. My parents were educators. My mom was a sixth-grade teacher and my dad worked as a professor's assistant for Cornell in the agronomy department.

My family lived in a small farmhouse; we had a barn and a lot of land.

Talk a bit about growing up on a farm.

At the age of ten I got on a tractor for the first time and I didn't get off of it until I was about twenty-one. I would wake up at 5 A.M., get on the tractor by 5:30, and I would drag, plow, harvest, plant, whatever until about 7:15 A.M. I would get back to the house, eat breakfast, get dressed for school, catch the bus, and go to school until about 2:30. Then I would go to soccer or basketball or baseball practice until about 4:30, go home, and get back on the tractor until about 11 at night.

Talk about your education off the tractor.

In high school I did the morning announcements for the school and everyone would tell me I had a great radio voice, so I started to think, "maybe this could become a career." When I graduated, I went to a very small local junior college for Radio and TV. My first year I focused on radio and I loved it. My second year I studied TV and fell in love with that even more than radio. My then girlfriend, now wife, was going to school in Boston, so I remember working so hard to get great grades so I could transfer to any school I wanted to go to. Sure enough, after my second year I had straight As and was summa cum laude of my class, with a full scholarship. I went to my guidance counselor and told him to get me into the best TV and film school in Boston and that happened to be at Emerson College, so that's where I went.

At Emerson, I focused on TV, but during the summer between my first and second year, I got the opportunity to work on a film shoot called *The Legend of Firefly Marsh* that my high school friend Gabe Torres was directing, and that experience changed my direction and my life. I switched my major to film and I ended up graduating magna cum laude from Emerson College.

Wow, what the hell happened to you on that movie set?

I found my calling. I was just a production assistant doing anything they asked. I was *slinging cable*, setting lights, *gripping*. Whatever they told me to do I did. I really got caught up in the energy on the set and working with so many smart, creative people.

So you had a degree in film and TV, you were at the top of your class. Now all you needed was a job.

I remember my mom got me a three-piece suit and I started pounding the pavement in Boston and I found out pretty quickly there were no jobs. I ended up swallowing my pride and took a job in a *rental house.* I was driving trucks because that's what I had done all my life on the farm. Then one day I realized that if I stayed in Boston the only way I was going to move up was if the guy ahead of me died. So I made my next move.

You killed the guy?

(Laughs) No, I packed up and moved to L.A. with my then fiancée, now wife.

I ended up getting a job at a rental house. The job paid $3.50 per hour, I could have made more by staying in Boston. Thankfully that job only lasted three months before a producer asked me to come and drive a grip truck for a company he worked for. It paid better, so I went.

One day I was driving this five-ton truck packed with about ten tons of equipment out to this set for a movie called *Phantasm 2*. I was *walkied* to set, and asked to bring a *flag* immediately. So I start running this thing in and I ran into a buddy of mine who was a USC cinematographer graduate. We were standing in front of this set made to look like a crematorium and he asks, "Would you be scared?"

I said, "What? Listen, I got to get this flag to set," but he said, "Look at the way the crematorium set is lit. If you were in the theater, would you be scared?" He pointed out that every nook and cranny was lit and there was no shadow.

It was like, *pow*! It just hit me and from that point on everything I looked at was light. Long story short, I went from a grip truck driver to a cinematographer in three years. I was on this high-speed bullet train to being a DP.

Can you give us some more details on your journey from grip to DP?

I gripped from 1988 until 1991. I started *key gripping* on low-budget movies, getting my chops. In my opinion, being a grip is a much better way to become a DP than being a gaffer is because a grip is actually shaping light and a gaffer is just turning it on. Then I started shooting music videos with a director named Daniel Pearl. Pearl basically built MTV on his images. This guy is the archetype for music videos. There is nothing that he can't dream up and bring to life. He was a quintessential mentor for how I shape light today.

Then there's Joseph Yacoe. Yacoe's strength was his sense of beauty and style. He was about cream and softness and elegant composition. He taught me how to make everything beautiful. Yacoe introduced me to the great Herb Ritts, who was an artisan and had the most amazing eye for composition. He could compose a shot like no other. My first gig with him was a *Vanity Fair* cover shoot, and I worked with him for the next five years. I lit many of the stills he took during that time.

Can you encapsulate the job of the cinematographer/DP?

A DP takes the director's vision and brings it to life in the visual sense. By using composition, specific lenses, lighting, and camera movement, if done right, he will assist the story and performances seamlessly.

How did you get hired as a DP on your first feature?

The first movie I DP'd was *The Rat Pack* for HBO. That movie was definitely a defining moment in my career. I didn't have much narrative experience at the time, so when the director, Rob Cohen, told HBO that he wanted to hire me, they were skeptical. I had to convince them that I was the right guy for the job. They asked what I had in mind for the look of the film. I laid out my vision, I was going to make the actors look like they were movie stars, it was going to be *Hurrell* everywhere they walked. The actors were going to have the perfect back light and the perfect key light and they were going to look like they were on stage no matter where they went throughout the entire movie. They loved it. So I got the job and I was nominated for an *ASC Award* for that project.

The Rat Pack led to other movies like *Drumline*, *The Greatest Game Ever Played,* and *Semi-Pro* with Will Ferrell. Can you tell us about those experiences?

Drumline was just an amazingly inspiring film. When I got on the set and saw the musicianship and the passion those kids brought, it was awe-inspiring. That was my first of two projects with the director Charles Stone.

Photographically, *The Greatest Game Ever Played* represents some of my best work. Bill Paxton is a talented and visionary director, and I feel everyone on that project fired on all cylinders. I embraced the time period, I loved the powerfully moving story.

Will Ferrell was a good sport on *Semi-Pro*. I remember putting him on a piece of half-inch Plexiglas and put a camera below him and shot his balls when he was taking a foul shot. It was a low-angle ball shot in slow motion so you see him doing this pumping motion and underneath you see his underwear and his ABA short-shorts. He called it the crotch cam, and he said it was his favorite shot in the movie. See, I'm very versatile. (Laughs)

How many people do you oversee on set?

On *Terminator Salvation* I had a crew of ninety-plus and I loved to challenge them and push them to their limits. I have what I've coined "lightmares," where I sit up in the middle of the night and have this epiphany. I had one on *Terminator Salvation*. I sat up in the middle of the night and I said out loud, "Tractor beams!" That's all that came to mind. So I called up my rigging gaffer, Scotty Graves, and he said, "What is it now Shane?" I told him when we shoot the Sky Net Testing Center scene I want a tractor beam to cut through this smoke to guide the transports down into the test facility center. He asked me how the hell I was planning on doing that and I said, "I want to get 600 sports fixtures, like the ones that light football stadiums, mount them to construction cranes and tilt them up and when that spaceship comes down I want to nuke the whole area, just fill it with blinding light."

"Are you kidding me?" he asked. I just told him, "We're doing it!"

There's a "beam me up Scotty" joke in there somewhere, but we'll leave it alone. So assuming Scotty didn't quit on the spot, did the shot come together?

You better believe it. I came in the next day and they had ten massive forklifts with racks of lights, 60 lights on each of them. Think about it, that's—600 lights. It was awesome looking, so cool. That is one of my favorite-looking scenes in the movie.

So what advice do you have for a newbie looking to break into your business?

The best way to become a great DP is to start at the bottom. Take a job, paid or unpaid, on any set, doing any job. Look at David Fincher, James Cameron, Tony and Ridley Scott, these are guys who know how to do everyone's job very well, and they are inspired film-makers. I know Fincher, I worked with him four or five times, and he would operate the smoke machine better than the smoke guy.

You came up on the technical side as a grip. Don't most people climb the ladder to DP by getting into the camera department?

Yes, the normal practice to get to DP is to come in on camera and be a loader, then a second assistant, then a first assistant, then an operator, then a cameraman. My personal belief is if you come up on the gripping and gaffing side and spin into being a DP you will be better formed, you'll know light very well and you will in turn be a much more confident and versatile DP. Also as far as efficiency and organization, you'll be a step ahead because you will know how to direct your team more effectively.

Are there specific characteristics or qualities a person should possess in order to be successful as a DP?

In order to be successful as a DP, you have to be an artist, feel the emotion of a scene, a character's mood, and translate that into light, mood, emotion, and elegance. Take something ordinary and make it extraordinary, be obsessed with the subtleties, then finish with an unstoppable work ethic and passion.

Well, your job sounds fun, but does it pay well?

You can make a very good living. As a DP, if you are a commercial shooter, you can make $2,500 to $6,000 per day. On feature films, on a project with a medium budget, you can make anywhere from $7,000 to $15,000 per week and on a large studio movie you're looking at $15,000 and up per week.

Excuse us for a second while we second-guess our entire careers. Finish this sentence: If I had known then what I know now . . .

I wouldn't be as good of a DP as I am today. You have to go through all the bumps in the road, and you can't pass up milestones, because they are what end up shaping you. There is no shortcut to hard work.

We have one final question that I am sure everyone reading your chapter has been dying for us to ask. What is one word that would best describe your high school picture?

(Short pause) Three words: Big hair. Corduroy.

A DAY IN THE LIFE OF SHANE HURLBUT

Marines commercial "For Us All," Washington D.C.

3:00 A.M.: Wake up, roll over, turn off iPhone alarm, why so early? Oh, I wanted the morning light.

3:30 A.M.: Greg Haggart, my producer, meets me in the lobby along with my elite team members.

4:00 A.M.: Arrive at set and help team unload the camera truck and start setting up our three-camera setup. I have a day's worth of shots to get in six hours.

5:30 A.M.: All cameras and the crane in place and we start finding the shot. Fix some technical problems and crane shuts down for no reason. Okay, we are back up, we find the shot. I am happy.

6:00 A.M.: Agency and client show up, I grab a coffee with them and take them over to the three cameras on the hill to discuss the setup.

6:34 A.M.: Sunrise, we shoot the Iwo Jima Memorial and then to the marines at the base of the memorial and a shot of a mom with her kids.

7:45 A.M.: Move from the hill down to the monument, and set up the dolly shot over the back of our mom and kids.

8:30 A.M.: Dolly and talent are ready. I go over and talk with the marines on the plinth. I give them some direction about why we are shooting here, what this means to the Marine Corps and how it will play out in the commercial.

9:00 A.M.: I move to the close-up of the mom and the son. I think the light looks great.

9:45 A.M.: Then, brilliance happens with the smile from the boy and mom. Priceless, agency and client are very happy. We look back at that magical take. Yeah, we got it, moving on.

10:00 A.M.: The sun breaks out, the sky is blue, now we shoot our brains out. We move to a shot of the Marines standing guard at the memorial.

10:30 A.M.: Greg, my producer, comes to me and gives me the news that we have one hour left. What? We keep shooting.

11:45 A.M.: I am over my hour deadline and we work out blocking next because Park Service will shut us down in fifteen minutes.

11:55 A.M.: I say, "Action" and the crane moves up, the couple crosses frame, the family moves in, and to cap it all off, her son points right at the camera. Amazing. Play back for agency and client, yes we got it. Whew, made it!

12:00 P.M.: Wrap up around memorial and grab some lunch.

1:00 P.M.–8:00 P.M.: All the gear is packed and we have a company move. We travel all day to South Carolina, which is our next location.

8:00 P.M.: We arrive, check in at the hotel, and get ready for the grind of the next day shoot.

9:00 P.M.: I call my family to say hello, I miss them, as I have been on the road for the last three weeks. I go over the shot list for tomorrow and check e-mail.

10:30 P.M.: Lights out.

LISA MELAMED
TV Writer/Producer

Photo credit: David Thomas, www.davethomasstudio.com

In 1968, the Beatles won over legions of fans with their stirring rock ballad, "Hey Jude." Twenty-two years later Lisa Melamed was among a team of writers who gave the world *Hey Dude*. What else does this nice Jewish girl from Brooklyn "sort of" have in common with four blokes from Liverpool? It turns out, absolutely nothing; unless you count a strong will to succeed in the entertainment biz.

Lisa's success story as a writer-producer began when she traded the comfort and security of her beloved Brooklyn for the bright lights of Hollywood. Her knack for assembling words on a page grabbed the attention of agents and producers, and it didn't take long for her career to take off. Nothing deterred this ambitious young writer, not even the humbling experience of having an entire script rewritten, but for one line, early on in her career. If anything, it educated her about the dreaded rewriting process and prepared her for what would come down the road. And what came were coveted staff jobs on many high-profile shows like *Lipstick Jungle*, *Mad About You*, *Party of Five*, and *Sisters*, not to mention pilots of her own.

In an industry that's often too eager to find the next great thing, Lisa has staying power and works continually. She's gained a lot of smarts over the years, which she's agreed to share with those who dream of their very own "written by" credit.

DIRECTOR OF DEVELOPMENT: He or she works with writers and producers to create TV show concepts to sell to the networks.

NOTE: A network executive assigned to a particular show will give notes or "comments" on every script they read, which may be addressed in the rewriting process.

SHOW RUNNER: The executive producer of a TV show, who is in charge of running that show. He or she oversees all the creative and is generally also a writer.

SPEC SCRIPT: A script you write in order to get work on a TV show. You don't get paid to write this script. You can write a spec for an existing show or it can be an original piece of work. It serves as your calling card.

WRITERS' ROOM: The place where the writers of a show spend much of their workday coming up with stories and breaking them down.

Was TV a big part of the Melamed household?

Oh, yes. The television was on constantly. That was the hearth. We weren't the family who said, "Turn it off; it's dinnertime." It was, "Make it louder so I can hear it over the forks and knives."

At what point in your life did you realize you had a gift for writing?

I knew from a very young age that words were going to be my currency. But I didn't know how exactly. I was always a good writer in school, but it was not a magical calling. And even as a kid I didn't go home and keep a diary, I didn't write a lot of stories or put on plays with the kids in the neighborhood. But I was very verbal and I listened to people. And I was drawn to people who spoke in interesting, funny, and quirky ways and so I think that more than the act of writing was the act of talking and listening.

So if writing wasn't a magical calling, what did you think you would do?

I didn't know. I knew for one thing I wasn't going to be a doctor, because I was squeamish. Once in a while my parents would walk past me and whisper the words "law school," but that never appealed to me. I guess I always knew it would have something to do with words. But it took me a long time to be brave enough to be "the writer." I always knew, like I said, that words were going to be the currency, but I thought that I would be more the midwife or the editor.

The "Writer Whisperer" if you will?

Yes.

Got it. So how does one get into the Writer Whispering business?

I went to Brooklyn College and started out as an English major, but switched over to the TV and Radio Department partway through. When I graduated I got a job with Scholastic Productions, an offshoot of Scholastic Magazines, which is a huge children's publishing company.

What did you do for them?

I was hired as an assistant. I was the "get coffee, read books" person. They had just started a film and television department where they wanted to take advantage of the books they had and adapt them for TV. So as well as being the person who typed my bosses' letters, I was reading books to see what would make a good show. It was a full-on immersion. By the time I left there, seven years later, I was *director of development.*

That must've been an incredible education.

Yes. I read hundreds of scripts. And at the time we had a deal with Universal Television, so we were trying to find writers they wouldn't know in L.A. There's a big community of playwrights in New York. And so I was reading a lot of plays and meeting a lot of these people. And I was helping them adjust their writing for television and figuring out how to sell shows. The more I did that, the more I began to really feel like, boy I want to be on the other side of this.

What finally pushed you to "the other side"?

After Scholastic, I worked at Universal as their East Coast development executive. It was basically me and an assistant in a lonely office on Park Avenue, and I just didn't like it. In fact, I was there for a year when the president of the TV division called to say what a lovely job I had been doing and what my bonus was going to be, and in the same conversation I said, "That's really nice, but please don't pick up my option." I was gracious as ever, but I basically quit.

With a plan?

With a hope. The big X factor was that I was beginning to realize I would have to move to L.A. After a while, my moment came when I got a phone call from an agent, Bob Levinson, who knew me as an executive at Scholastic. Bob said, "I have somebody who's doing a show called *Hey Dude* for Nickelodeon. And I thought maybe you'd like to write an episode." So I went in and met with the head writer of the show. I pitched some ideas, and they liked one of them and I went off and wrote the script and then they said, "come be one of our writers." I was still in New York but I had a guarantee to write two of the thirteen episodes. I thought, "It's now or never," so I made the move out to L.A. in 1990.

So you arrive at LAX . . .

I get to L.A. and I expected there would be people with a big banner that said, "your career this way." Guess what? That didn't happen.

Maybe they showed up at another airport. L.A.'s got a few of them. So what next?

I had this *Hey Dude* job, and they asked me to go live on location for a couple of months. I packed up the Camry and drove to Tucson, Arizona, where the show was shot.

What was it like?

Hot. It was September and 120 degrees. But what was so great about that experience was getting to see my stuff produced for the very first time and getting to know the actors I was writing for and learning how to write for them.

Describe the feeling that first time you ever heard your words coming out of their mouths.

Oh, absolutely thrilling. Crazy. And what was great about *Hey Dude* was that it was very much under the radar. It was Nickelodeon's first original sitcom. They didn't *note* us to death. I wrote eight episodes, ultimately, and they were shot pretty much word for word, which doesn't happen. And that really steeled me for the next job, where I wrote a script and there was only one sentence of what I had written left when it got on the air.

What show was that?

Brooklyn Bridge. It was Gary David Goldberg's (*Family Ties*) baby. It was based on his life; Marion Ross was playing his beloved grandma, and it was so personal to him. At the end of the day, he wanted to tell all the stories the way he wanted to tell all the stories, and that was immensely frustrating. But now I look back and I say, God bless you. You're Gary David Goldberg and you should have that.

This brings up a good point, actually. Other than having a thick skin, what does an aspiring TV writer need to know about the rewriting process?

Rewriting is going to happen whether you want it to or not. It's part of that process. I still hate it, but I understand that there needs to be one voice in charge and the *show runner* is entitled to make the script exactly what they want it to be. But on the other hand, when I'm a senior writer on a staff and I get a script from someone who I think didn't quite hit the mark, I have absolutely no problem going in and rewriting it to my specifications.

So let's talk about some of the other shows that were pivotal to your career.
Okay, well, coming off *Brooklyn Bridge* I was a person of interest for both *Roseanne*, and *Sisters*, a single-camera drama. And dumb good luck, because at the time I think *Roseanne* was the number one show on TV and I probably would've taken that job had I been offered it. Luckily they said no on Wednesday and *Sisters* said yes on Thursday. If it had been the other way around I might've said no to *Sisters*, which would've been terrible because I worked on the show for three years. I have twenty-one writing credits. It was an amazing experience.

Describe what it's like to interview for a writing gig on a show.
It's a blind date. You go in and they sniff you and they make sure you don't seem crazy or that your speaking voice isn't going to send them into seizures. You try to be charming and to basically tell them what you bring to the party and how you'll fit into their mix, but also how you will stand out as an individual.

What was the next pivotal show after *Sisters*?
Party of Five, which was complicated for me because it was a show about five kids whose parents were killed in a car accident and how they go on as a family, and right before I started, my father died,

and a year later my mother died. And I wasn't quite ready to address that in my writing, so it became a little bit strange for me. But it was a great show and it won the Golden Globe for best dramatic series and the fans loved it. It was also a great *writers' room*, and you looked forward to reading everyone's scripts. Everyone had their own take on it, and yet it all fit nicely under the umbrella of what the show was.

How stressful is the job of writer with that deadline hanging over your head?

You know, for me, the most stressful part is figuring out the story. I'm actually a fairly happy writer when I'm writing. I know there are some people who find that to be the excruciatingly difficult part. I'm a little bit the opposite, which is the plot challenges me. But once I have my outline I'm fairly good to go. And yes, it's stressful, because you have to be fresh and you have to come up with something that the other writers haven't come up with, and you have to hit your deadline. But it's so much fun. It's a great way to make a living.

Can you rattle off a few of the other shows you've worked on?

There was *Mad About You, Trinity, The Fugitive, Lipstick Jungle*, and I just came off a show for ABC called *Scoundrels*.

You've also created some pilots, correct?

Yes. I sold a father-son medical drama to CBS. And I did a pilot for Showtime called *The Ranch*, which was the most wonderful, exquisite, and frustrating experience of my career because it ultimately did not go to series. But I became very close with the cast; it probably was the highlight of my career. And then when it didn't cross the finish line to become a series, that was just absolute heartbreak.

What advice do you have for an aspiring writer?

To a kid, I say observe the world, make friends with someone who tells funny stories, tell your stories over and over, because those will become the things that end up in your work. For somebody who's got a *spec script* now or who's just started to do a script, I'd say make sure you watch a lot of shows and read a lot of plays and read a million magazines. Read weird books about strange pieces of information, because you never know when you're in the middle of a scene and something will occur to you. I think even in terrible times there are things to laugh about. That's another thing that makes you a writer. If in the worst moments of your life you can recognize what's funny and absurd and then file them away, great.

Right around the time my mother died my Uncle Ira, who's a real character, wasn't well, so he was unable to come to the funeral. My sister and I decided we would go and visit him. Lots of people had sent food, so we had a lot of leftovers. And we brought a tray of deli meats over to his house. Uncle Ira was eating a sandwich and he turned to us and he said, "I'm sorry your mother is dead and all, but this corned beef is delicious." I thought, "That is fantastic," and fourteen years later almost to the day I put that in a script.

I think we all have an Uncle Ira in the family. So can writing be learned or is it something you're born with?

I think it's both. You have to have the inclination to want to take life and analyze it in that way and take that argument you had in your real life and relive it between fictional characters. But when you write it, you get to be as articulate and witty and cutting as you wished you had been when it actually happened. You have to love language. You have to have read things that absolutely opened up your mind and stuck with you or movies or TV shows or plays or whatever that have meant so much to you that you can't believe you could've lived your life without knowing about them. If you're that person, then I think you have the instinct to be a writer. Then you have to learn structure, you have to learn to edit, you have to learn rhythm. And I think all of those are learnable skills, but you have to have the desire to do it.

What's the secret of your success?

Dumb good luck and the goods to back it up when the dumb good luck happened. I work very hard. I think you have to really care, and I care a lot. I still get excited when I see my name on screen. It is a weird little piece of immortality. And the idea that somebody's spending millions of dollars to put something I wrote on its feet is flattering and humbling, and I take it very seriously.

On that note, would you do us the honor of writing us out?

(Pause) And as she began to think back over everything she said and wonder how awful it actually sounded, we fade to black.

A DAY IN THE LIFE OF LISA MELAMED

8:00 A.M.: Alarm goes off. Who am I kidding?

10:15 A.M.: Change out of T-shirt and sweatpants I sleep in, into T-shirt and sweatpants I write in. Go downstairs. Have my first can of Tab for the day while checking e-mails and various websites, including *TV Tattle*, *Salon*, *The Futon Critic*, *The Daily Beast*, Facebook, and *Artnet*'s auction site.

11:10 A.M.: A quick look over the last few scenes I wrote yesterday before starting today's work. Change a few lines here and there, but I'll leave any major polishing/changing for when the script is complete. Read my outline to see what scene I need to write next. Write it. It goes well.

Next scene. A little more of a wrestling match, but I end up happy with what I end up with.

1:00 P.M.: Check and answer a few e-mails and any calls I let go to voice mail earlier. The phone calls are brief. I'm not a big talker when I'm writing.

1:20 P.M.: Next scene. Uh-oh. Hated it in the outline, hate it now. I realize that the scene is redundant and was just there to try to keep a character alive in this act. Curse the person who decided that one-hour dramas need to be broken up into six acts to accommodate that many commercial breaks. (When I first began writing, the structure was a brief teaser and four acts.) Decide to drop the scene from the episode, hope no one will miss it.

2:15 P.M.: Lunch. Read the *L.A. Times* and *Variety* over an egg-white and oatmeal frittata (and a Tab).

3:00 P.M.: Reread the scenes I've written so far today. Make a few changes. Some minor, some bigger. Debate whether I'm ready to tackle the next scene. I'm not. Take a TV break. And here, I must stop and tell a story about why writers should and must take breaks. Years ago, I was writing a pilot about a father and son who had a very difficult relationship. I was about to write a scene in which the son opens up about this to his wife late at night after having had a brutal argument with Dad. I knew this was a pivotal moment in the script, and since I didn't have my big idea yet, I turned on the television. The World Series was on. The game was tied, there was a runner on base, and a rookie came up to bat. The commentators talked about what an amazing and terrifying opportunity this was for the young player. He hit a sacrifice fly and tied the game. The stadium went nuts. And what crossed my mind as I watched him return to the dugout to receive his high-fives was the following: I wonder if that was good enough for his parents, or were they disappointed that he didn't get an actual hit and win the game. (We can get into why this was my first thought at another time. . . .) I *ran* to the computer and wrote the monologue that would become the centerpiece of the script. About the hard-to-please dad taking his son to a baseball game. And a rookie player coming up to bat with the score tied. . . .

4:30 P.M.: No such comparable revelations from channel surfing, but I'm ready to write a little more. Which I do.

5:45 P.M.: Shower, dress, go out to dinner. This is a last-minute thing. I never make plans when I'm on script, but if I feel like I've earned a couple of hours out of the house, I'll make a few calls and find someone to play with.

9:00 P.M.: Back home. Watch some news and anything I might have DVR'd.

10:30 P.M.: One last look at the last few scenes I wrote. One makes me very happy. One is definitely a place-holder. Decide that I've done enough writing today, and it will keep.

11:30 P.M.: Letterman. Sleep.

2:00 A.M.: Bolt upright in bed. I'm hit by a flash of knowing exactly what the place-holder scene needs to fix it. Debate for a second whether I'm going to drag my ass out of bed now and fix it. Of course I am.

2:50 A.M.: Much better. Back to bed.

8:00 A.M.: Alarm goes off. Who am I kidding?

CARLOS BARBOSA
Production Designer

Photo credit: Art Director Carlos Osorio on the set of *24*

Bogotá, Colombia, is roughly a seven-hour plane ride and a million miles from Hollywood. But when you're talented like Carlos Barbosa and you've got ambition to burn, that's a trip worth taking. Carlos took that trip, although his L.A. story didn't begin right away. On his way to becoming an award-winning production designer, he had a layover at Tulane University in New Orleans, where he earned a master's in architecture.

Sometime after graduating he ended up working for an architectural firm in Connecticut, where he found he didn't much care for the corporate lifestyle. To make matters worse, it was the dead of winter and his South American blood was rejecting the frigid cold. So in the blink of an eye, he called it quits and hit the road for sunny

California—without knowing a single soul. Now a funny thing happened on his way to L.A. A random encounter with a retired soap star resulted in his first job in the entertainment biz. That job led to another and another, and it wasn't long before he became a sought-after production designer.

In a career that spans two decades, Carlos has bounced between projects on both the big and small screens. Do the names *24* and *Lost* ring a bell? If you want to learn what it takes to have a career designing sets, read on. If you want to learn more about Bogotá, you should buy a guidebook.

ART DEPARTMENT COORDINATOR: He or she manages the art department office. The job includes everything from obtaining legal clearances for products and artwork appearing on screen, to researching information and tracking the department's budget. This is a noncreative administrative position.

COSTUME DESIGNER: He or she designs the wardrobe an actor or actress will wear in a film, TV show, or play.

LEADMAN: The leadman manages his crew, the swing gang. He's also the right hand man of the Set Decorator and deals with all the logistics of the set dressing department. He's responsible for tracking and keeping the budget for his department.

PILOT: The very first episode of a TV show that establishes the series. After the pilot has been shot, the network then decides whether or not to order more episodes. Most often, a pilot is tested by screening it to focus groups.

PROP MASTER/PROP GUYS: They're responsible for purchasing or manufacturing and, in some cases, operating any props needed on set.

SET DECORATOR: He or she is responsible for arranging the set dressing on a film or TV show. That includes things like furnishings, wallpaper, and lighting fixtures.

SWING GANG: The swing gang works under the direct command of the leadman, and their job is to do all the pick ups and returns of set dressing from vendors and prop houses, and to dress the sets in accordance with the set decorator's instructions.

UNION: Production designers are represented by IATSE, Local 800; the Art Directors Guild.

Let's start with the basics. Tell our readers what a production designer does.

A production designer is the person who creates a visual world for the script to unfold. So everything you see on the screen, all the locations, the sets, the colors, the textures, even the look when it comes to makeup and wardrobe is part of the task of the production designer.

Sounds highly creative. Was this something you wanted to do as a kid?

Actually, I wanted to be an architect. As a little kid I'd play with Legos and cardboard and I'd build homes and castles and forts and whatever, so I had that from as far back as I can remember. It was architecture I pursued first. In fact, most production designers are architects.

So, you grew up in Bogotá, Colombia?

I lived there during my formative years and I came to the states when I was twenty-one to study at Tulane University.

And after graduating you worked as an architect, right?

Yes. I worked for some really big firms.

What was the catalyst for making the switch to the entertainment biz?

I loved architecture, but I hated the business of architecture. Once I completed my studies and got my job, I found it to be a very regimented, corporate lifestyle. There were also all the permits and the city codes and the ordinances, so you spent a lot of time tangled in this web but not actually getting to see your work completed.

How many years were you in this tangled web before you decided to switch gears?

I'd say after five or six years a light bulb went off and I was like, okay, where else can I have the joy of architecture? It was obvious that it was in the movies because production design in a certain way is architecture for the movie, but we get to create worlds, entire universes. Also, the speed at which it happens is really fast because you start a movie and all of a sudden you've created twenty different environments, so it's a lot more gratifying. Plus I'd seen a million movies and had kind of a parallel love for them.

How did your first job in the industry come about?

I was working on a project in Connecticut and it was winter. I walked out to go to the studio and had to pour a bucket of water on the windshield to get the ice off and I was like, "What the hell am I doing here?" So just like that I decided I was going to pack up and leave. Two days later I was driving cross-country. Along the way I stopped in Yerington, Nevada, where I'd helped design a ranch house for some clients. We met and I told them I was going to L.A. because I wanted to get into the movies. They said, "Oh you should meet our next door neighbors." It turned out their neighbor was a retired soap opera actress from *Days of Our Lives* and her husband was a very established *costume designer*.

She asked if I knew anybody in the industry and I told her I didn't. She literally picked up the phone, made a call, and got me a job working construction on this movie in L.A. So that first movie I worked in construction, the second movie as an art director, and then the third I was the production designer and it just kind of started to click.

Wow, your life literally sounds like a movie script. You got your foot in the door and you took off.

For me it was just about learning who did what on a production and how it was put together, which is not a big deal. The rest, the design process, is really understanding that there's the script and there's a story you're going to create this world for. You also have to understand the characters; you have to understand the context and all the different layers to it. But once you understand that, it's just like any other design problem. So in a way it's the same approach as designing an architectural building.

Continue on your career track.

This is a funny story. I had done two or three movies as a designer, but it was hell getting the next job. I kept hearing, "Oh you don't have enough experience." I got so sick and tired of hearing this, I created a fake resume. I put down my four real credits and then I created all these things that I supposedly had done in Colombia and I used my architectural portfolio to create all the images. Every time I would get a new movie one of the fake ones would come off my resume until they were all real. This was before the days of the Internet.

How did you get into the *union*?

Well, I did a lot of movies of the week and it was all nonunion. I needed to figure out how to get into the union. I had met a producer who liked my work and he got a series called *Moloney*. They had a designer who was having a kid and couldn't be there full-time. So he offered me the job of art director and made me production designer when she left. That was how I got into the union. That was a pivotal moment.

Let's talk about *24*. How did you land that job?

I read the script and the one thing I got out of it, as a visual departure, was there was a mole in the organization and you didn't know who it was. So I asked myself, "How do you create architecture for a mole?" Well for me the answer was to create a sense of false security and false enclosure. Meaning, you've got walls but they're see-through, so you can always see everything. Everyone's looking at everyone. That created the fish bowl where Jack Bauer worked, and you could see him on the phone, but yet it was kind of private. You start to create that tension. So to me it was about creating an architecture of transparency. I pitched this concept and nailed it because it was kind of the perfect physical and environmental response to the needs of the story.

You worked a couple of seasons on *24*, correct?

I did the *pilot*, then I was asked back to do season eight because it was completely new. It was New York, but we shot it in L.A. They had money to build all the CTUs (Counter Terrorist Units) again, so

I pitched them a concept they really liked. I knew we needed the UN and we need the CTU. Where in New York is the CTU? Is it in a skyscraper, is it in an old abandoned power station, is it in Manhattan? Then I came up with the idea where I said, "Look, because of all the terrorism, I think it should be an underground facility and I think it should be right across from the United Nations on Roosevelt Island so it's got that medieval moat defense scheme. It's away from everything, it's underground, but we're going to pretend that it's linked to Manhattan by this old abandoned tunnel that could've been an old subway tunnel." It opened up all these possibilities for the story and they loved it.

How many people were on your crew?
At the peak I would say anywhere from 120 to 150 people.

While we're on the subject of crew, can you tell us some of the different jobs that exist within the art department?
There's the production designer, then your right-hand person is the art director. The production designer is the director of the art; the art director is the person who interprets the vision, and they have a lot of artistic input, of course, but they're more about logistics and coordinating the departments and making sure the drawings are done in time for construction. Then there are the set designers, who produce all the drawings for construction. You've got graphic designers, the *art department coordinator*, and production assistants. And that's kind of the nucleus of the department.

Then you have your construction coordinator, the *set decorator* who's the head of that department, his or her *leadman*, and the *swing gang*. You've got the *prop master* and your *prop guys*. Who else? Well, hair and makeup and wardrobe, not that we tell them exactly what to do, but again a good designer will give the broad strokes of the style and vibe we're trying to achieve.

Are you the person who hires the department heads?
Yes. And the department heads hire their own guys, and those guys hire their own guys, and so forth and so on. It's not like I hire every single soul.

Let's go back to some of the other tent poles in your career. You production-designed *Lost*, which is another huge show with an equally huge following. Can you talk about that experience?
You're going to love this story. They did the pilot, and then I met with them and they said they needed a permanent set. So they asked if I could build a beach on the stage, and I said, "Wait. You're going to Hawaii so you can build a beach on a sound stage?" That was funny to me. And then something hit me at that moment. I said, "I can suggest a direction that will take us to a permanent set. These characters are going to run out of water, so in their search for water they're going to get to these volcanic caves, which you find on these islands. What if we get to one of these places where there's a waterfall and remnants of another piece of airplane that fell in there? Then that becomes their home, which we can build on a stage." So they wrote that into the story.

Wow, from your mind to the screen. That's powerful.
Switching gears . . . we talked about what happens when you're in preproduction. What happens when you're in physical production?
When we're actually in production, we want to make sure the set is ready for that day. Either the art director or I will show up to open

the set, especially if it's the first time we're shooting, to make sure all the needs are met, then we move on. In the meantime we're prepping the next day, and the day after that, and the next week and breaking down the new scripts so we're always ahead.

So now that you've given us a general overview, what words of encouragement can you give someone who'd like to do what you do?

Well, look. It's really about your work and about finding a place where you can show or execute it. It's ultimately your product that's going to sell. If your product is good, they're going to come back. So that's number one.

Number two, how do you get that opportunity? For somebody who's starting from scratch, I wish there was a road map. I was really lucky. There are sites that list all the independent filmmakers and projects and stuff, like Mandy.com. There are USC, AFI, and UCLA film schools. I suggest trying to get into a thesis project. I don't care if they don't pay you, again it's about showing your work in the beginning. Go offer yourself and try to get into the art department to get to design something that you can document. That's how you get in. You've got to be resourceful. And you've got to create contacts.

What would you say to someone starting out about putting together a portfolio?

Be very critical and don't try to clutter it. Don't show everything. If you show everything, undoubtedly 25 percent of them are not going to be great. It's best to serve a little food that tastes terrific, and you want more than an all-you-can-eat crappy meal.

Can a person make a comfortable living as a production designer?

It's like anything. It's not the profession; it's the love for the profession and the passion you have for it and the quality of your work that will, as a consequence, give you the means to do it. If you're going into this to make money, go be a banker. Making money is not the objective. Making money is kind of an accidental reward of your labor and your love. You should never think about the money.

When you go to someone's house are you constantly redesigning each room in your mind?

Yeah. Actually, a home tells me everything about the person. And more than the home I usually head for the refrigerator. If I'm interested in a girl and she invites me home for the first time, I can't help it, I go in the fridge. Because it tells me everything I need to know.

What's in your fridge?

You can go have a look.

A DAY IN THE LIFE OF CARLOS BARBOSA

On the set of the TV show 24.

4:45 A.M.: Wake up. Exercise and shower. Get dressed, drink juice, and leave.

5:30 A.M.: Get in the car and onto the 101 freeway. Listen to morning news.

6:00 A.M.: Arrive at studio, park, and walk to stage.

6:15 A.M.: Review the set and make sure everything is ready for shooting. Walk through with director and DP.

6:45 A.M.: Get breakfast from catering truck and sit with my crew to review the plan for the day.

7:15 A.M.: Back on stage watching the first scene being shot.

8:15 A.M.: Walk to my office. Meet with my team and review drawings and details for sets coming up.

9:15 A.M.: Meet with construction coordinator and review new details of set under construction.

10:00 A.M.: Back in my office designing new sets for future episodes.

11:00 A.M.: Get in the van with director, UPM, and location manager to go downtown (Los Angeles) for a scout.

11:45 A.M.: Scout possible new locations for upcoming episodes.

12:45 P.M.: Nice lunch at Bottega Louie Downtown.

2:00 P.M.: Back to scouting new possible locations through downtown L.A.

4:00 P.M.: Back in the van and driving back to the studio in the middle of rush hour. Squeeze in a nap.

5:00 P.M.: Arrive at studio and go back to stage to check on the status of the shoot.

5:30 P.M.: Back to my office, meeting with my team (art director, set designers, graphic designer, Art Dept. coordinator) to plan and review our strategy for the following day and upcoming week.

6:30 P.M.: Get in my car and drive home. Listen to NPR for news of the day.

CECILIA CARDWELL
On-Set Tutor/Studio Teacher

Photo credit: Susan Friedman

Cecilia Cardwell grew up in Palo Alto, California. She was a per-former and dancer who graduated from college with a degree in the-ater and dance. She furthered her education by getting her teaching credentials. As an on-set tutor, she travels the world working with kids on the sets of major motion pictures and TV shows. Her non-traditional teaching career has taken her to places like Minorca, Spain, with the Douglases, Michael and Catherine Zeta, that is; the set of James Cameron's epic *Titanic*; and running alongside a van as her pupil, Abigail Breslin, was shooting a scene for *Little Miss Sunshine*.

Cecilia is a woman with a lot of ambition and an adventur-ous spirit, which is not suited to the traditional confines of a classroom. She's petite, a bit of a gypsy, and a fervent proponent of education. She also has zero tolerance for child actors who aren't serious about their studies and people who don't recycle. (We promised we would fit a green message somewhere in here.) While on set, Cecilia is not only responsible for teaching the child stars, she's also in charge of their well-being and making sure they are not overworked. Add to that the authority to give detention and this is one woman that nobody, not even the director, wants to mess with.

Let's begin today's lesson, shall we?

FLIP: When a TV show begins production as nonunion, then applies for union status. If the status is approved while the show is in production, all the nonunion workers become eligible for union hours.

LOCAL 844 UNION: As per the union website, "our commitment to caring for minors in the entertainment industry has continued since 1926, when the producers asked that teachers be provided so children could work during school hours."

PRINCIPAL PHOTOGRAPHY: The period when a movie is no longer in preproduction and is being shot. The action primarily includes all the major scenes featuring the lead actors and characters.

STUDIO TEACHER'S AGENCY: An organization that represents on-set tutors and submits them for jobs throughout the industry. If an agency secures work for an on-set tutor, it's customary that they're paid a 10 percent commission.

STUNT COORDINATOR: A current or former stunt person who hires other stunt people for film or TV jobs. He or she also choreographs the stunt sequence and maintains a safe working environment.

UNIT PRODUCTION MANAGER (UPM): A producer who is on set and responsible for a multitude of duties including budgets, scheduling, administration, hiring, and general supervision.

Can you please explain what your responsibilities are as an on-set tutor?

I teach child actors on the sets of movies and TV shows (child actors five to seventeen years old are required to attend class on set) and I make sure that when school is in session the kids are getting three hours of lessons per day. I also monitor the hours they are allowed to work on set and make sure they are not being put in any dangerous situations. Those, in a nutshell, are my responsibilities.

Let's learn about your career path. You started in theater and dance, then you became a teacher, then an on-set tutor. Can you connect the dots for us?

I was twenty-five years old living in California waiting tables and trying to get my dancing career off the ground. One day, I decided that life as a struggling performer was not for me and was definitely not a viable way to support myself, so I switched a gear. My mom had been a teacher, and I knew that teaching was a fairly solid profession with a good schedule, so I went back to school and got my teaching credentials. After I graduated, I tried to get a full-time teaching job, but in the early nineties the job market was much like it is today, recessionary. I was only able to find substitute teaching jobs where I taught all levels for different districts in my area. The teaching jobs were so infrequent that I had to waitress on the side. Things just weren't working out as I expected.

At this point you knew what *wasn't* for you, so how did you find your calling?

I was invited by a friend to work for the day as a production assistant on a TV set and realized how much I had missed the artistic environment. While I was on set I met the *unit production manager (UPM)*. In conversation, I told him I was a teacher. When he saw how much I loved being around production he suggested that I look into becoming a studio teacher and a light bulb went off. It sounded like the perfect job for me because I was always a little bit concerned about being stuck in a classroom and I loved to travel. I immediately signed up for a one-year program to get my on-set tutor teaching credential.

By this point you've experienced that a degree and credentials do not always equal work and getting hired, so how did you get your first job in Hollywood?

The *UPM* I met on the commercial gave me the name of a *studio teacher's agency* that he used to hire teachers, so I listed with that agency. Not many people who listed with the agency were fluent in French, but I was, and that really made me stand out when UPMs needed to hire tutors to teach French. I also had the good fortune of meeting the California Labor Commissioner, who introduced me to Betty King, who is now ninety years old, bless her heart. Betty was, and still is, my mentor. As a studio teacher she was president of the union back in the sixties, and she tutored Jodie Foster, Ron Howard, and Michael Jackson.

Wow, she must have had some great advice for you.

She was really instrumental in guiding me. She taught me to be professional, enforce the child labor laws, and the general basics of the job. Then, through a little persistence and a little luck I was hired on the movie *Titanic*.

Oh, the movie about the iceberg?

Yes, the small art house film; you've heard of it? I have to say I was terrified. I was calling Betty every day because that job was very chaotic at first. We were shooting in Mexico and there were a lot of variables, a lot of things that people didn't think about regarding the kids prior to beginning *principal photography*. I taught six background kids every day for six months, and I had a handful of the speaking-role kids who were thankfully not there the entire time.

So your career kicks off with a mammoth Academy Award–winner. Where did you go from there?

My next feature was a film directed by Wes Anderson, called *Rushmore*. I started off tutoring Jason Schwartzman, whose mom is the lovely Talia Shire and whose Uncle Frank is Francis Ford Coppola. Jason was seventeen years old when he shot that movie, so I was his first and last studio teacher. The sole reason I got that job was because Jason had French as one of his subjects.

Bill Murray was also in that movie and he speaks French fluently. Did you tutor him?

(Laughs) No, but he's a funny man. After *Rushmore* I was hired on the movie *Signs*. Once again, there was an actor who was studying French. One of the really great offshoots of that film was that I met Kim and Abigail Breslin and we became friends. I've worked on eight projects between Kim's two children since then, including *Little Miss Sunshine.*

So you taught Abigail, but you also had to look out for her well-being on the set. Do you have a *Little Miss Sunshine* story you can share with us?

One that comes to mind is the now-famous scene when Abby had to run alongside and jump into a moving van. This stunt made both her mom and me very nervous. Ultimately I let her do it for a couple of reasons. First, the stunt guy, Tommy Harper, is a great *stunt coordinator*, and second, I knew Kim really well, Abby's mom, and I knew she would never let her daughter do anything she didn't think Abby was capable of doing.

So Abigail was comfortable running alongside the van and jumping in?

She was totally comfortable with it. The entire stunt was very well thought out, planned, and rehearsed. She did great. Before any questionable scenes I always watch my kids, and if I see fear in their face I just step in and tell them that they don't have to do it. I've had to put my foot down and say "no" on numerous occasions.

Talk about the additional credentials and certifications needed to protect a child's welfare as an on-set tutor.

You need to get certified by the state you work in. First, a person would need two teaching credentials. Next, you need to become certified by the State Labor Commission by taking an extensive test where you memorize the state child labor laws. If you pass, you get a studio teacher state welfare worker card from the labor commission. The certification must be renewed every three years.

Have you had a situation on set where production wanted to go over the allotted time a child can legally work?

Oh, yeah. People try to do that all the time, but I don't allow it. It tends to happen more on the lower-budget projects. The lower the budget, the more people think they can bend the rules, because the people who work on lower-budget projects are generally people who just haven't been in the business very long. In the union film and TV world people understand the repercussions. The production can be fined and I can be fined.

How much is the fine?

I don't even know because, like I said, I don't allow it. I think it is in the area of $5,000. So a smart producer doesn't want a kid to work overtime either, there is just too much at risk.

What are some perks of the job?

At times very cool and unexpected things happen. On the movie *No Reservations* I met Catherine Zeta Jones and I ended up getting invited to Europe with her; her husband, Michael Douglas; and their five-year-old son to tutor him over the summer. I was in Minorca, Spain, and London for three months. I have to say it was surreal to be sitting across the table from Michael and Catherine at breakfast every morning in their villa.

Not something that a middle school teacher in, say, Des Moines gets to do every day. Are child actors held to the same standards as high school athletes, where they have to maintain a certain GPA?

It's a little different. A regular student must have a certain overall average, but for a child to get a work permit, the child must have a grade of a "C" or better in every subject. If there is one "D" on a report card the state of California will not issue the permit.

Have you ever been in a situation where a kid dropped below a "C" while working and had to be removed from the show?
I have been in situations where kids have had to be replaced.

Who flunked out?
Hey, I'm great with phone numbers and horrible with names, so even if I wanted to tell you I couldn't remember.

That's a great line. We've got to remember that one. So a normal school day is five or six hours, but on the set a child only needs three hours of schooling. Why is that?
Well it's based on instructional minutes, and in the state of California even though a child might attend school from 8:30 A.M. to 2:30 P.M. the actual time where they are being taught is only 240 minutes. So on-set teaching requires no less than 180 minutes of instruction. I get their current curriculum and I work with them on the same material that they would be studying if they weren't shooting a movie.

Have you ever put a student in detention?
I've threatened it.

Could you actually do that?
Sure, I could. Sometimes my strategy with the younger kids is to threaten that if they don't settle down and do their work, I'll tell the director that he can't use them in the movie. That always gets their attention.

Is there a law limiting the number of students you are allowed to teach at one time?

Yes, one person can have up to ten students. So if there is an eleventh, the production needs to bring in a second studio teacher. And then in the summer, when school is not in session, one person can oversee up to twenty kids.

Is it mandatory to become a member of the union?

Well, no, it's not mandatory, but if you want to work on a big feature film or a network TV show, you'd have to become union. If you are not in the *Local 844 Union* you can only work on cable TV and independent low-budget movies.

How did you get into the union?

A stroke of luck. I happened to work with Christopher Coppola on a nonunion movie called *The Creature from Sunny Brook Park*. I was talking to the producer and asking him if I could replace myself on the movie because I had another teaching opportunity that was going to go longer and I didn't want to pass it up. He told me that I might not want to do that because the Coppola movie was about to *flip* and go union, so when that happens the days you work are recognized by the union, and once you have sixty days you are allowed to work on union movies. You must work a certain number of days every six months or you can lose your union privileges. You also have annual dues you must pay.

What is an on-set tutor's salary range? Are you paid better than a regular schoolteacher?

There are ranges you make based on your experience and based on the project and whether it is a big studio film or an independent project. A low-budget 500k film pays around $150 to $300 per day. Some producers will try to hire people for less, but again it depends on experience and credits. A high-end rate is in the area of $450 to $500 per day. You do realize you are going to flood the on-set tutor market with this chapter, don't you? (Laughs)

Even if you've been in the business for years, you never know when you'll get another job or where it will take you. Is that frustrating?

You need to have a little bit of gypsy blood in you, which I do. You have to like traveling. You have to like change and variety, and you can't be attached to having an eight-to-three job like most teachers, with summers off. That goes out the window and you sacrifice regularity for better money, variety, and excitement. But it's not for everyone. Also, people shouldn't think my job is glamorous; it's not. The reality is sometimes you are in the trenches and other times you are on the red carpet. You have to be a pretty adaptable person.

What are the best parts of your job?

For me, personally, it's the variety and the stimulation and knowing that no two days are ever alike. I personally love that; it suits my personality and I never get bored.

One more question. May we go to the bathroom?

Yes. One at a time and take a pass.

A DAY IN THE LIFE OF CECILIA CARDWELL

Working on the ABC TV show No Ordinary Family.

6:00 A.M.: Wake up, make tea, take a shower and prepare for the drive to Burbank.

7:15 A.M.: Begin the drive to ABC/Disney Studios. Receive a message from the Second AD saying my student Jimmy Bennett's call time is changed from 8:00 A.M. to 9:00 A.M. Ugh! I could've slept another forty-five minutes.

8:00 A.M.: Stop at Patty's for breakfast in Burbank since I have time to kill.

8:45 A.M.: Arrive and day begins. Jimmy goes through hair and makeup, rehearses on set, then I get him for thirty minutes and we begin studies. Today it's Algebra I and English.

10:00 A.M.: Jimmy is back on the set. Over the next several hours I alternate between being on set with him and going back to the trailer for school studies. We have gotten in an hour and a half of school before lunch.

2:00 P.M.: The entire crew breaks for lunch. It's a hot day, so I head to the commissary for a salad and air conditioning, instead of walking across the studio lot to the catering truck.

2:30 P.M.: Lunch is over and Jimmy is back in school with me for the next thirty minutes while the crew sets up for the next shot.

3:00 P.M.: Jimmy returns to the set to film. I go with him and take breaks to warm up outside, as the studio is freezing.

3:45 P.M.: Receive a phone call about a feature film. The job would take me overseas and I'd work with an AD I worked with on the movie *No Reservations* (with Abigail Breslin). Very interesting offer. Hmmm.

4:30 P.M.: Another break in filming. I do thirty more minutes of schooling with Jimmy. Then we do thirty minutes of PE (throwing a football). Jimmy is fourteen years old with high energy. He needs to get out and be a kid.

5:30 P.M.: Go back to set. The scene is finished by 6:00 P.M. so I let Jimmy take his last thirty minutes of rest and recreation.

6:30 P.M.: Meet a friend for dinner in Burbank (the mom of a boy I tutored on *Heroes*). We had become good friends and I haven't seen her in a long time. It's great to catch up.

9:00 P.M.: Leave Burbank and have a nice drive home—no traffic. MacGyver (my cat) waits for me at the door.

10:00 P.M.: Make sure the lessons are planned for the next day, watch the tube, and go to bed, as I have a 7:00 A.M. call time tomorrow!

JOHN ROSENGRANT
Makeup Effects Artist/Co-owner of Legacy Effects

Photo credit: Legacy

John Rosengrant has worked with some of the scariest creatures in Hollywood. No, we're not talking about agents, that would be an insult to scary creatures. We kid, of course. These creatures we speak of have names like Predator, Alien, and Terminator, iconic figures who've scared up worldwide box office receipts in the billions of dollars. That's billions, with a B.

John's fascination with all things monster, sci-fi, and creepy can be traced back to his childhood, where in art class he'd draw creatures with gnarly fangs while other kids quietly sketched harmless bowls of fruit. Years later, he landed in Hollywood and captured the attention of Academy Award–winning special effects artist Stan Winston, who gave him his big break, not to mention job security for the next twenty-four years. John and a few partners went on to launch Legacy Effects, a cutting edge live-action and digital design house that's created some of the most memorable characters for film, TV, and commercials. Giants in the industry, their work can be seen in everything from Aflac to *Avatar*.

We met John at his facility deep in the San Fernando Valley, a facility that's so top secret we had to sign an agreement promising not to divulge its location. We're kidding. You can totally find it on MapQuest. We sat down with him, but not before getting a tour of his amazing playground.

ANIMATRONICS: A puppet that is mechanized and is remote-controlled or preprogrammed. Stan Winston Studio created an animatronic dinosaur in *Jurassic Park III*.

BORIS KARLOFF: An English-born actor who appeared in many movies, but is perhaps best known for his portrayal of Frankenstein's monster.

CG: Stands for "computer graphics," which are graphics or images created for film, TV, video games, or print with the help of a computer.

LON CHANEY JR.: An American actor, he is known for his work in *The Wolf Man*. His father was silent film star Lon Chaney.

MIXED MEDIA: A term that refers to a combination of different types of media to create a piece of art.

STAN WINSTON: Stan Winston is a legendary Academy Award–winning makeup, creature, and visual effects artist. He owned and ran Stan Winston Studio.

First of all, thanks for the tour. It's not every day you get up close and personal with the real Iron Man. Which leads to our first question. Do you ever stop to think how incredible it is to be making creatures for a living?

Yes. It happens the most when I go to see a film that I had a hand in and witness the audience's reaction. I'm fortunate to have had that feeling several times working on *Avatar*, *Jurassic Park*, and *Terminator*. I've been so fortunate to be involved with so many projects that are iconic.

It's probably a cliché to say you were into monsters as a kid, but you were into monsters as a kid, right?

Yes. It was a passion since I was little. I'd see a horror movie, whether it was *King Kong* or *The Bride of Frankenstein* or even *Abbott and Costello Meet Frankenstein* and I'd just be stopped in my tracks. I just couldn't take my eyes off of them. It was magic to me.

Did you have an inkling that you'd get into this business?

In elementary school those thoughts would cross my mind. My secret dream was to make monsters for movies. I wanted to be Jack Pearce, the guy who did the makeup on *Boris Karloff* and *Lon Chaney Jr*. And my parents were always very encouraging and one hundred percent supportive, but I don't think they knew how to help. Nobody did. They saw I had an aptitude for drawing, so they had me take some art classes, and the teacher would always say I was wandering off drawing monsters. Eventually she said, "You know what? I think enough with the still lifes, just let his imagination kind of run, he'll get the basics of it."

Was there anything in those early drawings that you thought might make a good project?
I always had a thing for werewolves, and I'm still waiting for the perfect werewolf project.

When that day comes, do you have a werewolf arsenal ready to unleash on the world?
I do.

So when there's a full moon it's all over.
(Laughs) It's all over. It's all coming out.

Did you continue your art education when you got older?
Yes. I ended up going to Louisiana State University as an art major. There were a couple of teachers who were really good, who helped teach real anatomy that I still rely on today. Because when you're making a creature you need to design it so that there's something familiar about it, something that suspends disbelief but is rooted in reality.

So you were getting an education, but you were a long way away from Hollywood. How did you keep the dream alive?
Well, what happened was I discovered that the classes offered were more about mood and feeling and less about the nuts and bolts of anatomy. I got to a point where I was a little frustrated. So I went to work full-time in a grocery store. And I think that actually helped me because it was such a mundane job. It made me realize that was not what I wanted to do the rest of my life. Then, *An American Werewolf in London* came out and *Alien* and those movies really triggered it. It was like, "Get me out of here! I'm missing things." It was the kick in

the butt that made me realize, you've got to do something or you're going to see all your dreams disappear.

So, California here you come?
Pretty much. I packed my car up with a U-Haul full of crap behind me. My saving grace was my grandmother, who lived in Pasadena, California, at a retirement place, and my aunt who was always there for me once I got to L.A. My uncle was an entertainment lawyer, so at least I knew some people out here. I stayed at this retirement place until I found a roach-infested apartment in North Hollywood. My uncle represented *Stan Winston*, and he said, "Well you should see Stan." And I said, "Oh my God. You know Stan?" So I actually got to see Stan because of my uncle.

What was that meeting like?
When I first met him, he took my portfolio and flipped through it really fast, and said, "Yup. Really good stuff. It reminds me of when I first started out. Why don't you have a look around? Take your time." And that was it. Game over. But I was fascinated; I must've stayed in his shop for over an hour. Looking at all his sculptures, artwork, molds. It was my first chance to look at anything like this. It was very inspirational.

Did he give you any advice?
Nothing. Nothing at all.

And you weren't knocked down?
I was okay because it felt like a huge first step. I asked him if I could stay in touch and show him my work. And he said sure, thinking he'd never see me again, probably. It actually was helpful to me

because I finally got a glimpse of the business, so it helped me to really focus.

What kept you going at this point?

Tenacity. I had the talent but I think I also had the tenacity to hang in there. I ended up getting an interview with a place called Makeup Effects Labs. They had done *Friday the 13th* part three, seven, four, I don't remember exactly, and they did some other low-budget films. I had a decent interview with those guys. But at the time they didn't have enough work to hire me. So I ended up getting a job at a supermarket. After six months, I finally got the call from Makeup Effects Labs and they hired me.

That must've been an exciting moment. What was the project?

It was called, *Metalstorm: The Destruction of Jared-Syn* in 3D.

What was your job?

It was a low-budget *Star Wars*–type movie, so I worked on different phases. They saw that I could paint pretty well, but I ended up doing lots of different things. I became part of that team. They were paying me $200 a week and working me at least sixty, seventy hours. But I was very excited and grateful for my first "movie job" opportunity.

How long did you end up working there?

About six months. And then the work ran out. But I met a lot of people who were working there. Your contacts are important because they move on and work somewhere else and they refer you. There was some other low-budget place and somebody who was working there remembered me, and I went down for an interview and I got hired and did some teenage college comedy called *Stitches*.

Because this industry is job to job to job, how important is your reputation?

It's everything. Word-of-mouth kept getting me hired. Also, during that period I kept in touch with Stan. And at one point in 1983, I actually offered myself up to work for him for free. Stan was doing a Styx video for the song "Mr. Roboto," and I ended up helping out on that.

Special Effects for big hair?

(Laughs) There was that whole robot costume and those masks. So I was helping make the masks for those guys. Then time passed and I would keep calling Stan, but there was nothing. Eventually I got a call from him because he was looking for people to work on this movie called *Terminator*. That's when I actually got hired for real.

What were some of the things you did on *Terminator*?

I helped construct the robot. I sanded all the parts on him and ended up doing work on all the heads of Arnold. I had my hands in everything. I went to set on that movie as well, that whole scene where he peels his eye out—that was a phone call in the afternoon from the set. They were like, "We have to get an eye made that we can cut and peel out." So I whipped something up out of a mold and ran it to set. It was fun stuff like that. It spoiled me forever.

What happened after *Terminator*?

After that, I never got another job. I stayed there for twenty-four years. I became part of the team that was Stan Winston Studio, and that was a big deal.

Can you talk about some of the different jobs involved in making a creature come to life?

You have the designers who work on what the creature's going to look like. That's the design phase. We also make sure that mechanically it's going to be sound and *animatronically* it's going to move right. Then it's sculpted. Once it's been sculpted it needs to be molded. The mold team makes the parts, whether it's foam rubber, silicone, hard fiberglass, or plastics. Then the fabrication team does the sewing and, for example, with the Iron Man suit, they figure out how it snaps together and how the under suit works. They're like high-tech tailors. It's a concert between all these groups until it gets to the end, when it's finished by a painter. Then you've got the hair department that's either tying these hairs into it if they're making a wig, or they're punching them in one hair at a time which is the only way you're going to get that realism.

How long did it take to go from design to completion of Iron Man?

Everything is four months now. It's the new number. Three to four months depending on the project.

Talk a little bit about working with the director, like James Cameron, for instance, who's known for his attention to detail.

I thank him every day. After you work with Jim you can work with anybody. I always want to bring my "A" game, but he makes you bring your "A-plus-plus" game. Because he never misses a beat. Starting with *Terminator*, I had no idea at the time who James Cameron was going to become, but I knew after reading his script and being on set with him that he was making a good movie. He had really good ideas. He cares about every aspect of it. I mean every aspect. There's nothing that isn't important to him.

What were some *Avatar* hoops you had to jump through?

We started out by designing the characters, whether they were avatars or they were the Na'vi, and Jim (Cameron) had ideas so what we did was help bring Jim's ideas into the flesh. And because of the digital age we were able to give him every variation under the sun. Sigourney Weaver was a challenge because he needed to see her as a thirty-year-old, so we had to move backward in time but still make her recognizable. Her facial structure with that broad nose and that lioness cat look wasn't working on her face because the minute we started adding that to her, we lost her. So if you go back, you'll see her nose and her facial structure are not in keeping with all of the others. But it was the only way to retain her look.

How does somebody work for Legacy Effects? Do you go to schools and recruit?

Yeah, the people we need to go recruit are the *mixed media* digital artists because we offer something that the video game companies and the *CG* companies don't, which is an interaction between CG and live action. The other artisans and mechanics we hire mostly come in by word-of-mouth.

What about entry-level jobs in your field?

They'd probably end up back in the mold shop doing things as simple as cleaning out molds. Grunt work basically. Helping the molders mix chemicals and other on-the-job training tasks. You look and see what their aptitudes are and you also figure out how much drive they have and what they're willing to do to excel. Will they sweep the floor?

Where's the broom? We want to work on *Avatar II*! So you've had a hand in shaping some of the most iconic movies of all time. What advice would you have for someone who'd like to have half the career you're having?

You have to pursue that dream. You have to take that chance. When I was in Louisiana getting ready to move to California I would say to myself the worst thing that could happen would be that I'd be back to square one. If I go out there, then I'll have no regrets. I will have tried it, given it a shot. That way you have no regrets.

What did you learn from the late, great Stan Winston?

Stan was an extraordinary guy. He was a great artist, charismatic, funny but also an astute businessman. A big thing I learned from Stan was the business side. Also his ethics and his way of looking at things. For example, when you would think, "I'm just exhausted and I can't take another minute of these schedule changes and all this stuff," he would say, "Well, how do you think the director feels? He's got all your problems and he's got all the other departments' problems too. So you've got it easy." That kind of wisdom makes you want to do this work and figure out how to get it done.

Final question. If someone had told you the Terminator would one day be the governor of California, what would you have said?

(Laughs) I would've laughed like I just did. Arnold's a super-smart guy, and I don't think people realize that about him, but I never would have thought that he would've ended up in politics.

A DAY IN THE LIFE OF JOHN ROSENGRANT
October 5, 2010

5:30 A.M.: Wake up and get ready, jump in the car and hit the L.A. freeways. I usually grab a coffee and something to eat on the way to work to save time. Today is a shop day, which is a shorter day for me, as opposed to working on set, which typically runs twelve to fourteen hours.

7:00 A.M.: Arrive at work before the official shop start time of 8 A.M. to catch up on e-mails and budgets before the craziness of the day begins.

8:00 A.M.: I get suited up into a suit we've built for an Orkin commercial, in which I'm playing the role of the featured rat. We tape a performance/rehearsal to send to the client to review work in progress.

9:00 A.M.: Clean up (wearing a creature is physical business, hot and uncomfortable, but in an offbeat and fun way) and meet with our lead designer, going over our concept art in preparation for a meeting with producers and a director for a new, big-budget film called *World War Z.*

10:00 A.M.: Review works-in-progress designs and digital sculptures with director and producers. We flesh out ideas and hone the direction of the designs.

11:30 A.M.: Do a shop walk-through and check on the various film and commercial projects, seeing how they are all coming along, chatting with the artists, mechanics, fabricators, and model and mold makers.

12:30 P.M.–3:00 P.M.: Shop breaks for lunch, I grab lunch at my desk, return phone calls, work on the business end of the business, budgeting creatures and effects for upcoming feature films and commercials. Get caught up with my partners on their projects and business in general.

3:00 P.M.–5:00 P.M.: Back out into the shop, once again checking progress on the work, making sure everything is headed in the right direction. Sit with designers and get updated on their progress as well.

5:00 P.M.: Do a little work preparing for an upcoming *Avatar* press junket I will be part of in conjunction with the extended DVD release. Talk with a producer we are developing a film script with.

6:00 P.M.: Decompress from the day by playing guitar for a bit before heading home.

7:00 P.M.: Return home.

HOWARD SUSSMAN
Costume Supervisor

Photo credit: Nancy Davis

If you've ever caught an episode of that celebrity juggernaut known as *Dancing with the Stars*, then you've definitely seen the work of costume supervisor Howard Sussman. Howard doesn't actually design the dresses worn by celebs, nor is he the person who painstakingly glues all those Swarovski crystals to them. He plays the most crucial role of all. He's the guy who directs the designers, seamstresses, and various assistants in a backstage dance of his own. It's called the "This better get done before we go live 'cause it's my butt on the line" dance. Oh, yeah, and it better come in on budget, too.

Good thing Howard's got a thick skin and an even thicker resume to back him up. He's worked on many other high-profile TV shows like *Mad About You* and *The King of Queens*, not to mention films like *Mission Impossible II.* He sat down with us to describe the job of costume supervisor, which he claims is more than just pretty clothes, flash bulbs, and red carpets. Although it's exciting, it's also hard work. There are many early morning calls, long hours, and stress-filled days. But he wouldn't have it any other way.

BOB MACKIE: A fashion designer best known for designing dresses for icons such as Cher, Diana Ross, Whitney Houston, and Tina Turner.

COSTUMER'S UNION: IATSE (International Alliance of Theatrical Stage Employees Local 705).

NONUNION: Many projects are nonunion, meaning the production companies are not signatories to the major unions like SAG, Aftra, and IATSE. Rates are often a lot less on nonunion productions.

PRODUCTION MEETING: A meeting once a week with all the department heads of a particular show to discuss the needs of an upcoming episode and answer any questions.

SEASON: A season in the real world can be spring, summer, winter, or fall. In television it refers to the period of time a show is on the air.

So before we get into your backstory, tell us what it's like to be on one of the hottest shows on TV.

I feel privileged to be a part of something that's so familiar to so many. It's a rare day when someone I meet doesn't know *Dancing with the Stars.* I would say it's a bit like living in a bubble. A big, celebrity-filled bubble.

How did you end up as the boy in the bubble?
I was working on a show called *The Class*, which everyone thought was going to be a successful series. But it didn't get picked up. So I was at a point of, "What am I going to do?" when I got a phone call from a colleague who heard they were looking for a new supervisor on *Dancing with the Stars*. I knew the concept of the show and I thought, it can't hurt to go interview with them. And the designer was a great guy. He's a Libra, and I'm a Libra and the assistant was a Libra and I liked all that. The producers were young English people who were kind of groovy, and I liked them, too. I walked out of there feeling like it was my job if I wanted it.

Always nice to be wanted. So take us through a typical week on *Dancing with the Stars*.
Okay. Monday night is a live show and then Tuesday night is our result show, when a couple goes home. The remaining couples consult with the designer and conceptualize their look once they have their music for their next dance. Then our designer and his assistants go downtown to the garment district to shop and they come back with bags of fabric and go over the designs with the woman who runs our workroom. She then hands off the fabric and the sketch to a sewer and it's their job to start creating the dress our designers sketched. That's on Wednesday and Thursday. Then on Friday all the talent come in for their first fittings. Once they're happy with the structural parts, then the beading and the fringe happens. We apply Swarovski crystals individually with glue; it's very labor intensive. There have been up to 15,000 on one dress. Then on Sunday we have a full day of fittings with all the celebrities, because Monday we're live again. Monday afternoon is the first time they get to wear the clothes they're going to be seen in that night.

Do you sit down with the celebrities ahead of time to discuss style and address concerns?

Absolutely. At the start of every *season* the costume designer and I have a consultation with every female celebrity.

Tell us what it's like when that last crystal is applied right up to the second you go live. Are there moments of holding your breath?

Many, many moments. The first time the women are wearing their dresses is at dress rehearsal, so if we see something that's too long or a strap that has to be fixed, that happens between dress rehearsal and the show, which literally is a window of two hours. So it's about getting them undressed, getting the dresses upstairs to the workroom, and getting it fixed. That pressure is ridiculous.

But isn't that what you signed on for when you took the job?

Well, initially *Dancing with the Stars* was done as a six-episode throwaway series and it's now become a phenomenon, so with that growth the pressure has gone up exponentially. It's unlike anything I've ever done.

Okay, so now might be a good time to tell us what you *have* done.

Well, after high school I went to Syracuse for a minute and a half then transferred to the Philadelphia College of Textiles and Science, which is where my undergraduate degree is from. Then I went to F.I.T. (Fashion Institute of Technology) in New York for a couple of classes. I moved to New York in 1981 and got into the Macy's executive training program.

Did you aspire to work in fashion when you were younger?

Yeah, I was voted best dressed in my high school, and best hair. Fashion and clothing were always something I had an association with. And I went to school for merchandising.

Did you ever think your fashion sense, education, and great hair would one day land you a job in the entertainment biz?

Never. I moved to Los Angeles because of a relationship, not knowing what I was going to do, frankly. My boyfriend was in a production of *La Cage aux Folles* at the Pantages Theater, and the hairdresser on *La Cage* said to me, "Well, if you know clothing, why don't you do costumes?" And I honestly had no idea what he meant. I mean, I was in a couple of things as a young kid in theater, but I never did anything in costumes. So he said, "Let me get in touch with my friend Bob and see if he can help you out," and Bob was *Bob Mackie*, so within three months of moving to L.A. I was working with Bob Mackie.

Not a bad start. What was the job?

I worked in Bob's rental facility where all of the clothing from productions he had done, like *The Carol Burnett Show* and *The Donny and Marie Show*, were stored. I would then interact with designers who would come in to rent the stock of old costumes, tuxedoes, and dresses. In doing that I got into the *costumer's union*. I spent almost a year there and met many designers including the designer from *Moonlighting*, who eventually gave me a job as an assistant on that show.

What does an assistant in the costume department of *Moonlighting* do?

I was a shopper. I would go to buy the fabrics because we made everything that Cybill Shepherd wore on the show. Getting out of the costume house onto a show took the dynamic of my job to another level.

Was *Moonlighting* a good learning experience?

I definitely saw it as a place where I could learn a lot but also apply my knowledge of fabrics and merchandising. So it was a learning experience, but it was also a growing point. You get in on a show and you work your way up from assisting to supervising, and I could've become a designer if I had those aspirations.

For the wardrobe-impaired, can you explain the difference between a costume designer and a costume supervisor?

A costume supervisor works as the liaison for production. I'm about the budget, the hiring, and making it all happen. I'm not the creative. Designers are all about the fluff, and I'm about the foundation. Although I've been fluffy at times!

Who hasn't? How many people do you oversee?

Dancing with the Stars is a huge production. I have my own workroom of ladies who are sewing. So I have dressers, I have shoppers, I have sewers, I have a designer and assistant designers, all of whose comings and goings are overseen by me.

So you worked on *Moonlighting*. Then what?

The first show I supervised was *Evening Shade* with Burt Reynolds. After that I worked on other sitcoms like *Mad About You* and *King of Queens* and *The Class*, which was created by David Crane and Jeffrey Klarik, from *Friends* and *Mad About You*.

What does a costume supervisor do on a sitcom?

Some sitcoms don't have a designer, they just have a supervisor. Or they may have a supervisor for the men and a supervisor for the women, in which case it's that supervisor's responsibility to shop, which is where much of my merchandising experience had come into play.

So you're handed a script . . .

I'm handed a script and I break it down and do a budget. How many days? How many people do I have to dress? What season are we in? What are the needs of the character? Sometimes writers will have opinions of what their characters should look like so we'll go over that in the weekly *production meetings*. Then I head out and make it happen. Whether I go to a costume shop to rent a particular look or buy something at a retail store.

Will the producers give you a budget and say, "This is what you have to spend, make it happen"?

Most shows have a budget, but it varies from show to show. Of course, on a show like *Sex and the City* where the wardrobe plays a big part it's going to be different than *King of Queens* where the main character basically wears a uniform. *Dancing with the Stars* is a little different in that I'm not given a weekly budget—it's more about, "Don't spend more than this at the end of the day."

Do you ever have a moment where you stop and think, "Wow. I work in the entertainment industry. How cool!"

I do remember when I first got the job supervising *Evening Shade* that I'd never seen a Burt Reynolds movie and I didn't know the magnitude of his celebrity. Spending the next four years of my life with him and his inner circle, there were moments of being in places like a suburban record store in Florida with him on a movie one summer and watching the throngs of people starting to gather. Or years later going to the Academy Awards with him and his girlfriend when he was nominated for *Boogie Nights*. And other moments of realizing you're in it big was on *Dancing with the Stars* when we had a security breach and somebody was coming after one of the celebrities and security had to shut us down. You went from just living your life to all of a sudden we were shut down by security. There have been times where the celebrity gets in the way of what I know life to be.

Many people have come through the doors of that show. Was there anyone you were really taken with?
Yeah. I can't believe that L'il Kim—this outrageous rapper chick and I bonded the first time I ever hung out with her. Wayne Newton was the most generous and delightful man. I never imagined knowing any of these people. So when I meet these people and I know them, especially on *Dancing with the Stars*, I see them completely stripped down after they've rehearsed for ten hours and they're exhausted. Seeing them and knowing them as real people is actually kind of refreshing because I'm often turned off by the bigness of Hollywood,

Do you have an agent?
Nope. Never have. But designers often do have agents.

So how do you find jobs?
I get rehired based on my relationships with producers, mostly. I think you have to work well with people and by well that means not

only staying within budget and producing a good-looking show, but also getting along with everyone like the hair and makeup department, the transportation people. It's a team effort.

What makes a good costume supervisor?

If you're going to lead other people, I think you have to be confident about who you are and the job that you're doing. That brings out the better qualities of the people who are working with you.

What words of wisdom can you pass on to someone who wants to get into your line of work?

My advice would be to stay positive and don't give up on it. Try every avenue. Costume houses are one way to get into the union, which is how it happened for me. So when someone calls me I'll tell them to contact the union because they'll give you information on the various ways of getting in as well as the requirements. Also, you might want to just get in the trenches in the *nonunion* world to be sure it's even something you want to do before you start pursuing it. Get some experience.

What are the misconceptions about your job?

The glamorous end of it. People think it's just pretty clothes and moments of red carpets and flash bulbs. There are segments of costuming and styling that are that. I mean, stylists dress people for the red carpet all the time; that has more elements of glamour. But costumes and Hollywood filmmaking and television shows, it's much more arduous than that and it's much longer hours. There are a lot of early morning calls and dressing a hundred extras off the back of a truck. It's not just all about shopping at Neiman Marcus.

What do you like about it?

I get to run the show from my perspective. I get to oversee and then be proud of what we've put out. We put out hundreds and hundreds of costumes over the run of the season and there may be one or two that were questionable from an aesthetic point of view, but I think for the most part we put out a really quality product.

We started this interview talking about *Dancing with the Stars*, so it feels right to end with that. You have a loincloth and two safety pins. Which actor is in that fitting with you?

Gilles Marini, Samantha's hot next-door neighbor in the *Sex and the City* movie and *Dancing with the Stars* season eight runner-up.

A DAY IN THE LIFE OF HOWARD SUSSMAN

Show day on Dancing with the Stars.

Sunrise: Gotta do some yoga!

7:30 A.M.: Off to the office. It's quieter when no one is around and I can get my thoughts and papers in order for the day.

8:00 A.M.: My crew arrives; we go over the day's challenges.

8:30 A.M.: Meet with hair and makeup departments to go over looks for each contestant.

9:00 A.M.: Check in with the workroom, where all costumes are sewn, to check on progress.

10:00 A.M.: Set the line-up of costumes for the show!

11:00 A.M.: Meet with sound department to have wires and microphone packs put into the costumes.

12:00 noon: Be sure all costumes are accessorized . . . i.e., bracelets, hosiery, earrings, socks, belts, etc.

12:30 P.M.: Lunch.

1:30 P.M.: Dress rehearsal.

3:30 P.M.: End of dress rehearsal. Any costumes that need altering or adjusting go back up to the workroom for attention.

4:00 P.M.: Begin setting the talent trailers with costumes for the show.

5:00 P.M.: Show is live to the East Coast.

7:00 P.M.: End of show. All talent does press.

8:00 P.M.: All costumes are wrapped from trailers.

ZACH KANE
Craft Service

Zach Kane was born in Denver, Colorado, and raised in Salt Lake City, Utah. According to him he had a simple childhood: riding his bike, eating a lot of pizza (his mom owned thirty-six Domino's Pizza stores), and getting harassed by his two older sisters.

Zach's single passion in life is baseball. He never aspired to work in the entertainment industry, and growing up, the closest he came to being exposed to Hollywood was accidentally driving by the set of *Touched by an Angel* on his way to play baseball. Little did he know that when he grew up he would be chatting with Matthew McConaughey, making Katherine Heigl gag, and winding up on the receiving end of a flirtatious January Jones.

In order to be a craft service professional, one must never get tired of answering the question, "What the hell is craft service?" It is our hope that if you ever cross paths with Zach, you'll spare him that question because after reading this chapter you will fully understand the craft behind craft service.

DAY PLAY: When a person or department is hired to work on the set of a movie or a TV show for a single day. That person is referred to as a day player.

EXTRAS: Actors who appear in the background of a scene and do not have lines. Also referred to as background actors.

KEY: The word *key* is used to describe the head or leader of any given department on set.

LOCAL UNION 479: The local workers union that is specific to entertainment in Georgia. The union represents all the "below-the-line" technicians covering several departments including craft service.

ON-SET DRESSER: The person who works within the art department and is responsible for placing the set pieces and props on the set to make the shot look as authentic as possible.

PERIOD MOVIE: A movie that is set during a historical time period.

SHOWMANCE: A romance that begins on the set of a TV show or film between two crew members that can, at times, lead to marriage.

Zach, care to answer this question one more time? What is craft service?

I can tell you what it's not. Craft service is not breakfast and it's not lunch. There are caterers who provide those meals. Craft service is the "in-between," the people who supply coffee and drinks, healthy snacks, and a variety of treats and comfort foods on the set of a movie, TV show, or commercial. At times, the craft service person will even carry medical supplies.

Wow, you provide peanut M&Ms *and* a defibrillator?

No, more along the lines of Band-Aids and tweezers.

Tell us a little bit about young Zach.

I was born in Denver, Colorado, and moved to Salt Lake City, Utah. My mom ran thirty-six Domino's Pizza stores. I had two older sisters and we had a pretty simple childhood. I played baseball throughout my childhood and through college. I was scouted and might have gone pro, but an injury my senior year ruined my chances.

Was there a certain point while you were at college when you realized you wanted to work in the entertainment industry?

Entertainment was never even a thought in my mind. I always wanted to play baseball. Salt Lake had a couple of shows shooting locally when I was growing up like *Touched by an Angel* and *The Sand Lot*. Park City was also the home of the Sundance Film Festival, but I never went.

Then how did you go from college graduate to the guy doing craft service?

It was kind of a fluke. I had a really depressing job interview in Jacksonville, Florida, to be a financial advisor with a major bank.

I got the job, but just realized that I didn't want to be strapped in a cube for the rest of my life. So I turned it down and ended up moving to Atlanta where my dad lived. My dad mentioned that a friend of a friend was looking for some help doing something called craft service on a movie set. He said the movie was called *We Are Marshall* and starred Matthew McConaughey, Matthew Fox, and January Jones. And I was like, "Ohhhhhh, yeah! That sounds really cool, I'm in!" To this day, it was the easiest job I ever got. I just made a phone call at the right time and she needed my help so I started the next day.

So what were some of the ups and downs of your first days on the job?

Well, for one, I didn't know what I was doing. Luckily I am laid back and was able to roll with it. The lady who hired me would go on store runs and be gone for hours and leave me alone to handle everything. *We Are Marshall* was the best and the worst to have as my first job because I had to learn very quickly what to do. The cast and crew were massive. We had 60 football players and about 1,200 *extras* every day. It was a *period movie*, so everyone was wearing wool clothing and it was 112-degree summer heat in Georgia. Just trying to keep the coolers filled with bottled water and ice was a constant pressure, not to mention all the food.

So were you wishing you had taken the cubicle job at this point?

No, it was hard, but I was loving it.

It is widely known in the biz that people on set will hang around the craft service area all the time. Do you find that you perform the role of shrink some of the time?

I think I am well on my way to having my degree in psychology. And here's the funny part—I'm not much of a talker. In social settings I usually keep to myself. My wife finds it so funny because I go on a movie set and I try to be quiet and do my job and people come up to me and just start talking. I'm like, "Why are you talking to me? I'm just the craft service guy!"

Have you ever had a star-struck moment?

I'm really not a star-struck kind of guy I guess, but on *We Are Marshall* we were outside at night filming the plane crash scene and this blonde woman came up to me and started talking. My boss was there, so I was trying to be polite, but at the same time I just continued working. The woman is just hanging out and talking to me and asking me questions and finally she just walked away. My boss asked if I realized that the girl was flirting with me, and I did a little bit. She asked if I recognized the girl and I said no. It was January Jones. And I was like, "Oh, (pause) damn it."

If you hadn't been such a "nose-to-the-grindstone" kind of guy and took a minute to notice, you might have ended up dating January Jones. Oh, well. So tell us, what makes a good craft service person?

I think for someone who wants to be good and get hired regularly, you really need to be focused on craft service specifically. So many times people on set do one job with hopes of getting to another. Craft service doesn't really lead to anything else, so focus on the task. It is a strange job because you work in the industry at times, but you're not really exclusive to the business. I can take my rig to a construction site or any other job site and do what I do. I don't consider myself a part of the film industry, I just work in it.

Let's talk for a second about working locally. Most people think all production is in Los Angeles or New York, but you have a fairly steady flow in Georgia and you work quite a bit throughout the year, right?

I have done well. I work about three or four movies a year and each movie runs for about twelve weeks. Then I also *day play* on commercials and TV pilots as well. If you work hard you can do well. I bought a house two months after I wrapped *We Are Marshall*. I saved up enough money because I didn't do anything but work sixteen-hour days. I didn't have time to spend money.

The film business is all about relationships and referrals. What do you do to ensure you are the guy who gets the jobs when production comes to town as opposed to your competition?

First, I make sure to get featured in a book about Hollywood success stories. (Laughs) I'm joking. The key thing is to be polite at all times. Another very important part of the job is to always be there. You need to make sure you're on set all the time. A big complaint in the film industry is that a UPM will hire a craft service person as a *key* and that person will disappear. The key will get the job and then just rotate assistants in and out during the entire shoot. This is a problem because UPMs like having faces they recognize. So I like to be polite and be visible.

How can you expand your business if you always have to be on one show?

That's an interesting catch-22 in my business. People keep telling me I should get more trucks and get more people working on multiple movies, but there is only one of me. I've seen craft service people come in with multiple trucks and multiple crews and for a couple of jobs maybe they'll be okay, but eventually the UPMs stop putting up with it. They figure they are paying you a good day rate and they expect you to be on their set, and you can't be two places at once.

Let's talk about the hourly rate for someone in your line of work.
I am part of *Local Union 479,* which is the union here in Georgia. We run an hourly rate like the rest of the crew. Movies pay about $26 an hour and an assistant would make about $24 an hour. We typically work twelve-hour days. Overtime can really add up. After the first eight hours of work we make time and a half and from twelve hours and above we make double time.

Have you ever gotten a big fat tip from somebody on set?
A tip? Yeah. "Make something without gluten." (Laughs)

People in the business often need to spend their own money and invest in their job somehow. Whether they buy tools or a trailer hitch or . . .
A twenty-foot Honda box truck that was fully equipped for $25,000.

Wow, that's a considerable investment.
If you want to be a key craft service person you need a truck or a trailer, but either will cost you. My first truck had a six-foot commercial refrigerator. On the left side there were plastic bins for the deli meats and all the cheeses, lettuce, tomato, and onions. There was a freezer, commercial coffee maker, espresso maker, hot

water maker, ten air pods, three six-foot tables, a propane oven, and storage shelves. The right side was set up like a convenience store. There were wire racks to put all the snacks in so they were organized.

That sounds pretty cool. You are literally, meals on wheels.

It was cool until the engine died. I ended up having to buy a new rig and this time I got a trailer, which I recommend over a truck. There is not as much upkeep on a trailer, on a truck you need expensive tires, the oil, gas, there's too much that can go wrong. The trailer is the way to go.

How physically demanding is your job?

It ranges. If you're on a sound stage, it isn't so bad. But if you're at a rock quarry shooting *The Walking Dead* in 110 degrees where you have to run coolers filled with ice up to the top of the hill, it can suck.

Can you give us a list of perks that come with the job?

The money is good, I'm my own boss, I'm not stuck in a cubicle, every day is different, I meet a ton of good people, and I met my wife on set.

Fishing off the company pier?

Yup, a *showmance*. She was an *on-set dresser* on the movie *Three Can Play at That Game*. We've worked on a few shows together, but since we got married we haven't worked together at all, so we don't see each other much.

You've been busy working on set with some big-name talent like Owen Wilson, Ashton Kutcher, and Katherine Heigl. Is there a celebrity moment you'd like to share? Any snack or treat that a specific celebrity prefers?

Actually yeah, on the movie *Killers* Katherine Heigl was talking to me about how much she loved this chili red pepper hot chocolate she had at her wedding. She wanted me to make it for the cast and crew, so she had a couple cases shipped down from New York. It was shipped as a dry powder and when I got it I had to add some spices and milk and heat it up. Simple, right? . . . Wrong! To this day I don't know what happened, but my assistant and I prepared it like six or seven different ways and it was the most awful hot chocolate we'd ever tasted. We tried it with regular milk, water, skim milk, two percent, I mean we tried it with whatever we could and it tasted god-awful.

Did you dare give it to Katherine?

After over an hour of trying, Katherine's assistant came over and asked if the hot chocolate was done. My assistant thought I should take it to Katherine because I'm a guy and she didn't think Katherine would get mad if a guy brought her bad hot chocolate. I thought my assistant should take it because she couldn't get mad at an assistant. In the end, I took about two or three samples, she sipped each one, gagged a little bit, and told me it was awful. But we were laughing and she was sweet about it.

Last question. Do you know CPR and have you ever had to Heimlich anyone who was choking on a snack?

(Laughs) Yes, I do know CPR, and no, I have not had to do that. And thankfully we have a medic on the set to take care of that should it ever happen.

A DAY IN THE LIFE OF ZACH KANE
While filming the TV series The Walking Dead.

4:30 A.M.: Wake up and get dressed in the dark.

5:00 A.M.: Pick up supplies for the day at the grocery store. Ice, hand fruit, soda, milk, etc.

6:00 A.M.: Arrive at set and begin to set up. Today I am on a rooftop and need to cart everything from my truck to the roof. Make coffee. Fill the coolers with drinks. Fill the snack baskets and set the craft service table up.

7:00 A.M.: The company begins to arrive.

7:30 A.M.: Already have gone through 200 pounds of ice.

9:30 A.M.: The crew ate breakfast two hours ago, so it's time for me to make a snack and pass it around for the crew. We serve a platter of green grape quesadillas with guacamole, butler style (where food is passed around on a tray) to the crew.

10:30 A.M.: I bring sandwiches to the people who special ordered them. I also make the leads two protein shakes with a spoonful of peanut butter, per their request.

11:00 A.M.: Send my assistant to the store for another 400 pounds of ice.

1:00 P.M.: While the crew is at lunch we reorganize for the second part of the day. Clean around the area and restock everything. Drain the coolers and refill with ice and beverages.

3:30 P.M.: It's time for another butler-style snack—this time it's buffalo chicken Caesar wraps and two more protein shakes with peanut butter.

4:30 P.M.: Another restock and a store run to get more supplies.

6:00 P.M.: The crew eats second meal.

7:00 P.M.: I restock coolers and snacks.

8:00 P.M.: Begin break down and clean up. I review the stock so I know what I need to buy tomorrow. Today I went through: sixty cases of water, twelve cases of Gatorade, 2,000 pounds of ice.

9:30 P.M.: That's a wrap.

11:00 P.M.: I depart location.

11:30 P.M.: I get home and go to bed. Tomorrow's call time is 6 A.M.

DAVID JANOLLARI
Head of Programming, MTV

Photo credit: Scott Gries/Picture Group

David Janollari grew up in Rhode Island. He was a popular guy who had a lot of friends. He went to Boston College for two years then transferred to NYU film school. He turned his sights on Hollywood, and a few of his loyal friends went along for the ride. David owes a lot to these friends, especially Rachel, Phoebe, Joey, Chandler, Monica, and Ross. Do we need to play this out any further or have you figured out by now that Mr. Janollari had a hand in creating the hit show, *M*A*S*H*? Kidding, he was the studio exec who helped get *Friends* on the air.

David is as unique in his work philosophy as he is successful. While a lot of his peers work themselves into the ground, literally, David takes time off to recharge his batteries and clear his head. We're not talking about a week or two, we're talking years. For most, such a departure would be career death. But for David, well, he did end up *Six Feet Under*, the only difference was he was holding an Emmy!

In a career that has spanned nearly three decades, David has seen the business from every angle. He's gone from studio executive to network president to cofounder of a successful production company to his latest endeavor as head of programming at MTV. In this chapter, David doesn't hold back. He talks about the time Academy Award–winner Alan Ball delivered the perfect script, how a career-changing revelation occurred at Tavern on the Green, and how Jami Gertz and Tea Leoni turned down starring roles in one of the biggest shows in TV history. He even opens up about Jennifer Aniston's taste in men.

AMERICAN BEAUTY: A 1999 movie written by Alan Ball and directed by Sam Mendes. Ball was nominated for an Oscar in the Best Screenplay category.

DEVELOPMENT: Every studio, network, and production company has a development department that "develops" material with the goal of getting it on the air. There are often separate drama, comedy, and reality development departments under the same roof.

OVERALL DEAL: A writer, producer, or actor can be signed to an overall deal by a production company or studio. That artist is then locked in for a period of time during which he or she develops material exclusively for that company or studio with the hope of making a sale.

PITCH: A writer or producer "pitches" or proposes his or her idea for a TV show to the studio and/or network with the hope of making a sale.

PRODUCTION ASSISTANT (PA): An entry-level position in the TV and film business, also known as a gofer. There are office PAs and set PAs. In general they assist production in every capacity, from delivering scripts to getting coffee for the director.

PRODUCTION COMPANY: In TV, a production company is an independent entity that develops material to sell to networks. That company is then responsible for the day-to-day production of a TV show. For example, the hit show *Law & Order* is produced by Dick Wolf Productions.

SITCOM: This is short for "situation comedy," which is a TV show that's often thirty minutes in length.

SUPER 8: A film format first released in 1965 by Kodak that improved upon the older "regular" 8 mm home movie format.

UPFRONTS: A once-a-year event where TV network executives announce their Fall primetime schedule to advertisers, who are all gathered in New York City. This typically occurs during the third week of May.

You grew up in Rhode Island, which is famous for, uh, well, it's famous for the fact that you grew up there. Was there a defining moment during your youth when you were drawn to the entertainment world?

I was one of those guys who always had a camera in his hand. I always envisioned myself in the entertainment industry. I think very specifically I thought I was a feature film director. That was kind of the goal. So I made little films and read *Super 8* filmmaker magazines and even started a film club in my high school.

Talk about your first job.

Back in 1984, while I was a student at NYU film school, I got the proverbial "foot in the door" with Nederlander Television and Film Productions, which was an offshoot of the iconic theater organization. I was an intern in their TV department making forty bucks a week and did everything from getting coffee for executives to running errands to answering phones. It was an amazing experience because I was able to observe and learn and it didn't take long for me to rise up through the ranks. After five years I became head of their *development* department and my career as a TV executive began.

Did you find that working within this organization known mostly for theater gave you a certain edge?

Approaching TV through theater was actually one of the things that helped set us apart from others in the creative community who were pitching and developing TV shows at that time. I was in a unique position to learn the business and forge relationships from a different point of view. At the time, we were attempting to develop and sell comedy projects. Because the Nederlander organization was rooted in theater, I had this entrée into theater writers, a niche pool of writers who weren't necessarily being mined by Hollywood. I ended up working with playwrights Chris Durang and Wendy Wasserstein and the young up-and-comers like Marta Kauffman and David Crane.

So you met Marta and David while they were still playwrights. Thank you for pulling them over to TV. Could you imagine if *Friends* was a play on Broadway? [The scary thing is, you know someone in Hollywood just read this and thought, *Friends* on Broadway, what a great idea!]

(Laughs) You're welcome. I was deeply rooted in the theater world and would see theater five, six nights a week. It gave me such an incredible base of understanding of a really particular group of writers and actors who had previously been untapped.

In 1989 you decided to forgo both the hustle and the bustle of New York and you headed out to Los Angeles. What motivated the move?

I realized that the business was mostly in Los Angeles. So I left my job with Nederlander Television and Film Productions when I was twenty-five and moved to L.A. I called a bunch of my contacts and had four job interviews set up, and I got four job offers. The one I chose was director of comedy development at Fox. I spent two years there, and that was a great way, in terms of profile and platform, to meet as many people as quickly as possible. I grew my profile in the community, and then Les Moonves, who was running what was Lorimar Productions, which would then become part of Warner Brothers Television, hired me. They had shows like *Full House* and *Step by Step* and *Family Matters*, and Les wanted me to get them a bigger comedy presence. Ultimately I spent six years at Lorimar and it was there that I got the opportunity to put on *Hangin' with Mr. Cooper* and *Living Single*, among other hits.

Your New York relationships started to pay off as well. Talk about how *Friends* came about.

It was the early nineties and *Melrose Place* was the big hit on Fox at the time, and I loved it; I couldn't miss an episode. I kept saying, "This is really cool, there should be a comedy version of this." So Marta Kauffman and David Crane came up with *Friends*, and it was completely based on their circle of friends growing up in the early days in New York City. They came up with the *pitch* and it was truly one of the great pitches of all time. Because they came from theater they were very performance-oriented and they pitched like nobody else. We actually pitched it to Fox first because they were the younger-skewing network. They liked it, they got it, but they just didn't step up to the plate and make the right offer, so we took it to NBC and there was just no looking back. That was the perfect home for the show. I don't think we pitched it anywhere else after NBC.

Can you talk about the casting process?

As the development executive I was involved with every aspect of the show. Once the script was developed we had the daunting task of casting it. Up to that point in my career, casting *Friends* was one of the hardest shows I'd had to cast. Matthew Perry and Jennifer Aniston were the last two we found. Jon Cryer was first considered for the role of Chandler. He was very good. We offered the role of Monica to Tea Leoni and offered Rachel to Jamie Gertz. Both of them passed. We saw Courtney Cox as Rachel, but she kept insisting she was Monica. She'd tell us, I *am* Monica, I'm this mother figure in real life. And I remember looking at the producers at one point and I said, "Look, why don't we just have her come in and read for Monica?" Then I got a call from them after seeing her and they went, "Courtney's right. She *is* Monica." The rest of the story everyone knows. The show went on to become one of the most successful *sitcoms* of all time. It was on air for ten years, won five Emmys and a Golden Globe. It sent the careers of the six principal actors into the stratosphere.

After *Friends* you headed up other big hits like *The Drew Carey Show* and *Suddenly Susan.* Then you made a pretty bold move.

Bold, but exciting. I started my own *production company* with my friend Bob Greenblatt, who's currently chairman of NBC Entertainment. Bob and I were sitting at the *upfront* celebration in New York at Tavern on the Green in 1997. At that time Bob was executive vice president at Fox and I had just put two shows on the Fox schedule. We were both at this party and we kind of looked at each other and said, "This should seem like more fun." You know, I was running Warner Brothers studio and he was running the network. The demand of our jobs called for us to have so many shows in development, so many pilots, and we were both running around trying to service everything. It's impossible to really get as much in the trenches as you'd like when you are spread so thin. We thought there's got to be a better way to do this, to build a better machine that concentrates on fewer projects but gives those projects extra attention. So the idea for the Greenblatt Janollari Studio came out of that conversation.

You were developing and selling shows and also partnering with some pretty amazing talent. Tell us about your partnership with Alan Ball.

We signed Alan to an *overall deal*. We sat down with him to talk about the kind of shows he wanted to do and we turned him loose. He went off and wrote a pilot for a show called *Oh Grow Up*, which we sold to ABC. We made thirteen episodes, but the series was cancelled before all the episodes aired. That show was Alan's baby and he took the cancellation really hard. Alan took a month off after the cancellation and went back to his home in Georgia. When he came back to L.A. he had the pilot for *Six Feet Under* written.

We ended up taking the show to HBO at around the same time *American Beauty* was nominated for best screenplay. The day after the Oscar nominations came out, HBO called us and said they wanted to make the pilot. Bob and I were shocked; this never happens. Usually a pilot has to go through an entire process before it gets picked up. We told HBO that we can't just make a pilot; *Six Feet Under* was a big piece of business. So they stepped up and made a substantial deal.

Chris Albrecht, who was president at the time, approved thirteen episodes. Bob and I were astonished; they weren't even going to test it. They told us they loved it and wanted us to make the series immediately. That was a real conviction of passion.

After a good run, you and Bob decided to amicably part ways, and you moved on to become the president of the WB Network.
I became president in 2004, of the network, which was a joint venture between Warner Brothers and Tribune Broadcasting. I think I was, in a way, their last-ditch effort to kind of drum up some kind of success on the programming front. I wish I'd known how dire the situation was before I began. I launched shows like *Supernatural* and *Beauty and the Geek*, which were fairly big hits for the network, but ultimately, the network shut down in 2006 and merged with UPN to become what is now the CW Television Network.

So you took some time off and then started your newest venture as the head of scripted development for MTV. You were quickly promoted to head of programming. Are you enjoying it so far?
MTV is a new and fun adventure in my career. I love the brand, I grew up on the brand. We're in a world now where the network has evolved largely into a reality destination and the idea is to get back to its roots.

So you're going to start airing music videos again?
(Laughs) No, we're getting back into creating more scripted content. Our theory is, let's put the MTV brand on some scripted series and

see if we can offer our audience, who looks to MTV to be ahead of the curve, some entertainment on all fronts.

What advice do you have for anyone out there wanting to be the next David Janollari?

If you are starting out and you want to be an executive in the TV business, there are multiple ways to go about it. Get a *production assistant* job any way you can. Get your foot in the door and start observing the process. You can learn a lot of things in film school but the practicality of how the business works and the dynamics between agents and producers and managers and how they all work together you really have to learn from inside to understand it.

What characteristics should a person possess who is looking to get into your field?

First and foremost, you really have to have a passion and you have to really believe this is what you want. This is a very competitive business, with a lot of people who want to be in it from every angle—actor, director, producer, executive. You have to be decisive. Identify what aspect you're most interested in, then get on that track as soon as you can. If you go the executive route, you have to know that the business is filled with fragile yet strong egos. Actors and writers are putting themselves out there, and I think the mistake too many people make is that they need to speak the language of the artist as opposed to the language of the network or studio. You have to foster creative dialogue, and that's something you learn by trial and error.

A lot of people in entertainment never unplug or decompress from the grind of the business. You have a different philosophy. Can you discuss your approach?

The theory is there's more to life than just slaving away. I have traveled around the world numerous times. After the WB went down, I took a lot of time off. For the better part of four years I traveled the world extensively. It was fun and relaxing in a kind of "take a deep breath" way. I got to reconnect with friends and family. I was very fortunate that I'd done well enough in those years that I could afford to take off. I totally acknowledge that. I think it should be part of everybody's thinking to some degree to really step back and enjoy and to take a picture of life. I think it only adds to your creativity. If nothing else, it refreshes you in a way that you can get re-energized and be creative again.

Last but not least, if Jennifer Aniston were a cartoon, would she date Beavis or Butthead?

(Laughs) Neither.

A DAY IN THE LIFE OF DAVID JANOLLARI

The following is an excerpt from David's schedule for one weekday in 2010.

7:00 A.M.: Woke up. Viewed recent cut of *Teen Wolf*, gave notes. Read recent draft of *I Just Want My Pants Back* (new scripted show in development at MTV) to prepare for casting session.

9:00 A.M.: Joined the daily commuters of Los Angeles for my trip to the office and "rolled calls" from the car.

10:00 A.M.: Development meeting with staff. Covered "weekend read" and status of projects in development.

11:00 A.M.: Attended the bi-coastal macro programming senior management weekly meeting via videoconference.

12:15 P.M.: *Emmy* magazine phone interview (from the car en route to lunch) regarding the rebranding and reconfiguring of MTV.

12:30 P.M.: Lunch with Randy Jackson.

2:30 P.M.: Pitch meeting with Bo Burnham, a young rising-star comedian. Great idea!

3:30 P.M.: Marketing update meeting with press and marketing department representatives regarding our comedy series *The Hard Times of RJ Berger*.

5:00 P.M.: Viewed *Skins* pilot cut to give notes.

9:00 P.M.: *Jersey Shore* wrap party.

TAMMY ADER GREEN
Show Runner/Executive Producer/Writer

Tammy Ader Green always knew she wanted to write. She was the kid who wrote plays and staged them in her backyard and the teenager who went off to college to become an English Lit major. That's where her story takes a bit of a left turn.

While at college she switched majors, became pre-med, got accepted to med school, then quit in under a week. Heard this story before? We didn't think so.

Yes, on the road to becoming a successful TV writer and show runner, Tammy made a pit stop at med school. And although she didn't become a doctor, it turns out the medical profession has played a big part in her life. For one thing, it provided the backdrop for what is arguably her greatest professional triumph—the hit medical drama

Strong Medicine. It also played a lead role in introducing her to the Johns Hopkins ER doctor who would eventually become her husband. If you want more details you're going to have to read her story. Who knows? It might inspire you to fill out a med school application and begin your own journey toward becoming a successful TV writer and show runner.

AGENT: A person who secures jobs and negotiates deals on behalf of their client. They receive a 10 percent commission for their services.

BREAKING A STORY: The process of laying out the story of an episode in acts. What are the major story points in each act? How does each act lead to the next? Etc.

EXECUTIVE PRODUCER: In television, the executive producer is generally the CEO of the company. He or she is usually a writer who moved up through the ranks and may also have been the creator of the show he or she is executive producing.

EXECUTIVE STORY EDITOR: A staff writing job that typically comes after the staff writer and story editor positions.

FREELANCE: A freelance writer is generally not part of the writing staff on a particular TV show. He or she typically works up a pitch to land a job freelancing a script for an existing series.

HIP-POCKETED: Being informally represented as a writer by a literary agent without signing with that agent. The agent will attempt to get the writer work, and if successful, may sign him or her to the agency.

PITCH MEETINGS: Meetings where a writer attempts to sell an idea. This may be a pitch made to an executive producer of an existing show for an episode or a pitch to a network executive to sell a new TV show.

PRODUCER, SUPERVISING PRODUCER, COEXECU-TIVE PRODUCER: These are all staff writing positions that have a certain hierarchy. Once you've been a producer on a show, your next job can be supervising producer and so on. All of these promotions come with a bigger paycheck.

PRODUCTION COORDINATOR: A production office position in the TV and film business. A production coordinator is the link between the production office and the set. Among other tasks, he or she makes sure everyone has copies of the latest script, puts out schedules, orders equipment, and coordinates travel and accommodations for actors.

STAFF JOB: As a writer, a staff job means you are signed on to work for a certain period of time, at which point the executive producer may terminate your employment or keep you on indefinitely.

SYNDICATE: To be sold to multiple individual stations outside of a broadcast network. It used to be that a TV show would syndicate after 100 episodes, but that has since changed.

TRADES: Magazines and other industry publications such as *Variety* or *The Hollywood Reporter* that report on the goings-on in the industry from a business and a creative standpoint.

Tell us the story of Tammy Ader Green from "fade-in."

Well, I think I always knew I wanted to be a writer. I grew up in Los Angeles, and as a kid I was the one writing plays, casting the neighborhood kids, staging them in my back yard, and charging their parents a quarter to see them.

That'd probably be $5 in today's market, right?

At least. So I had a typical childhood, grew up and went to Brandeis University, where I was an English Lit major. But at a certain point I switched majors and became pre-med.

Pre-med? Strange choice for someone who wants to become a writer, no?

Well, I wanted to be a writer, but I had no idea how to do that. Everyone at college was either going to become a lawyer or a doctor or go into the family business, and I was very driven and very ambitious and I knew I wanted to succeed. I had no idea how to become a writer, but it was crystal clear how to become a doctor. So I switched majors, continued for two more years, got accepted to a school in Chicago and drove cross-country with my dad in my little blue Mazda.

What happened next?

Well, I'm normally a very happy person. From the second I got my first acceptance to med school I immediately got depressed. Then, sitting in class my first week I was completely overwhelmed by the feeling that I'd made a huge mistake. I looked around the room and realized that everyone there wanted to be a doctor more than anything else, but I wanted to be a writer. My professor handed out the syllabus and said you need to read to chapter whatever by Friday, and I thought to myself, *No I don't because by Friday I won't be here.* With the syllabus in hand I got up, walked out, went straight into the bathroom and threw up. And here's the funny part: I was so distraught I didn't even realize I'd walked into the men's room. Then, I went to the dean's office and quit. Later, and this is a metaphor for my life at that exact moment, I walked into the parking structure sobbing, unable to find my car. I walked in circles for what seemed like hours wondering where I was supposed to be.

You obviously found your way out. What then?

I called my parents. My dad flew to Chicago to try to change my mind. He couldn't. I don't think he forgave me until he saw my first "written by" credit on screen. My mother, on the other hand, never thought I wanted to be a doctor. When I asked her why she didn't tell me that in the first place, she said, "When your daughter tells you she wants to go to medical school, you don't try and stop her."

So did you have a game plan at this point?

I was determined to write in television, so I got a job as a waitress and I would read the *trades* every day. But I wouldn't go to the jobs section because everyone was doing that. Instead I'd read the articles to find out who was starting something or what producer just got an overall deal at some studio. Then I'd call that person and ask if they were hiring. In the end I landed a production assistant job through an old college friend who happened to come into the restaurant where I was working. This college friend, Caroline Baron, who today is a producer with credits like *Capote* among other things, knew some people in the entertainment industry. She helped get me a job with a company that mostly did low-budget films. I worked on a movie there and I ended up meeting people who ultimately became producers of *The Wonder Years*. They hired me to be the *production coordinator* of that show.

So in a year you went from med school student to waitress to production coordinator. At what point did you add writer to your resume?

While I was working on *The Wonder Years*, I wrote my first spec script for the show *thirtysomething*. When I was done, I showed my script to Neal Marlens and Carol Black, who were the executive producers of *The Wonder Years*, and they told me it was good. Up to that point, no one had ever told me that I was good at writing. They gave me a note here and there on the script, but mostly they gave me confidence that I could do this. And then, Jeff Silver, who was a producer on my show, knew Marshall Herskovitz, the cocreator of *thirtysomething*, and got my script to him.

It pays to know people. We're guessing that was a good move?

It was. One day, I was sitting at my desk in the production office when the receptionist yelled out, "Marshall Herskovitz is on the phone for you!" I picked up the phone and there he was on the other end, telling me that he doesn't like anything, but he liked my script. He then went on to say that they just hired an actress by the name of Patricia Kalember, who was going to play the girlfriend of Peter Horton, one of the principal characters. After she was hired, and much to everyone's surprise, they found out she was pregnant. So they needed to write a script that took her pregnancy into account, and since all the other writers were off writing other episodes, he wanted to give me the job. So I worked with Marshall on the outline, went home, and wrote two drafts, and then they told me to go away and completely rewrote the script.

I would tell any budding TV writer to be prepared to be completely rewritten. That was devastating to me, but that's how it works. The bottom line, however, is that phone call changed my life and the experience taught me a lot about structure, story, and character that I still use today. That was really the start of my writing career. I left *The Wonder Years*; actually they jokingly "fired" me and told me to go home and write.

Did you get an *agent* at that point?

Yes. And here's a little piece of advice. After my first script, I was *hip-pocketed* by two different agents. But I came to find out you're never supposed to work with two agents from competing agencies. One day I got a phone call from John Wells, show runner for series like

E.R. and *The West Wing.* He had read my *thirtysomething* script and wanted to talk to me about writing for his show *China Beach*, but he didn't know who to call because my script appeared on his desk from two different agents. So he decided to call me directly. I didn't get the writing gig. What I got instead was a scolding by my agents.

Ultimately, I went with Beth Uffner from an agency called Broder, Kurland, Webb and Uffner, who I stayed with for a number of years. Right away, Beth got me *pitch meetings* for *freelance* work. The first freelance episode I sold was for *Quantum Leap.* I ended up selling eight scripts that year, which is a lot. I've since learned, having been on both sides of a pitch, that pitching is really an important skill and something every writer needs to learn how to do well.

So you've been schooled by your agent and you're pitching your heart out. We're sensing another big break.

That year led to my first *staff job* on *Manhattan Nights*, which was created by my dear friend Robin Green, who I'm still friends with today. Robin was one of the executive producers of *The Sopranos*, and has many other credits, including *Blue Bloods* on CBS. My second staff-writing job was on a show called *WIOU*, which lasted a season, and then I landed a job as an *executive story editor* on *The Commish*, a successful police drama starring Michael Chiklis. I remember my first day of work there very well. *The Commish* was produced by Stephen J. Cannell Productions, the same company that was doing male-centric shows like *The A-Team* and *Wiseguy*. Here I was, this young female writer and this was my first big staff writing job. I was all excited, and I walked into the building, not knowing where I was going. A security guard stopped me and I said, "I'm here for my first day of work." He pointed me to Human Resources assuming I was hired to be a secretary. For the next eight years I moved up the ladder from executive story editor to *coproducer* to *supervising producer* to *coexecutive producer*.

I wrote for popular shows like *Sisters* and *Party of Five*, and other lesser-known shows like *Going to Extremes* and *The Big Easy*.

How did *Strong Medicine* come about?

In 1999, I was in the writers' room of *Party of Five* breaking a story when my agent called and told me Whoopi Goldberg wanted to meet me. She had an overall deal at Sony, as did I, and she wanted to discuss an idea she had for a show. So I went to her house and Whoopi, who was extremely gracious, discussed her idea of creating a medical drama that focused on women and women's health issues. She wanted to create a show that focused on women at a time when gender-specific medicine was booming. The more I thought about it, the more interested I became.

I went off and worked up a pitch, and then, largely because of Whoopi's schedule, I don't think I met with her again until the following year. She liked the pitch, and we went to Lifetime, where I sold it in the room. I wrote the pilot episode that summer, we shot it, of course not knowing if it would go to series. Then, a little while later, I was in my kitchen when I got the phone call from Dawn Ostroff, then head of programming at Lifetime, who said she loved the pilot and wanted to go ahead with the series. She said she thought they had the next hit show and believed it would become the signature show for the network. She was right. It became the highest-rated basic cable drama, the first cable show to *syndicate*, and the first to go more than 100 episodes.

Creating a successful series must be incredibly rewarding. What was that experience like for you?

Really incredible. Being a show runner is like being a CEO of a huge company. You've got hundreds of people working for you. There are incredible highs and incredible lows. Working with Whoopi was also great. She was wonderfully supportive. She was there for anything I wanted, she did publicity for the show, gave me her thoughts and notes, but she never wanted to step on my toes. In fact, when it came time for credits I remember Whoopi saying, "Couldn't it just read, 'created by Tammy Ader from a notion by Whoopi Goldberg?'" In the end, the credits read, "created by Tammy Ader and developed by Whoopi Goldberg."

We teased it a bit in your intro, so can you tell readers how *Strong Medicine* led to your meeting the doctor who would become your husband?

I was writing an episode and I needed some information for an ER scene, fast. So I called the best ER in the country, Johns Hopkins in Baltimore, and I kid you not, my future husband answered the phone. That random phone call led to many more phone calls, to finally meeting and starting up a cross-country relationship. Eventually, we got married. I always say I met my husband literally sitting at my desk, and that was the only way I could have met him because I was working so hard, I never left my desk.

What's ahead for you?

I live in Baltimore now, but I keep my career alive by coming to L.A. every so often and pitching show ideas. I also keep my creative self fulfilled with smaller niche projects. I teach writing classes, for example. But my focus now is on family. We've adopted a baby.

Sounds like a Hollywood ending. What advice do you have for someone who would love to do what you do for a living?

The great thing about writing is you just need a desk and a computer. So my first piece of advice to any writer is to just write. Get your hands on some scripts to learn the format, study the show you want to write for, learn the characters inside and out, and figure out the kinds of stories they tell. Make sure that the first script you show people in the industry is the best one you've ever written. And it should be the best, because it'll come from the heart. If it's really good, I believe you're going to work. TV is an insatiable machine that constantly needs to be fed.

One last question. How would you have fared as a doctor?

The world is lucky I became a writer instead.

A DAY IN THE LIFE OF TAMMY ADER GREEN

A day on Strong Medicine.

5:30–8:00 A.M.: Wake up. Work on a script. (I have to do all my writing before I get to work, because I never have time once I get there.)

9:00 A.M.: Arrive at work.

9:30 A.M.–1:00 P.M.: Have a story meeting with the writers. (We break a story, meaning we figure out what would happen in a particular episode.)

1:00 P.M.–2:00 P.M.: Have lunch with the crew on set.

2:00 P.M.–3:00 P.M.: Have a tone meeting with director John Flynn. (A tone meeting is where you go over every single scene and every word in an upcoming script to ensure the director understands what is intended.)

3:00 P.M.–3:30 P.M.: Sit in on a casting session for an upcoming episode with casting director Lori Sugar.

3:30 P.M.–4:00 P.M.: Meet with Janine Turner (star of the show) to talk about a story point in an upcoming episode.

4:10 P.M.: Take a call from a network executive who works in broadcast standards to say he has concerns about a scene in an upcoming script.

4:15 P.M.–6:00 P.M.: Work with the editor and Joe DiOlivera, post-production producer, on a show that has already shot.

6:00 P.M.–6:30 P.M.: Have dinner.

7:00 P.M.–8:30 P.M.: Go to the set to watch a scene with a very good new young actress. (Turns out it was Dakota Fanning. This was her first line on film.)

9:00 P.M.: Go home.

KEVIN CLASH
Puppeteer/Creator and Voice of Elmo

Photo credit: TM and © Sesame Workshop. All Rights Reserved.
Photo credit: Nate Langford.

Kevin Clash grew up in Baltimore, Maryland. He was an average kid who did average kid things. He went to school, studied, built puppets, and while still in his teens was performing on *The Great Space Coaster*, *Captain Kangaroo,* and *Sesame Street*. You know, average kid stuff.

To say that Kevin is the rock star of the puppeteering world is to not give him enough credit. He's Elvis! His claim to fame fits in a carry-on bag and was nothing more than an ensemble Muppet on *Sesame Street* before Kevin got a hold of him and literally brought this character to life. For the last twenty-five years, Elmo and Kevin have been inseparable. Whether they are performing with major celebrities like Robert De Niro or traveling the world meeting fans of all ages, they are both making history.

Some people in the entertainment industry have all the luck, and things are dropped in their lap. Kevin's story is different . . . he's worked hard to get where he is, even though he was always poised for greatness. For the record, Elmo wasn't dropped in his lap either . . . he was thrown at him from across a room.

IMPROV: Short for "improvisation." This is the art of reacting in the moment and playing out a scene or situation without the use of a script.

MUPPETS: Muppets are puppet characters that were built and created by legendary puppeteer Jim Henson. It has been reported that Jim created the word by combining *marionette* and *puppet*. Others report that Jim fabricated the story and really just liked the way "Muppet" sounded.

VOICE LESSONS: Classes taken by singers, voice-over artists, and other professionals who rely on speaking or singing. The lessons include, but are not limited to: voice warm-ups, voice technique, strengthening exercises, breathing techniques, microphone technique, and vocal health care.

Kevin, let's start with the story of how you and the little red monster met.

Elmo, Elmo, Elmo. Here's how it happened. One of the main Muppeteers for Jim Henson, named Richard Hunt, was given the red one by another fellow puppeteer who left to pursue his acting and writing career. Richard didn't like performing the youngness of the character and his plate was already full performing other *Muppets*. So one day I was alone in the Muppeteer greenroom, where we would all hang out, and Richard walked in. He said to me, "You think you got a voice for this? and I said, "I'll try something." So he tossed this fur ball across the room, I caught him and put him on, and did the falsetto voice, that was it.

That's the same way Sonny met Cher. What about the voice? Did it take you months to come up with what Elmo would sound like?

Immediate, it was immediate. There is no crystal ball, it either clicks or it doesn't. With Elmo and me, it clicked. I came up with the voice right there and Richard took me to Lisa Simon, the producer at the time, and I did the voice for her and she was fine with it. That's how I got Elmo. Fortunately for me, everyone who was watching the show at the time connected with the character. The only thing that has changed with Elmo was the primitive way he spoke. When I first started with him his speech was really broken up and very simple. Now he speaks in full sentences.

What was the motivation for the change?

For teaching purposes, so the children can really understand what Elmo's saying and the children learn from Elmo while he is learning.

Talk to us about your childhood and your influences as a kid.

Growing up I was watching a lot of Warner Brothers cartoons, *Captain Kangaroo*, and then locally in Maryland, a show called *Hodge, Podge, Lodge*, but my main focus was watching *Sesame Street*. I was ten years old when it came on PBS in 1969/70.

Sesame Street really glued me to the TV and got me interested in puppets. I was interested in performing with them, but I also wanted to learn how to build them. I began building puppets at ten, and I taught myself how to use them and then began performing live shows around my neighborhood and incorporating my puppets into school projects.

So you started making a name for yourself?

I was just having fun with it, but it just so happened that the principal's secretary at my school saw me perform and told one of her friends, a writer at the local newspaper, about me. I was interviewed, and when the article came out people started calling me to do shows. I started to perform at the Heritage Fair and City Fair, and all around Baltimore. Lucky for me, a very talented man by the name of Stu Kerr saw me perform and asked my mom if I could come in and audition for him for a new local children's program called *Caboose*. That audition turned into my first job on TV.

That had to have been exciting being on TV at such a young age.

It was a blast, and Stu was a great teacher. Every Friday my dad would drive me to the studio, and I would perform my puppets on the show and it just took off from there. Stu ended up getting a tape of my work to a friend of his in New York, who just happened to be Bob Keeshan (Captain Kangaroo). Bob and his writers liked what they saw and asked me to do some guest spots on the show. I loved working on *Captain Kangaroo*, but I still had my sights set on *Sesame Street*. Locally I watched a show called *Call It Macaroni*, and Kermit Love, one of Jim Henson's colleagues who helped design and build Snuffleupagus and Big Bird, was featured on the show. I asked my mom if she would call PBS and track Kermit down so I could call him. She was great, she got the number and I left him a message, and believe it or not, Kermit called me back. He said whenever I am in New York I could come over to the studio and meet him. Fortunately, in twelfth grade I took a class trip to New York and I met with him. They had already cast the puppeteers for the season, so he told me he would keep me in mind for the next year.

Forget about climbing the ladder to success, you were on an escalator. From back yards, to street fairs, to local TV, and then national TV, all before you graduated high school.

I was juggling a lot. I had regular guest spots on *Captain* and was going up to New York all the time to tape. Kermit had kept his word about keeping me in mind, because the people from *Sesame Street* invited me up to do a couple of shows. Then shortly after, Kermit turned me on to another program that was starting called *The Great Space Coaster*, and I started doing puppets for them as well. At the age of like nineteen I actually had three shows I was working on simultaneously.

At the age of nineteen Keith was trying to keep his acne flare-ups in check, but we digress. So talk a bit about your experience as the new guy on the *Street*.

I would perform with whatever puppet they needed me to work. I could get a pig one day and a monster the next. Around the same time I started, Jim Henson and Frank Oz were already doing *The Muppet Show* and getting ready to get into the movie business, so they weren't really at *Sesame Street* that much. I was hired because Jim was looking to groom a new crop of young puppeteers. The show was trying out new characters on us. There was Hoots the Owl, a seventy-five-year-old jazz musician who just happened to be an owl. I did pretty good with him, but they would constantly have us try out new characters.

Talk about your process for developing characters and finding the voice.

The process is a little different each time. When I got Hoots that was a voice that was in my range and that I thought was hip and fun for an older jazz musician. For Elmo, the writers were saying in the scripts he was very young, so I knew it had to be kind of a high falsetto voice. Baby Sinclair on the TV show *Dinosaurs* was a brat, so that voice had to have a little mischievousness to it. When I did Splinter for *The Mutant Ninja Turtles* I knew he was a *very* old man from Japan so I took Edward James Olmos's coolness from *Miami Vice* and a bit of Pat Morita's sense of humor from *Karate Kid* and I put those two characters together. Richard Hunt, again that main puppeteer from *Sesame Street*, was really funny. He would say, "I'm going to do voice number fifty-six of my repertoire of voices," and we would all laugh knowing we all only have about five voices, which we change around.

What are some of the voices?

Basically, I have a falsetto voice, a gravelly voice, a little boy's voice, a little girl's voice, and a couple of monster voices. That's my base, and from those voices I can create different-sounding voices. Take Frank Oz. Frank could do Miss Piggy and then he'll put a little gravelly voice on it and it sounds like Grover. One good piece of advice that I learned from Jim Henson is the voice is always secondary to the character. Jim explained that the personality of the character comes first and then the voice.

As part of Elmo's character you made him laugh a lot, but there was a producer on staff who wanted you to eliminate the laugh. How did that go down?

I went out to lunch with the producer, Lisa Simon, and she said point blank, "I think the laugh you are doing is too much." So

I said okay and came back and worked the character, and I just couldn't have that character *not* laugh. I respected her opinion, but I kept the laugh!

Yeah, Tickle Me Elmo without the laughter would just be sad. Share some good advice you received.

The best advice I received was from Frank Oz, who told me not to hold back from being silly, not to worry about the lines, and have as much fun as I possibly can.

Talk about some of the demanding aspects of your job.

The puppeteer is not to be seen so that always puts us in challenging positions. Oscar the Grouch lives in a trash can, that means that Carroll Spinny is in there also. Snuffy is worked by two puppeteers, mainly performed by Martin P. Robinson, and the back end of Snuffy is performed by Bryant Young. Not the easiest puppet to perform.

The year during the Tickle Me Elmo craze I was doing a lot of press interviews and it was very cold out. I was running around nonstop, and I was having difficulties doing Elmo's voice. I saw a vocal coach, showed a tape of how I perform, and she said, "Oh my God, you can't do that." I said, "Well, I can't be a puppeteer if I can't do that," and she replied, "You're closing up here" and blah, blah, blah. I said, "That's how you puppeteer!" She told me, "Well, you won't be able to do that for long!" (Laughs)

I'm still doing it. I do have limits, though, I can only do Elmo's voice for three hours before the falsetto starts to not sound right. You find ways to make it work so you're not permanently damaging yourself.

Who are some memorable celebrities you encountered working on *Sesame Street*?

It's really a lot of fun meeting celebrities through *Sesame Street* because nine times out of ten they either grew up watching the show or they found the show again because now they have kids. Even Robert De Niro came to the set to tape a segment and brought his kids with him. They got a chance to look around and were in awe. He'd say, "That's Mr. Hooper's store; oh, that's Oscar's can! Look, there's Big Bird's nest!" What other show provides that sort of connection and welcoming environment? So it's really cool, there's never any attitude because they already know this is not Hollywood, it's *Sesame Street*!

There have been some wonderful moments. Tracy Chapman came in to sing and she was so happy she started crying while she was singing. Danny DeVito stopped everything and got on the steps of "123" and thanked the crew and the cast for all we had done for his children over the years. They come in with this wonderful love for the show and we appreciate it.

Arguably one of the most classic moments was with Paul Simon and this little child sitting on the steps of "123" singing "Me and Julio Down by the School Yard." Paul's playing and all of a sudden this little girl starts riffing off of the song and just shuts him up. He continued on the guitar and she just felt the music. It was an amazing moment that gives me chills just talking about it. On the set we all felt the buzz and the raw energy of that moment and afterwards the crew started clapping and Simon, he was just blown away by her. Nobody expected it, it wasn't scripted, it just happened. You can't write that. The essence of a child is right there, all you can do is get out of the way and let it happen.

You have one of the coolest jobs in the business. So how should someone prepare who wants to get into your line of work?

There are some very practical things that someone can do. Get a camera and connect the camera to your TV so you can watch your puppet on your TV. That is how you learn to perfect performing a puppet for television. I also recommend acting lessons, *voice lessons*, *improv*, all are important. The key is to expose yourself to as many forms of entertainment as you can. That will help you with all the different things you have to do to create a character.

Do people in your profession make a fairly good living being a puppeteer?

Yes. I think in the seventies and eighties there was more happening in the way of puppets on children's programming, but there has always been a fairly steady amount of work. You can definitely make a comfortable living.

Is there such a thing as an apprenticeship in your line of work?

We don't really have an apprentice program. The best way to let us know about you is by sending a DVD of your work. I get a kick out of seeing kids out there who really want to do this for a living.

Kevin you have been talking nonstop. Why don't you take a break so we can have some time with Elmo. Do you mind?

No, not at all. Here he is.

Hey, Elmo, nice to meet you. We have been talking to Kevin for quite a bit and we were hoping to get some last words from you. Any last words?

Elmo: Any last words? (Stops talking, pauses, and giggles.) Let Elmo see. He loves all of you very, very much. And always have fun with whatever you do, it's very important. (Laughs)

Would Elmo like to share any secrets he has about Kevin?

Elmo: Sometimes Kevin's hands are cold. (Laughs) Elmo has tried to tell him about that, but he doesn't listen.

On that note, we'll say goodbye. Thank you, Elmo.

Elmo: You're welcome. Bye, bye. (Laughs)

A DAY IN THE LIFE OF KEVIN CLASH

5:30 A.M.: Get a call from trainer at home. Ignore call.

5:35 A.M.: Get a call from trainer on cell phone. Ignore call.

6:00 A.M.: Wake up, brush teeth. Avoid looking at self in the mirror.

6:30 A.M.: Eat breakfast that nutritionist advised me not to eat.

7:00 A.M.: Watch *The Today Show*.

8:00 A.M.: Call with my personal assistant, Kimi, to go through that day's schedule.

9:30 A.M.: Get picked up and head to the recording studio to record audio tracks for new toys.

11:30 A.M.: Break to eat lunch—something that tastes good. Think of nutritionist again.

1:00 P.M.: Head to Sesame Workshop for edits on outreach content.

3:00 P.M.: Meet with international coproducers to discuss upcoming *Sesame* projects around the world.

4:00 P.M.: Meet with Sesame Workshop's public relations team to discuss upcoming appearances and events.

4:30 P.M.: Meet with *Sesame Street*'s executive producer, Carol-Lynn Parente, to discuss the new season.

5:00 P.M.: Go home. Turn on the Food Network and order some dinner.

9:45 P.M.: Say goodnight to my daughter, Shannon.

10:00 P.M.: Brush my teeth. Ask myself to make an honest attempt to train and eat well tomorrow. Amen.

LEONARD MALTIN
Film Historian and Movie Critic

Photo credit: Becky Sapp

Leonard Maltin gets paid to be opinionated. And he's got a few opinions about movies. Actually, he's got at least 17,000 of them. That's the number of reviews that appear in his latest annual movie guide, a critically acclaimed, *New York Times* bestseller which is famous for its star rating system and economy of words. The guide first came out in 1969 while Leonard was a freshman at New York University. If you think that's young for a published author, consider this: Leonard had his own magazine at the age of fifteen, and before that he had his own newspaper at the age when most young boys had newspaper routes.

Leonard's love of movies and movie history goes back to his childhood. Growing up in Teaneck, New Jersey, he'd often take the bus over the George Washington Bridge to Manhattan, where he'd head to a movie theater or browse the movie memorabilia shops. He devoured books on movie history, which gave him an education that helped shape the film historian and critic he'd become later in life. He's written numerous books, been the resident critic on *Entertainment Tonight*, and hosted *Maltin on Movies* on ReelzChannel. We got him in between movie screenings, and he stayed until his popcorn ran out. In this interview he tells about one of the best days of his life. He also shares the secret of his success and discusses how you, too, can become a critic.

THE TELLURIDE FILM FESTIVAL: Established in 1974, this four-day festival is held every year in Telluride, Colorado. The festival is known for discovering new films and filmmakers.

What's your earliest movie memory?
Seeing the last scene of *Snow White and the Seven Dwarfs*.

The last scene?
Yes. I was maybe four and a half years old. In those days theaters used to show films on a continuous basis and they didn't clear out the auditorium, so you could stay and watch the movie over and over again. I remember my mom taking me by the hand into the theater as everyone was leaving the previous show. It was the last shot when the prince takes Snow White off into that golden sun in the sky to "happily ever after." So that's my first movie memory: seeing the last scene of *Snow White*.

What did you think after you saw it from the beginning?

It had an impact on me because I became hooked on all things Disney. It was around that same time that Walt Disney started hosting his own TV show, which became a weekly ritual for me. Then in 1958 a movie came out called *The Golden Age of Comedy*. It was a compilation of film clips of great silent comedy shorts with Laurel and Hardy, Charlie Chaplin, and Buster Keaton, among others. All these things fired my interest, and my imagination, and they still do all these years later.

Before we get to "all these years later," tell us, where did you grow up?

I was born in Manhattan and when I was four my family moved to the suburbs of Teaneck, New Jersey, just over the George Washington Bridge. By the time I was twelve and getting seriously hooked on movies, and movie history, my parents would let me take the bus over the bridge to Manhattan by myself or with my friends to spend the day.

So while other kids were off playing football or baseball, you were learning about the greats like Charlie Chaplin and Buster Keaton?

Yes. I'd go to my local library to take out every book I could. There weren't that many at the time, but I read every one of them. I kept borrowing them, taking them back after thirty days, then taking them out again to reread.

Did you ever consider that this education might pay off down the road?

No, I had no plan. I had no particular goal. But I did like to write. When I was in fifth grade, my best friend and I started a form of a newspaper together. We lived in Bergen County, New Jersey, and we called it the *Bergen Bulletin*. Later on a cousin of my father's gave us a used mimeograph machine, which was a little more professional, although you got ink underneath your fingernails. We started publishing every week with an issue of that and distributed it to schoolmates and friends. That eventually became a more magazine-like publication called *Profile*, because I was interested in movie history and I wanted to write about Buster Keaton and Laurel and Hardy and all those subjects that interested me.

When I was thirteen I started reading a magazine called *Famous Monsters of Filmland*. It was all about classic horror films and science fiction films. In one issue there was an article all about "fanzines." Today they would be blogs, but back then they were amateur magazines. There were two in particular that interested me, so I wrote to the editors of those magazines and offered myself as a writer. They both accepted my first submissions, so at thirteen I became a regular contributor to *The 8mm Collector*, published in Indiana, Pennsylvania, and *Film Fan Monthly*, published in Vancouver by a guy who was nineteen. After contributing to *Film Fan Monthly* for two years, the editor wrote to me and said, "I've got a full-time job now and I just can't keep up with the magazine. Would you want to take it over?" So when I was fifteen years old I inherited this magazine and its mailing list.

Wow. A mini media mogul. When did your first issue come out?

In May of 1966. I edited and published that magazine for the next nine years, every month. It was my whole life. Schoolwork took a distant second from that point on. At first I wrote all the articles and I would buy stills from the memorabilia stores to illustrate the articles. Then some people started contacting me offering contributions.

Pretty soon I had some good writers, some of whom were legitimate published authors who were looking for a place to write about film-buff topics they cared about.

Was there ever a light bulb moment where you thought, "I could do this for a living?"

No, the light bulb was turned on by someone else. When I was in twelfth grade an English teacher at Teaneck High School stopped me in the hall one day and said, "I have a friend in New York who's an editor at Signet books and I think the two of you would really hit it off. I want you to call him and one day after school go to Manhattan and meet him." So I met this man named Patrick O'Connor, and I brought a wad of my magazines with me. We were breaking the ice and he asked, "What's that?" And I said, "This is the magazine I edit and publish." And he said, "That's your magazine? I love your magazine!" He had somehow seen it before, which kind of surprised me.

So you'd already made an impression on the New York publishing world and didn't even know it!

I guess so. He went on to ask if I knew this book called *Movies on TV* by Steven Scheuer. He had a syndicated column at the time, writing up highlights of what was on TV that night, and he had a catalog of movie reviews that were collected into a paperback book. Of course, I had this book. He asked what I thought of it and I said, "I think it's good, as far as it goes." He asked, "What would you do differently?" I said, "Well, I'd put in more cast names. I'd list the director, I'd say whether it was in black and white or color and I'd give the original running time." I rattled off all these things, because I really knew that book inside and out. Then he told me he was looking to do a rival book and asked if I'd like to write it. I said, "Sure."

Let's get this straight. You're in the twelfth grade at this point, correct?

Yes, I'm seventeen years old. In fact, he decided not to tell his superiors he was hiring a seventeen-year-old kid. When I turned in a chunk of the book and he was pleased, he then told them the truth, but it didn't matter; they liked what they had seen. He had me include a star rating for each film; I didn't want to do it, but he said, "It's a shorthand people respond to," and he was right. He also said, "You have to write it in a telegraphic style. You can't do full sentences; you have to make them really terse so you can fit a lot in." I hired people to help me do it, because he said, "You can't do this alone." Again, he was right. What really made the book work was that they hired a proofreader and a film expert to go over it to find mistakes and make suggestions. I found then that the secret to a book of this kind is rewriting, editing, and fact checking.

Were these movie reviews?

Yes. They were reviews. It's the same book I do today.

Oh, so this was the precursor to your annual movie guide?

Yes. The first edition came out in 1969 when I was a freshman at NYU.

What did you think when you first laid eyes on it?

All I saw were the mistakes and shortcomings, and I thought, "This is the end of my career." But people seemed to like it. It got my foot in the door with this publishing company, and I immediately sold a second book. And then a third. Every summer off from NYU I'd be working on a book. It was five years before they asked for another edition of the movie guide, and it was another four years before they asked for it again. Then they said they wanted to do it every other year. So it became a bi-annual until the mid-eighties when, with the rise of home video, it seemed to all of us to make sense to put it out annually.

It's really become a bible for so many movie lovers. When did it become *Leonard Maltin's Movie Guide*?

When I got on TV. That was one of the great days of my life. I got hired by *Entertainment Tonight*, and sometime later I got a call from my editor, who said, "We want to put your name above the title and your photo on the cover." That was the happiest outcome of my getting on television. It changed my publisher's view of me and changed the public's perception of the book.

Speaking of *Entertainment Tonight*, how did you land that job of resident critic?

Whenever a book of mine came out, I would always do publicity. I'd gotten on *The Today Show* one time and they had me back when I wrote a book called *The Great Movie Comedians* in the spring of 1982. I was interviewed by Gene Shalit, who was their film critic. Unbeknownst to me, someone here in Los Angeles at Paramount Television named Gary Hart saw that interview and called Jim Bellows, the newly installed executive producer of *Entertainment Tonight*. He had one of his producers call me in New York to ask if I'd be willing to audition to appear on the show. I said, "Sure."

They booked me on a plane out of Kennedy the next day and I went to the studio, Merv Griffin's old headquarters on Vine Street in

Los Angeles. They wanted me to do two movie reviews—which they hadn't told me ahead of time. The next day they asked me to come in before they did their regular show taping at 8:30 in the morning. They apparently had been auditioning other people, and one of the challenges was, after cueing a clip, we had to turn from camera slightly to the right to pretend to be looking at an imaginary movie screen. They would then cut to an over-the-shoulder shot of me and they would matte in the screen, showing the film clip. Apparently, several people with whom they had tried this couldn't get that right, and I did. They were full of praise for my being able to master this feat.

Who would've thought the ability to glance to the right would be instrumental in landing a TV gig? What happened next?
I kept waiting for a definitive answer, but I never got one. They'd fly me out every few weeks to do reviews, pay all my expenses—hotel, rental car, all of that—and everyone was very nice to work with. I did that for a year and a half. That's how I got hired on *Entertainment Tonight*.

How did you learn the job of film critiquing?
I think I just read enough reviews that I had a sense of how to write one, but I have to add, I was not writing for a newspaper or a magazine. I was not writing in depth. My reviews were brief, and I knew how to do that. I think I would've been more greatly challenged had I been asked to write essay-length reviews for a newspaper or a magazine. I probably could've acquired that skill set too, but it would've taken more time.

As a film critic, what do you look for in a movie?
Originality scores big points with me. Something fresh, or a fresh take on an old idea. Beyond that, I don't go with a checklist. I try to

take each movie on its own terms. If you're going to see a high school movie, don't expect *King Lear.*

For someone reading your chapter and saying, "I admire this man, I want to try to do this," what would you tell them?
I always tell aspiring critics to start writing, first and foremost. Before the Internet came along my advice was to get published somewhere, anywhere. If there's a local shopping weekly in your community, get printed there, because even in those shopper weeklies you have a deadline and you have a space requirement. There are going to be certain fundamentals that give you some basic experience.

A girl approached me at *The Telluride Film Festival* and said, "I'd love to do something like what you do but I don't how to get started." I said, "Well, maybe your public library would like to have a classic film series that you could organize where you screen films on the weekend and have a discussion afterwards. You could program that, lead the discussion, and possibly build a local reputation as somebody who knows and cares about this material." There are simple ways of trying to get your foot in the door in terms of building some reputation.

What's the secret to your success?
(Pause) Luck and timing. And I work hard. It helps that I love what I do.

We'd like to close your interview by asking if you'd give us a movie critic quote that we can use to market our book?
I've read a lot of books, but this is the most recent.

A DAY IN THE LIFE OF LEONARD MALTIN

My days vary, of course. I teach at USC on Thursday nights, and it's not every day that requires me to run to two screenings. Every other Wednesday I leave my house at 7:00 A.M., head for Los Angeles Airport and take a 9:15 A.M. flight to Albuquerque, where a staffer picks me up and we head to the Albuquerque Studios. That's where ReelzChannel is housed. When I get there I eat a quick lunch while rereading my two scripts for the day. We tape one episode, take a short break, and then do the second. That usually leaves me time to check e-mails, sometimes take a short nap, and then head back to the airport for an 8:35 P.M. flight back to L.A., which usually gets me home at about 10 P.M.

7:15 A.M.: Woke up and worked out with my trainer for an hour, while watching bonus features on the new DVD of *One Flew Over the Cuckoo's Nest.*

8:45 A.M.: Checked e-mail, tried to whittle down the number of messages in my inbox. If I can keep it under twenty I feel okay.

9:30 A.M.: Began writing for the day: new movie reviews and essays for my website, hoping to cover a week's worth. I try to stay ahead but it's a constant struggle. Then I had to tackle scripts for next week's episode of *Maltin on Movies* (on ReelzChannel). I nearly finished one episode's worth yesterday; I have to write two episodes at a time, as that's how we tape them.

1:15 P.M.: Left the house for 2 P.M. screening of Stephen Frears's new movie *Tamara Drewe* in West Hollywood.

4:45 P.M.: Home again, back to e-mails. I try to sneak in a catnap before early dinner, to recharge my batteries. Tonight's screening is way across town, and I have to leave a lot of time to get there.

6:00 P.M.: Left for the Sony lot in Culver City to see *The Social Network*. I should have allowed more time; traffic in L.A. is so unpredictable . . . but I made it just in time.

10:00 P.M.: Home from the screening, and outside to my office to do one last sweep of e-mails and make a few notes on the films I've screened today.

PAULA DAVIS
Senior Talent Producer for Conan O'Brien

Photo credit: Molly Moormeier

Paula Davis was born on an island called Manhattan. She was a good student and a college graduate, but as you're about to read, she learned far more outside school than she did in the classroom. Do they teach you how to sneak onto the set of *SNL* when you're thirteen years old? No. Can you read a book on how to land Academy Award–winner Meryl Streep as a guest on your show? Not in any book we've read. And has a teacher ever told a student to entrust their livelihood to a six-foot-four-inch freckled man with a big poof of fiery red hair?

Paula's career began as a talent assistant on the Emmy Award–winning show *Saturday Night Live*. She went on to talent-book HBO's *Def Comedy Jam*, then landed a gig on *Late Night with Conan O'Brien*, *The Tonight Show with Conan O'Brien*, and now simply,

Conan. She has been with Conan for the past eighteen years (that's the equivalent of 114 Hollywood years).

According to Paula, her job is not all glamorous. Yes, she knows a ton of A-list celebrities, and yes, she works on a hit show with cool people, and yes, she lives in sunny California on a golf course, but she swears there are some unglamorous moments. We sat down with her to find out what life as a powerful senior talent booker is like. We'll let you judge whether it's glamorous or not.

CALL TIMES: The time an actor or a crew member must be on set and ready to work.

PAGE PROGRAMS: NBC started the Page Program in New York in 1933 as a way to groom young professionals who had recently graduated from college and had little to no practical experience. The program allows participants to work in various departments in order to learn the inner workings of the network.

"PEOPLE OF EARTH" LETTER: This was an open letter that Conan wrote to his fans in response to the late-night situation at NBC.

PITCH: In the talent world this is done primarily by PR people who want to get a celebrity they represent on a talk show. They pitch ideas they hope the talent booker will find interesting. A pitch is also used internally by the talent department in explaining to the host and the executive producer their proposals for guests that they want to book.

PRODUCTION COORDINATING: A noncreative position that supports the production manager. Functions include: equipment rentals and reservations, location releases, insur-

ance certificates, permitting, and other tasks that support production.

PRODUCTION SCHEDULE: A document that clearly dis-
plays the days, times, and locations of physical production.

RUN-THROUGH: The process of starting at the beginning of
a show and going through the script in its entirety. This process
helps in adjusting show length, rewriting material, and allowing
the actors to rehearse, camera operators to block each scene,
and lighting and art departments to make last-minute adjustments. When the cast is in full costume and makeup, this is
called a full-dress run-through or dress rehearsal.

SEGMENT: A portion of a talk show that usually takes
place from one commercial break to another. Any given talk
show is comprised of individual segments strung together.
Examples of segments are: show open, first guest, second
guest, sketch, band, close.

If you would, please give us a description of your job.

I am responsible for the booking of guests, as well as the entire
department. We book celebrities, authors, politicians, and stand-up
comics. I do not oversee the booking of the bands, but I love music.

**Tell us about your childhood, where you grew up, and the
first time you were exposed to the magical world of entertainment.**

I grew up in Manhattan and both my parents worked in the television business, so I was exposed early on when I was seven years old.
My first exposure to TV production was when I visited my mom on
set of the game show *He Said, She Said*. She was the cue card woman.

So your mom gave you your first taste of what it was like to be on a set. What was your next taste?

When I was thirteen, I'm about to date myself, my best friend Toby and I watched the first episode of *SNL* on TV. I loved the show so much, it was a life-changing experience. Toby and I did some research and found out the show was broadcast at 30 Rockefeller Plaza, in the same building where my mom worked, on a different floor. So we took the train in one day by ourselves, found the set, and snuck into the studio to watch the show rehearsal. It was so easy; there were hardly any security guards, and we kept going week after week. We actually ended up becoming very friendly with the cast (Laraine Newman, John Belushi, Jane Curtin, Gilda Radner, Dan Aykroyd, Garrett Morris, and Chevy Chase) and many of the writers and producers. Everyone on the show got to know us, and we became known as "the girls." After a while we even started getting little job assignments. Once, Dan Aykroyd sent us off to buy a train set for John Belushi's birthday.

After high school you had great contacts at *SNL* and some production experience; did you go off to college?

I have to say I almost bypassed college. I just wanted to start working in the business, but wisely my parents told me it would be a good idea if I went to college.

For the purposes of this book, we'll just say you graduated top of your class. What was the first thing you did after graduation?

I called my mentor from *SNL*, Anne Beatts, who I knew from those early days of sneaking in. She knew I wanted to work for the show, but unfortunately there was nothing for me at the time. She did, however, hire me as her personal assistant for a small weekly stipend.

She said some of the job would have to do with the business and some of it would have to do with her laundry, and I said, "I'll take it." So I was in the business, sort of.

At least you didn't have to sneak onto the set anymore!
I didn't have to sneak on the set, which was the biggest perk. I told anyone who would listen that all I wanted to do was work on *SNL*, so when a job finally opened up in the talent department I was given the opportunity to interview for it and I got it.

Wow, huge break. What happened next career-wise?
I was promoted to talent associate, and my responsibilities shifted to booking all the extras on the show. I'll explain.

On *SNL* the sketch scripts were selected Wednesday night after the *read-through* by Lorne and a small group of writers and producers. Then those scripts were distributed to all the various departments. So I was in charge of booking extras, also known as background actors, for all the sketches. Extras would be placed in the background of the sketch to make the situation appear more real, whether it was a restaurant scene, or a park, a street scene, whatever.

Did you interact with other departments?
Yes, we all interacted. Because the show was live and there were so many moving parts, we all had to work together seamlessly. It was stressful, but highly rewarding. I met Conan on *SNL*. He was one of the young writers. We were really friendly and got along great. He was very young when we met, I think like twenty-four years old. We had a nice working relationship. He was very funny!

Eventually you left *SNL*. Talk about what motivated you to leave your dream job and what you did next.

I was a talent associate for three years and I felt like I needed to make a change. Sometimes when you take a job as an assistant, you're always looked upon as an assistant. To this day, I still get a little nervous when I see Lorne Michaels, assistant-like nervous.

I left there in 1989 and I went freelance and started *production coordinating* on commercials, which I didn't particularly love. Thankfully, Jeff Ross called me. He was a producer at Lorne Michaels's company, Broadway Video. He was doing a show for HBO called *Def Comedy Jam* and he needed a talent coordinator. I jumped at the chance. It was a racy, raunchy show and the *production schedule* was hectic. Meanwhile, NBC asked Lorne Michaels to help out with the 12:30 P.M. spot on their schedule. They wanted to develop a late-night show because David Letterman left NBC and went to CBS, so Lorne suggested Conan, and they hired him. Lorne was executive producer and Jeff was the producer. I knew Lorne, Jeff, and Conan and very much wanted to work on their new show. After interviewing with Jeff and Conan, I was hired as a talent booker.

In 1993 *Late Night with Conan O'Brien* premieres. Talk about your job and the process of putting a show together from a talent-booking standpoint.

I was booking celebrities, authors, politicians, and stand-up comics and was helping produce the stand-up segments as well. All the bookers would meet and go through names and ideas and we would try to generate ideas for guests we wanted to book. We would watch tons of tape, take *pitches* from PR people, and generate our own wish list of people we wanted to book. We'd reach out to the movie stu-

dios to determine movie releases and who they were sending out to
publicize the movies.

You talked about generating ideas when booking, can you elaborate on that?

Generating ideas means that if we are in a talent meeting and we
decide to book a cooking segment, we would approach that segment a different way. Where other shows might really want to teach
the viewer about the recipe, we didn't really care about the recipe.
We wanted the personalities to shine and the *segment* to comically
go wherever it wanted to go. We had Chef Gordon Ramsay on,
and we purposely booked Norm MacDonald as the other guest just
so he would participate and ransack the segment. If you didn't see
it, look it up, it was a perfect mess! You don't know 100 percent if
sparks are going to fly, but you put the players in place and hope
for magic.

Is there an art to knowing whom to book and when?

It's difficult. In a perfect world you never want to book an actress
back to back with another actress, and you don't want to have a TV
star as your first guest and follow with another TV star. If we are
leading with, say, a politician, we want to have something funny after
that. We always strive for funny.

Who has been your most favorite booking?

I would say my most favorite booking, the one I dreamt about and
I finally got, was Meryl Streep. Brad Pitt is a close second. I don't
want to sound jaded, but it's weird, it is kind of a machine. You book
them, they do the show, and you are on to the next. Meryl Streep was
a thrill for me, and she is just so lovely and sweet.

Late Night ended, and in 2009 Conan and his entire staff moved to the West Coast for a little Tonight Show action. Talk about that.

Well, the deal was actually presented and announced to Conan five years earlier, in 2004. We were, of course, all thrilled for Conan. It did raise a question with my family about the move, but the thing about my job is, it's not "a job" to me, it's the fabric of my being. If it were just a job I would have quit, found another one, and stayed in New York. But this was a shot to work on *The Tonight Show* and stay with Conan.

And what was it like?

It was very exciting, it was very dreamlike. I moved to Los Angeles ahead of my family to begin working. It was *The Tonight Show*, and it was a very exciting time, full of hope and promise. Conan was psyched, and it was fun just watching him be so happy and enthusiastic. On the talent-booking front we expanded our department, which was great because we hired someone to do politicians and sports figures and someone to just book comedians. So it was much more do-able.

And then, almost as soon as it began, it was over.

I will say that was personally devastating. Not so much from the standpoint of uprooting our family and making the move; that was in the background for me. It was watching Conan be so hurt. It was very hard to watch. Conan really put on a brave face and soldiered on. He was concerned for his entire staff, and reassured us that everything would be all right and it would all work out. He really urged us to stay focused on creating great TV, and it was inspiring to watch him go through it. And then he wrote the *"People of Earth"* letter and we were all so solidly behind him for doing what was right. Conan is very smart, and he is a great writer, and his letter was concise and it hit the right tone and you just couldn't quarrel with it. He is just so genuine, a true class act. He was right; we have another home and a new show.

Right, now you are on TBS with *Conan*, and loving every minute of it we're sure.

Every second.

Conan is funny on and off camera. What is the flat-out funniest thing he's ever said to you?

Oh my God, there are so many. One time I was in his office with the door closed (starts laughing) and his assistant, who had a very low-key personality, opened the door, poked her head in and said, "It's one o'clock," and then she shut the door, and Conan says, "I've had her do that ever since my cuckoo clock broke" (huge laughter).

What advice do you have for someone who wants to do what you do for a living?

Intern on a show to get a feel for all the different departments, the different jobs, and generally how TV works. Try to get an entry-level assistant position in any department so you can learn. Definitely be a fan of celebrities, TV, movies, pop culture, and tabloids. You have to hunger for it. Become a page. Networks have great *page programs* and you can land jobs that way. Countless people on our staff began as NBC pages.

Let's talk nuts and bolts, brass tacks, and whatever other hardware term we are leaving out. Talk about the characteristics necessary to do your job.

First, you have to know who you are booking for. Have a level head and get all the information on every prospective booking. Another characteristic is more human than work related but people forget about it: Be friendly with everyone. Every publicist who is pitching, every manager, every talent, the talent's entourage, everyone. Treat everybody with respect. Don't take anything personally. Be clear, direct, honest, and discreet! Whatever you hear, do not repeat it. Remain humble and level-headed.

Any job interviewing tips?

Know the show you are interviewing for. Let's use our show as an example. Here are the things I would look for in an entry-level hire: a good sense of humor, the right sense of humor. I want someone who has a sensibility that is cohesive with the show. If I asked what your favorite TV shows were, and you gave me examples of solid and current comedies like *Glee*, *30 Rock*, *Modern Family*, that would be a good answer. Have a solid knowledge of pop culture, and know what's hot on the web. Be able to talk about people we have booked on the show and give feedback as to who did well and which guests weren't so hot. I personally expect much more from an assistant than just answering the phone. Talent has got to be their life.

Did you ever have an off-putting moment with talent that made you bite your tongue or wonder if talent booking was the right career for you?

I can't answer that until I retire.

Okay, then how about this. Is there a misconception about your job from the outside looking in?

That it's glamorous. It's not *always* glamorous. If Sarah Jessica Parker wants a tea and I'm the one who is in the room with her, guess who has to go fetch the tea? Me.

Speaking of fetching, before we go can you fetch us a half-lemonade, half-sparkling water with a twist of lime and a splash of grenadine for color?

No.

Okay, we'll just grab a Tab on the way out.

A DAY IN THE LIFE OF PAULA DAVIS

6:00 A.M.: Wake up, make coffee, read paper, read e-mails, empty the dishwasher, and make kids' lunches.

7:30 A.M.: Yoga.

8:30 A.M.: Get dressed, head to work. Checking e-mails constantly at this point.

10:00 A.M.: Arrive to work (thanks L.A. traffic, you're great!). Check in, read e-mails, go to production meeting.

10:30 A.M.–1:00 P.M.: Work to book guests, send and return e-mails about guests, chat with our segment producers about the day's shows, go over future guest considerations with my staff, watch a string-out of talk show clips to see how different celebrities do on the show and what people are talking about.

1:00 P.M.: Lunch from the commissary on the lot. Bring the food back to my desk and eat while I peruse celebrity gossip websites.

2:00 P.M.: After lunch more of the same; e-mails, phone calls, my staff in and out of my office.

4:30 P.M.: Go down to the studio and say hello to guests and publicists.

5:00 P.M.–6:00 P.M.: Watch the show. Cross my fingers that the guests are good and that CO'B and the audience like them and that all the plugs are correct.

6:00 P.M.–6:30 P.M.: Postmortem meeting with host, EP, segment producer, head writer, and director.

6:30 P.M.–7:30 P.M.: Back to my office. Return phone calls, e-mails. Hopefully next day's guests are set so we can all go home and do it all over again tomorrow.

*If there's a guest issue, I'll stay at the office late while my husband calls to make guest suggestions.

MICHAEL GELMAN
Executive Producer Live with Regis and Kelly

Photo credit: Disney-ABC Domestic Television

When you see Michael Gelman walking toward you, as we did when we met him to conduct this interview, it is painfully difficult to not yell, "*Gelman!*" à la Regis Philbin. After watching him on TV all these years, you can't help but feel like you know the guy. Sitting with him in person, we were quick to learn that he is just as affable in real life as he appears on the set of *Live with Regis and Kelly*.

Gelman, sorry, Michael, has produced literally thousands of hours of live TV over his twenty-seven years with ABC. He has an enviable career, working with some of the biggest names in television. He's such a good sport that he's even willing to appear in sketches in full drag when comedy comes calling.

As the executive producer of a hit show you would think that
Michael might have a huge staff, but actually it's only made up of
twenty-two people. You would think that he'd have a plush office
on the fiftieth floor with a view of the Empire State Building and
Central Park, but he really just has a desk in the middle of a large
open space, newsroom style. You would think that he and his hosts
are very close and he admires them as people and talent; well, on that
point, you'd be right.

It is our hope that this chapter will put the guy who usually sits
off camera in the spotlight so he can share his path from ski bum to
running one of the most successful shows on television.

ASSOCIATE PRODUCER: This position is one step above
the PA. The job function is to assist the producer in the office,
on set and in the field. The job often involves a vast amount of
research and planning.

COORDINATING PRODUCER: This is usually a noncreative
position that supports the production manager. Functions
include: equipment rentals and reservations, location releases,
insurance certificates, permitting, and other tasks that support
production.

NATIONALLY SYNDICATED: Not airing on a broadcast network but instead sold to individual affiliate stations
in various markets.

POSTMORTEM: Production meeting following the airing or
completed production of a show. Attended by the writers and
producers, the meeting is designed to review what worked
and what didn't work.

REMOTES PRODUCER: This person is not based in an
office or on the home base set; instead, he or she is in the
field at various locations. The remotes producer must oversee

talent, camera, and story. If the remote is live they must serve as a link between the control room and the field crew.

SUPERVISING PRODUCER: Depending on the genre—scripted or nonscripted and talk or variety—a supervising producer serves as the intermediary between the executive producer and the rest of the staff. In some instances the process is creative as in reviewing scripts and handing out assignments. Another aspect is more technical in staffing and scheduling.

Please share with everyone what an executive producer does.
My job is to be blamed for everything. Whatever goes wrong is my fault.

Wow, all those years of Regis yelling at you have taken a toll, haven't they?
(Laughs) It's hard to describe what an executive producer does because they do so much, and on each show the job description is a little different. For example, most shows have multiple producer layers and staff several EPs, *supervising producers, coordinating producers*, and so on. But on *Live* it is me then my producers and an assistant; that is it. I'm very hands on. As the EP, I oversee the creative side, so I'm responsible for coming up with ideas for the show as well as vetting ideas my producers pitch me. And I oversee the financial end, which is our operating budget. The job is very right-brain, left-brain. The EP has to pull it all together.

Where did you grow up?

My dad was in sales and we would move every four to six years when I was growing up, so I grew up in the New York area, New Jersey, Long Island, then we moved to the Chicago suburbs. Then we moved back to Long Island my senior year of high school. I went to college in Colorado then moved back to New York and have been here ever since.

Maybe we should have asked where you *didn't* grow up. Can you talk about any early entertainment industry influences?

My father was in the photographic equipment business, so he made still cameras and also imported movie cameras. Since I was exposed to cameras early on, I started to play with them and even took courses when I was in elementary school. Then when I got to high school I got into theater. Gary Sinise and a lot of great actors have come out of the program that I was in. I took Acting 101, and halfway through Shakespeare I realized acting wasn't for me. I was not good at being natural and I also wasn't great at memorizing lines.

Other than those two details you would have been a superb actor.

A regular De Niro. When it came time for college, I always had a dream to go to school in Colorado. I was a big skier, mountain climber, rock climber, and just loved the outdoors. So that is where I went.

Powder wins out over academics every time.

I was able to combine my passion for film with my passion for skiing when I landed an internship as a cameraman for the U.S. Ski Association. Basically, they sent me around the country shooting pre-Olympic races. It was a great resume piece and fun at the same time.

I ended up getting a degree in journalism and broadcast production management and a minor in political science and film.

Before you graduated did you intern anywhere else?

I did a mass mailing of my resume to find an internship in New York, with no luck. Then, through a contact that my father had, I connected with a person at ABC who forwarded my resume to the appropriate person, and ended up getting the internship with WABC.

Ah, the importance of finding a contact versus a blind mass mailing.

It is absolutely key to find someone on the inside any way you can. I worked on a show called *Good Morning New York* hosted by Judy Licht and Doug Johnson. I worked my tail off for them and tried to make myself indispensable. By the end of the summer, I had become like a member of the staff. I found news stories and was pitching them and helping to produce some of the stories. They really came to depend on me. I had one more year at school, but the contacts I made during my internship became instrumental to launching my career.

So how did you make these contacts work for you?

Right before I was about to graduate, I arranged a meeting with Pat Caso, the executive producer of *Good Morning New York*. When I came in for my meeting I noticed Pat was pregnant. She said, "I'm sorry, I wanted to hire you when you graduated, but I'm leaving. I'll pass on your name to the new producer." Well, as you know, in this business it's all who you know and timing.

Yes, regime changes and timing can make or break you.

So I went from a guaranteed job out of school, to I'll pass your name on.

Back to square one.

Yup, I began networking and meeting friends of friends. I landed work. And I can tell you that was very humbling. I was a glorified messenger boy. I thought I had worked up impressive credits and I would land a job with ease out of school and that's just not how it works. I was commuting to the city from Long Island for minimum wage to do menial work, then I got a call from one of the producers that I used to work with. He was working on a new version of the old show I had interned on with Cyndy Garvey and Regis Philbin. I started off freelancing, but eventually got hired as a full-time *PA*.

So you are back at ABC after all?

Yes. Actually, I'm a bit of an anomaly in this business. Where I sat as an intern is within ten feet of where I sit today. Twenty-seven years later.

You must be so sick of the ABC commissary. Continuing on the career path, can you share more defining moments?

A year later I got promoted to an *associate producer*. A big moment for me was being left in charge when the EP was out or on vacation. That was when I first started getting noticed by Regis. We started to forge a really good working relationship. Another pinnacle point came when I decided to leave the show. I was not really getting along with the EP. He was not a very beloved fellow.

Did you have another job in the wings?

No. Regis at the time had another show he was hosting and executive producing for Lifetime called *Regis Philbin's Lifestyles*. He was looking for a producer and knew I was leaving, so he asked if I would be interested in becoming his producer.

Of course you turned him down.

Yeah, not interested. No, it was great. Career-wise, I made the jump from an AP to a full-fledged producer and got to keep working with Regis, whom I loved. We worked on that show for a season, and then it was cancelled, but Regis turned me on to a friend of his, Rick Rosner, who was producing the new version of *Hollywood Squares*. Rick hired me as their *remotes producer*. I was put on assignment to do the game show in front of the largest live game show audience ever at Radio City Music Hall. So, ABC in New York was airing the show and, you won't believe this, but the production ended up renting out office space for me on my old floor right next to all my buddies.

You just can't get away from this office, can you? It's almost creepy! Where did the *Hollywood Squares* job lead?

Back to Regis. The producer job opened up on Regis's local morning show. That was a huge opportunity for me.

How did you score the job?

I got clever. While they were deciding if they wanted to hire me I was still freelancing on *Hollywood Squares*, and I happened to be putting copy up on the ticker in Times Square for the show. So I wrote on the ticker, "Gelman gets job as morning show producer." I filmed it and sent them the tape of the ticker in Times Square and a note that read, "Wow, I didn't know I got the job." It worked. About a year and a half after I was hired we took the show from a local show to *nationally syndicated*, and that is when it really took off.

A little ingenuity goes a long way. For someone reading this book who might be thinking, "I want to be an executive producer one day," what advice do you have?

You want to focus on what job you want, then you need to train yourself in that area by getting internships while in college. Remember, it's not just who you know, but who you know that is impressed with you! I'd say start in a small market, where it's easier to get a job and you have the freedoms to be creative and try anything. You might be the writer, the producer, the director, and the cameraman all in one. Then you jump to bigger markets and eventually get to New York or Los Angeles.

Talk about your on-camera role.

Over the years my experience has been very different than other EPs because Regis started putting me on camera. Since Regis always likes to complain to someone, he needed someone to vent to, enter Gelman. So then my off-camera job became known on-camera. I started playing this sort of on-camera character.

Can you talk us through a typical creative meeting?

We have a meeting after every show. In that meeting we go over the ratings for the previous day. We look at what rated well and what didn't and we try to learn from it. Then we go over a *postmortem* on that particular day's show. A lot of times ideas start to percolate in these meetings. We then go over the upcoming show. So we discuss what the guest segment will be and how it will be structured.

How do you manage your staff and the show?

I still get to micromanage a lot of the show. Nothing goes on air that I don't know is happening. I try to let the producers do their thing because if I didn't, the show couldn't get on air. So the producers are incredible, and I have had the same staff for many, many years. I don't have a private office. I choose to work in more of a bullpen-style situation. I am in earshot at all times. When I want someone I just scream for them. I can hear them on the phone and if I don't like what they are saying I will chime in and tell them what to say. We have such a quick turnaround that we don't have time to go down the wrong road.

What are some of the stresses involved with your job?

I have been doing it for so long I don't know if there is a problem I haven't come across or solved at this point. I can say that it is unrelenting. It's an everyday show. Five hours a week of live airtime must be filled. We call it a creative black hole.

You've hired a lot of people. Do you have interviewing advice?

I interview people all the time and I ask them what they want to do and the response I get a lot is "I'll do anything. I just really want to work on the show." I have to say while the good intention is there, that is a really bad answer because if you do everything then you are going to produce nothing. Everyone wants to do something, but you need to narrow it down and know what it is you are good at and more importantly how you can be of service to the person who is hiring you.

What characteristics and skills do you look for in a person when you are hiring?

I want a smart, organized, and ambitious person. Organization is key. Common sense is key. Good judgment is key, and we can't teach those things, a person will either have them or not. I want someone who knows the show and can come up with ideas that fit what we are doing here and knows the TV business. Someone with a little practical experience who will be able to handle the pressure that comes with the job.

Have you gotten some sage advice that you would like to pass on?

Have a deep passion for your work, but keep it in perspective with your life. You need to have a balance and live your life fully. The experiences you have outside of work will allow you to be more creative and productive at work.

If you weren't running this show, what would you be doing?

Years ago, I had an idea to make a hybrid shopping show where you'd sell things on TV. So I could have been the father of the infomercial and been a multibillionaire.

A DAY IN THE LIFE OF MICHAEL GELMAN

December, 2010

5:30 A.M.: Wake up, check e-mails, and go to online news and entertainment websites looking for stories.

6:00 A.M.: Have a triple-shot latte and eat breakfast.

7:00 A.M.: Arrive at WABC on the Upper West Side of Manhattan. Head up to our fifth-floor production offices and sit down with one of the producers to go through the day's newspapers for possible host chat items.

8:00 A.M.: Head down to Kelly's dressing room to say hello, chat, and go over the show with our guests, Gwyneth Paltrow and Paula Abdul.

8:15 A.M.: Walk down to the *Live* studio for a walk-through of that day's "Happy New You" segment about saving money in the New Year.

8:25 A.M.: Rehearse new contest, "Blizzard Blast Travel Trivia."

8:35 A.M.: Take the elevator to the fifth floor, to Regis's office to go over the morning news stories and potential host chat items.

8:45 A.M.: Regis and I grab the elevator down to the backstage dressing rooms, where the producers and I go over last-minute details about the show and the guests for the day.

8:50 A.M.: Say a quick hello to Paula Abdul.

8:54 A.M.: Stage manager, Julian Abo, cues me to walk into the studio for the audience warm-up.

8:55 A.M.: Walk onto the *Live* set to warm up the audience.

9:00 A.M.: (announcer) ". . . Regis Philbin and Kelly Ripa!" as our hosts walk onto the set. The start of another live show, *Live*'s signature host chat commences.

10:00 A.M.: Another completed show.

10:02 A.M.: Record promos with hosts in the studio.

10:10 A.M.: Tape an interview with Roseanne Barr for a show later in the week.

10:20 A.M.: Head back upstairs to the office for my daily production meeting and review that day's show with the staff. Then we look ahead to the rest of the week, month, and February sweeps.

12:00 noon: I eat soup at my desk for lunch while going over upcoming theme week with a producer.

12:30 P.M.: I interview a freelance producer for an upcoming special project.

1:30 P.M.: I have a meeting re: "Run across America" project.

2:30 P.M.: I meet with Disney marketing and sales people.

3:30 P.M.: I meet with our talent bookers re: guest bookings.

5:00 P.M.–6:00 P.M.: Individual meetings with producers on all of our upcoming initiatives, publicity issues, ideas, etc.

6:45 P.M.: Head home.

CAROL ANN SUSI
Character Actress

Photo credit: Rick Stockwell

Carol Ann Susi has got chutzpah. Correction, she's got New York–style chutzpah. How else can you explain someone sneaking into the final callback of a major Broadway musical without ever having auditioned for a musical before in her life? Or years later, while waiting tables, asking the president of NBC if she could kiss his bald head for luck? Most people would never dare to be so brazen. But most people aren't Carol Ann Susi.

While many aspiring actors come to L.A., only a tiny percentage ever achieve stardom. Carol Ann figured out early on that she wasn't going to get the parts that went to Meryl Streep or Julia Roberts, so she needed to do what she did best. In her case, that meant sticking closely to her Brooklyn roots and squeezing out every last drop of that thick New York accent. In short, she'd be herself.

It turns out she's made a nice living "being herself." Her credits include everything from the loud-mouthed mom on the hit show *The Big Bang Theory*, to George's nightmare-of-a-date on *Seinfeld*, to Michael J. Fox's secretary in *The Secret of My Success*. She's got some great advice for aspiring actors. Most importantly, she says, "Be true to yourself." She's living proof of that. After all, you can take the girl out of Brooklyn . . . you know the rest.

CALLBACK: You've impressed the casting director enough in your initial audition to be asked back for another round. You may be called back numerous times before a final decision is made.

SAG: Screen Actors Guild. The union that represents actors. According to their website their mission is "to enhance actors' working conditions, compensation, and benefits and to be a powerful, unified voice on behalf of artists' rights."

Did you always know you wanted to be an actress?
From the minute I could talk. Actually, I wanted to be an actress-singer-dancer. And I went to tap dancing school, "Theodora School of the Dance." I was the funniest little fat girl, but I didn't care. I didn't know I was fat. I didn't know until I got to California.

What did people think about your ambition to be an actress? Sorry, actress/singer/dancer?
To everybody in Brooklyn, it was hilarious. They made fun of me. My uncles would be like, "She's a little fat girl. How the fuck is she going

to be an actress?" And then when I was eleven this church was doing
The King and I and my cousin Andrea was in it. I don't know why, she
couldn't talk. I was so jealous that I slapped her and said, "Give me that
costume, bitch. You don't want to be in it, let me be in it."

**You're not going to tell us that a heavy spotlight mysteriously
fell on cousin Andrea, are you?**
(Laughs) No. But I was pretty fierce.

So you went to dance school. What about acting school?
Oh yes. I went to "HB Studio" in Manhattan. I was thirteen, and I'd
take the train to the city by myself, every Saturday.

What was that like?
It was great. I was in the teenage workshop on Saturday afternoons.
I was there for three years and then I went on to adult acting classes
and learned the Method. I quit high school when I was about sixteen and went on every audition I could. I ended up in the Jewish
Theatrical Repertory. I didn't know what I was doing there, I cer-
tainly wasn't Jewish, but it didn't matter. I ended up doing a play. I
also met other people who were doing plays. So I was in acting class
constantly because that's what I wanted to do. I was young and pos-
sessed.

What next?
I was about eighteen and I hooked up with a guy who would become
my best friend, James Kelly Baron. Jimmy was also an actor. And
Jimmy became my gay significant other for like twenty years until he
passed away. So one time, there was an audition I will never forget
in my entire life. We met Harvey Milk, who wasn't "Harvey Milk" at

the time. He was the assistant to Tom O'Horgan who directed *Jesus Christ Superstar* on Broadway. And Harvey Milk says to us, "Oh my God, you should come audition. I'll get you in." So he did. He got us into the *callbacks* of *Jesus Christ Superstar.*

You're talking the original *Jesus Christ Superstar* on Broadway? You just sailed right into the callbacks?

Yeah, yeah. I don't know where my head was, but I really thought, "I'm getting this job." So we rehearsed. We were singing and rehearsing and here we were at the eighth or ninth callback at the Mark Hellinger Theater. I walk on stage, I have no fear. I go, "Hi, everybody. How ya doing?" And I stood there and I adjusted and I went, (singing) "Christ you know I love you, yeah, did you see I waved, yeah?" And the accompanist went to me, "Excuse me, Miss. What key are you in?" And I said, "I don't know, can't you just follow me?" And I hear laughing in the front and in the back. The director Tom O'Horgan said to me, "Darling, if this were a comedy, I would hire you on the spot."

Nothing funny about *Superstar*.

No, and I was semi-humiliated.

Something tells us you got over it. Is it safe to assume you didn't get the part?

Yes. Plus, up to that point I thought I was going to do drama until that director said what he did. So at that point I realized, I'm probably funny.

That must have been a pivotal moment for you.

One of them, yeah.

So how did you end up in L.A.?

I came out to Los Angeles when I was twenty-one on vacation. November 5, 1973. I remember the exact date. I was only supposed to be here for two weeks.

How did you get your first break?

I was working as a waitress at Hamburger Hamlet, waiting on tons of movie stars. I mean tons, all the agents, everybody. But I never told anyone I was an actress. Then one night I was waiting on Darren McGavin who was doing the show *The Night Stalker*. He asked me if I was an actor and I said, "No." He said, "That's a shame because there's a part for you." This other girl came over and said, "She's a pain in the ass, she doesn't like to tell people, but she is an actress." Then he said he'd love for me to come to Universal Studios and audition for a part on the show. And I went in and read for it and I was there for a couple of hours and Darren McGavin came out and he looked at me and said, "Kid, you got the job." It was a recurring character on *The Night Stalker*. I didn't have an agent. I wasn't even in *SAG*.

How often does something like that happen?

Never. It's a different business today. It's totally, totally different. So I was really lucky. I went on to do three episodes of *The Night Stalker*, and now the show is a cult favorite. After that they'd call me up at Universal to come in and do two lines here, two lines there in a movie. No audition. They just called me up. And that went on for a while.

What do you think won over the Night Stalker that day at Hamburger Hamlet?

He was sitting with the head of NBC, who had a bald head and I said, "Can I kiss your head for luck?" And he just cracked up.

So once again, the comedy thing gets their attention. At what point did you get an agent?

I had gotten an agent early on, but they weren't very good because I was getting myself the jobs and they would say, "Well, you got the job, you still have to give us 10 percent."

You were the one out there hustling, getting the work.

Exactly. They weren't really getting it for me. So I didn't really have an agent again until the mid-eighties. Before that I was getting everything from Universal on my own, but you can only do that for so long.

Talk about the audition process. How do you prepare for an audition and what advice do you have for an aspiring actor?

I usually make a choice about how I'm going to play the character and I go in and I'm not afraid. You've got to take command of the room. You've got to walk in and look people directly in the face and say, "Hi, how are you today?" You can't be intimidated. If you're intimidated, they know it, they smell it and you're gone. Here's what they're trying to figure out. They're trying to figure out if they want to spend the week with you. They want to see if you can deliver. And I can tell everybody reading this right now one thing, it's go out and audition for everything. Do not turn anything down. In the eighties you could turn things down, but it's not okay anymore.

You've got many credits to your name. Can you rattle off some of the movies and TV shows you've been in?

Sure. Movies, I was in *Outrageous Fortune*, *The Secret of My Success*, *Death Becomes Her*. I've done TV shows like *Who's the Boss?*, *Murphy Brown*, *Seinfeld*, *Ugly Betty*. Oh, I'm in an Adam Sandler movie called *Just Go with It*. I play his mother. I'm in a couple of scenes with him and Jennifer Aniston.

Great credits. Talk about your *Seinfeld* experience. You played the daughter of a woman at the unemployment office whom George dates to extend his benefits.

Yes. I went in to read for Larry David and I kind of knew in the room they liked me, because the choice I made was really specific and maybe no one else made that choice. I played her as this despicable human being. I was a nightmare. I couldn't believe that got me the job, but it did. *Seinfeld* was such a huge thing. People were stopping me on the street afterward going, "Oh my God, you were just so funny."

What about some of your other TV roles?

Ugly Betty was fabulous. I played Betty's teacher from Queens. It was kind of perfect. And then when I got the job they told me they needed me for three or four days and I went, "Why? It's only one scene." They said, "No, you're going to be in a fashion show. You're going to be a model." I jumped. I jumped so high. I've always wanted to be a model. And I had a fabulous time on *Ugly Betty*. Good people.

And now you're on the hit show *The Big Bang Theory*.

Yes.

You play one of the leads' mom, who's never seen, only heard. What's that like for an actress?

It's great. I love it. I might not have liked it ten years ago, but let me tell you, I'm loving it now.

How did that job come about?

It came about when the show first started. My agent called and told me to go in and read for the casting director. This was a costarring role. So I went in and read for the casting director and she called me back and I read for the producers and I got the job. The first year it was just two episodes, and I only worked a couple of days. Then, after the second show of the second season Chuck Lorre, the producer said, "Let me ask you a question. You don't mind never seeing hair and makeup for the next ten years do you?" I said, "No. As long as you're going to pay me, I don't mind it at all."

Not bad to be on Chuck Lorre's radar. He's made a couple of shows. *Two and a Half Men* and *Dharma and Greg* come to mind.

Yeah, he's great. And I love it. I'm working and I couldn't be happier.

There are a lot of actors in this town. But you have this niche, this New York thing that's a bit of a calling card. For an actor who's coming here and doesn't have a "thing," what would you recommend?

Just be who you are. Be who you are, in every sense of the word. Look at the character and bring to the character what you, yourself, would do. That's the most you can do.

Does being a character actor open you up to more work?

Absolutely. Much more than a leading lady. A couple of years ago I met this strange woman who said to me in her English accent, "When did you make the transition to character actress?" and I looked at her and I said, "What are you, fucking nuts? I was born a character actress. What transition?" When you weigh five pounds more than Nicole Kidman, you're a character actor.

What's the best part of your job?

Getting the paycheck. Oh no, I shouldn't say that. I've got to make it more dramatic than that. I actually do like it when I make people laugh. I like when people tell me I'm funny. That makes me happy.

What are the worst parts of the job?

Not getting the part. I was up for the part of Tony's sister in *The Sopranos*. I almost died over not getting it.

Final question. We're in Brooklyn right now, and your mother's calling you in for dinner. What does that sound like?

"Carol, get in this fucking house right now or I'm going to break your head."

A DAY IN THE LIFE OF CAROL ANN SUSI

Workday on CBS's The Big Bang Theory.

6:00 A.M.: Up, write my morning letter to God. I've done this for twenty years. Have coffee, check e-mails, and clean up house.

7:45 A.M.: I take the bus so I have to leave early.

9:00 A.M.: Get to Warner Brothers lot. I'm early, so I have breakfast.

10:00 A.M.–2:00 P.M.: Rehearsal and run through for producers and writers.

3:00 P.M.: Out. Back on the bus home to West Hollywood.

4:15 P.M.: Run errands, shop, post office.

5:30 P.M.: Back home. Check e-mails and other mail. Cook dinner. Return phone calls.

6:30 P.M.: Eat dinner.

7:00 P.M.: Watch TV.

9:30/10:00 P.M.: Asleep.

DEBBIE WILLIAMS
Head Stage Manager

Photo credit: Jac Flanders

American Idol, So You Think You Can Dance, The Jerry Lewis MDA Labor Day Telethon, and *America's Got Talent.* Most of us have just watched these shows on TV. Debbie Williams actually brought them to life as the head stage manager, making sure each show went off without a hitch. And they did. Well, most of the time.

To think she started out as a child performer in a traveling ice show, then became a dancer on the *Donny and Marie Show* before switching gears to become the first female head stage manager to do live TV.

To read Debbie's words on the page doesn't do her big personality justice. So in order to capture her energy, imagine this entire chapter in **boldface** and ALL CAPS, with a lot of laugher laced throughout.

She has had a remarkable career, with no signs of slowing down, and man, does she have stories to share. They include almost dying on the set of *American Idol*, high-kicking behind Donny and Marie Osmond, feeling up Brad Pitt in front of millions, working twenty hours straight with Jerry Lewis, and managing to maintain her femininity at work while being thought of as just another one of the guys!

> **GUILD SCALE:** Guild scale refers to the minimum wage that is accepted by the union representing the American film and television worker. The union, as pertains to this chapter, is the Directors Guild of America (DGA).

Debbie, where did you grow up and when were you first exposed to the entertainment industry?
My parents were gold medal ice skaters and I was born on the road, on the ice skating show circuit. When I was two I performed in the show and we traveled and moved every week of my life until I was fifteen years old. I lived on the road with a band of gypsies, I was home schooled for most of my life, and we would just travel and work, travel and work.

But you really didn't know any different, right?
Right, that was my reality. When I was interviewed as a kid people would ask me if I wished I lived a normal life and I'd say, "I think this *is* normal. If there is a normal, I mean life is pretty crazy!"

So once you were fifteen and finished with the skating tours what did you do?

I'm a pretty free spirit. I am one of these, "wherever the wind takes me" type of people, especially when I was younger.

Where *did* the wind take you?

When I was nineteen, my first stop was San Francisco, where I sold coats at I. Magnin, then I moved to Sun Valley, Idaho. When I got there I met a choreographer who was doing a Peggy Fleming ice-skating show that was going to Europe. I didn't really want to skate anymore, but I wanted to go to Europe. So he hired me to do the Europe tour. That same choreographer ended up doing the *Donny and Marie* TV series, which was on in the 1970s. He needed twelve girls who could skate and dance, so he hired me to do that show, and I packed up and moved to Los Angeles.

You are like the twelfth person we have interviewed for this book with the same story. Please continue with your predictable path.

Ha, right. That show was a trip. I was on for all four years that it was on air. And everybody appeared on that show, from Lucille Ball to Fred Astaire to Bob Hope, I mean everybody. Back then when you did a variety show, it took six to seven days to shoot it. The performance numbers were so involved; they were massive productions.

So when you came to Los Angeles, you were in front of the camera as a performer?

Yes, that was all I knew, but when I started dancing in the shows, I would watch all the people, and I was intrigued. I saw how collaborative it was, and I really liked that. Up until this point it had always been about me, my talent and my look, and that was a lot of pressure. I liked sharing the burden with other people and working in a collaborative world. So in the summers, when the show was on hiatus, I would work little production jobs.

So you were getting your feet wet?

Yes, and then I got pregnant. I ended up staying home, but I really wanted to work. So my husband at the time said, "You've been a performer and you understand the performer, you know a lot of directors, why don't you stage manage?" He was right, all the directors I had worked with were all directing really big variety shows. So I contacted them and they gave me a shot.

Was there a feeling at that point that you had found your calling?

No, I didn't like it in the beginning. Then the more I did it, the more I liked it. And I liked the challenge and the pace of it. So I thought, *if I am going to do this, I'm going to work on the biggest shows or I'm not going to do it at all.* I started to network and meet different directors, and they started to hire me to do bigger shows. Then I got into doing big variety specials. I liked that a lot. It was like being in the eye of the storm and there were so many moving pieces. I was a real adrenaline junkie. In the beginning I took all the jobs that the other, more established stage managers didn't want. It was a major boys club, all guys.

Explain the ins and outs of the stage manager job.

Simply put, we are the link for the director to the stage. On movies the director is on the set, but in TV the director is not on the stage, he's in a booth, so I serve as his eyes and ears. I wear a headset so I can hear the director and everybody else talking to me.

I am making all the moving parts behind the scenes happen that pertain to what the viewing audience sees on stage. I have to work out how every set move works, every transition, every talent cue. For instance, on *The Jerry Lewis MDA Labor Day Telethon* I worked twenty hours straight. I was in charge of blocking and determining who stands where so that it worked for the cameras.

It's a jigsaw puzzle, and I like putting the jigsaw puzzle together. I have to work with a lot of different personalities and that is part of the game. My forte is working with difficult men.

Talk a little bit about that, the challenges of being a woman in your line of work.

I am the only woman in my line of work. There are no lead females in variety to this day. Not a one. And that is hard. Come on all you ladies out there, step it up. I can't do this forever! Being a woman was the hardest part in the beginning. That, and not having a full grasp of the job. I was really up against it. And you know, I'm a feminine girlie girl. So I would wear cowboy boots, put a baseball cap on my head, and I would play it down and play the part. That's all part of the game, too.

Do you have a crew, and if so, how many people are there?

It depends on the show. On a telethon I have eleven or twelve stage managers. I did the *MTV Movie Awards* one year where I had a team of twenty-seven. It is very dissected when you do variety TV. You have someone who leads the talent department, and they figure out the flow for all the talent. Then you have certain people who are assigned to overseeing the sets and all the set moves. There are certain people who just cue the talent out to the podium. That's how you get a variety show done.

And you oversee all of this?

Yes, I put that all together.

So you are on the set of *American Idol* standing next to Ryan Seacrest and you are forty seconds from coming back from commercial and going live. What are you doing?

On that show, it's a little different. We do a lot of last-minute stuff. We fly by the seat of our pants. If we're forty seconds coming back from break a lot of times Ryan and I will see someone in the audience and come up with something.

During a results show one year we were on commercial break before we announced who was eliminated that week and I saw Brad Garrett sitting in the audience and said to Ryan, "Why don't we put him on the couch and pretend he's going home?" And Ryan goes, "Let's do it." So now it's like thirty-five seconds back, so I say to the booth, "Quick, we're putting Brad on the couch and Ryan is going to do a joke with him." And we walk over to Nigel, the executive producer, and ask if it is okay and Nigel says, "Yeah." So we have Brad on the couch and we come back from break and I'm counting backwards, five, four, three, and we are on. Ryan says, "The next one going home is . . . Brad Garrett," and it was great and it got a big laugh and we threw Brad out. And that entire setup happened in thirty-five seconds. That happens all the time. Ryan and I are always looking.

You had a scary fall on the *American Idol* set. Care to relive that horror for our reading pleasure?

I'd love to. We were doing a dress rehearsal and I was at the top of a very steep set piece made up of metal retractable stairs. I usually tell the crew when to retract the stairs, but this day we were in a rush and I didn't tell them. Once they saw Ryan walk down and clear the steps, they started to retract the stairs. Problem was, I was at the top trapped, with nowhere to go, about twenty feet above the stage.

I'm thinking, "*Oh my God*." There was nothing to hold on to, but I saw this little railing off to the one side and I very quickly thought that I would grab the railing. I was scared I was going to get sucked under the set and be crushed. So they retracted all the way and now I'm hanging by the railing. One of my arms dropped and then I lost my grip and fell. A metal corner caught my leg and cut it open. I needed fifty stitches, and I think I blacked out for a second. The next thing I knew Ryan was holding my head and going, "Don't move, don't move." I was telling them it was just my leg and I was pissed because we were behind and we had a live show to get on the air. So I'm lying there barking orders. Then I realized I was wearing these really expensive French jeans that I loved and they were getting all bloody.

That's a sad on-set story. How about a happy one? Can you tell the Brad Pitt Story?

Oh, that was silly. Brad had been backstage at the Kodak Theater for *Idol Gives Back*, and he was supposed to walk out and intro a videotaped package. So he is introduced and he goes out on stage. The crowd goes nuts and he starts talking. Audio starts going in my ear, "We don't have him, we don't have him. Mic is dead, mic is dead." And I'm going, "Oh my God." So it's my job to stop the show. I walk out and I ask him where his mic was and he says, "Oh, I put it in my pocket, I was making a phone call." I start trying to put it on him and I could just feel the entire theater looking at me. So I had to do it, I have a button and I can talk to the entire house. And I say, "I just came out to touch him, nothing else." It got the hugest laugh. So big in fact, Nigel kept it in the show.

Great story. What sort of range can someone expect to make in your line of work starting out?

Our pay is based on *DGA scale.* Scale is $789 a day, minimum, for twelve hours. But those of us who have been doing it for so long, we don't work for scale. Then there's overtime on top of that. Another benefit of DGA is first class airfare and paid travel days to and from out of town locations, and of course, per diem. It's been a wonderful thing for me, and it has given me a very comfortable paycheck with a lot of time off.

What are the characteristics or qualities of a good stage manager?

You can't be afraid. You have to be confident, or at least appear confident. Multitasking and being detail oriented is also important. And I can tell you in my own life I am not a detail-oriented person. I can't find my car keys, but I can tell you every cue in a show. Your personality has to do a lot with your success. If you're someone who has no problem meeting strangers, talking to people, being tactful and can sprinkle in a sense of humor, you'll do all right. Having a thick skin and not taking anything personally is also part of it. You have to logically be able to figure things out. Everything has logic, nothing is rocket science. I don't know how I do it to be honest, because I can't do that in life.

Could it be the $789-plus day rate?

It could be.

Someone off the bus wants to become a stage manager, what should he or she do?

There is no set rule on how to become a stage manager in television. If I were to give advice to someone, I would suggest starting as a stage manager at a theater. The technical aspects of running a stage in theater are very beneficial. Get as much experience as you can (high school, college, regional theater) until you are comfortable on a stage. Next, work at a television studio, either in local TV or at a cable network. You can learn about camera positioning and how the "floor" of a studio works. If you have to be a runner, gofer, or coffee-fetcher, do it. Use the time on the set to observe and learn. You will pick up on the terminology and how each department functions.

What is the secret of your success?
Working hard and having a passion for what I do. Also the drive to be the best at what I do. Being open to learning new things and taking risks. I never stop, I always strive to be better.

At the end of *American Idol* Ryan would say, "Seacrest out." How do you want to sign off from this interview?
Oh, Debbie is not out. I don't hope to ever be out. I will probably work until I drop dead. Then I'll be out!

A DAY IN THE LIFE OF DEBBIE WILLIAMS

6:00 A.M.: Wake up with my teenage daughter, get breakfast, read mail, feed the dogs.

7:00 A.M.: Drive my daughter to school, then go to work, listen to talk radio and sometimes FM radio and a certain host I work with, who never sleeps. Oh, and fight the L.A. traffic, which never ends!

8:00 A.M.: Arrive at work, look over schedule, sit down with associate director and block the show on paper with the script. Talk to crew, have coffee, meet with stage managers about notes, prepare rundown with director notes.

9:00 A.M.: Start blocking on camera with stand-ins as idols and judges. Place stage marks and positions for host and create the show's cold open with director.

10:00 A.M.: Music and camera rehearsal begins for *Idol* contestants. Three camera passes per person and then to makeup/hair/wardrobe.

10:30 A.M.: Rehearsal continues with idols. Music changes are made. Camera's scripted with camera shots, and voice coaches give notes. I attempt to keep us on schedule and deal with idol meltdowns and insecurities . . . being a mom transcends into work too!

11:00 A.M.: Last-minute break for orchestra and crew. I go up to the producer's office to see if there are any changes (there are always changes). Change is what keeps the show fresh!

11:30 A.M.: Still rehearsing with *Idol* contestants on camera.

12:30 P.M.: Lunch. I catch up on format, script, and schedule changes. I eat at a conference table with the singing coaches, band members, director, AD, and discuss life, work, and who is going to do well that evening in the live show, based on what we just saw in rehearsals. Sometimes we're surprised at those who are pulled through and those who don't make it. Lunch is a nice social time, I love the people I work with!

12:45 P.M.: I get script changes once the read-through with host is completed. Then I head down to the stage to do a dress rehearsal in front of a live audience.

1:00 P.M.: I greet the audience and explain what we are about to do. I introduce the host to the audience and proceed with a dress rehearsal from top to bottom.

2:30 P.M.: Finish dress rehearsal, release dress audience to allow ushers to open the house for the live show audience. I go to the director's booth to get notes, then go to idols and give them notes from the director. Judges get hair and makeup done and the idols get hair and makeup touch-ups. I find out about changes for live show and inform the crew, band, wardrobe, whoever needs to know about the changes. We talk through last-minute things with my team of stage managers, and then I go to craft service for a little protein before the live show . . . a must!

4:45 P.M.: Warm-ups begin for audience, while the stage managers get the judges/idols/band and all talent to the stage for the live show. I talk with the director about last-minute details and let them know if there are celebrities in audience for us to shoot. I let them know of information I might have received from the producers. Then I go on stage and introduce the judges, the host, and then the idols to the audience. I call for places and start the countdown to the live broadcast.

5:00 P.M.: Go on air live to East Coast.

5:15 P.M.: We are on air but I still might be getting changes to implement during the live show.

6:00 P.M.: If it's a one-hour show . . . we're off the air. If it's a two-hour show, we're halfway through the show.

6:20 P.M.: We're watching the clock and coming up with things to do to either stretch or shrink time on air. We're more than likely over on time, so we find places within the show to shave in an attempt to bring the show in on time.

7:00 P.M.: If it was a two-hour show, we are done. I go to the office and find out about the schedule for next morning. I talk with producers about the result show mechanics. We discuss problems and issues we might have had and we make tweaks for the next day's show. I have a bite to eat.

8:30 P.M.: I go down to the stage and rehearse the group song and choreography with the choreographers and the idols.

10:00 P.M.: Group song and choreography is finished and ready for tomorrow's show. It's time to drive home. I stop at grocery store and pick up whatever might be missing in the fridge . . . a mother's work never ends!

11:00 P.M.: *Home!* I kiss and talk to my daughter and catch up on her day. Then I feed dogs, check phone messages, check e-mail, write status on Facebook, have a glass of wine, take a bath, get in bed and watch the news. I attempt to sleep while the dogs are crowding me out of the bed.

11:30 P.M.: I'm still awake, so I cruise the channels and perhaps watch something mindless like the *Real Housewives of* . . . somewhere, and wonder if a show called "Real Housewives Who Work" will ever be done, maybe it is too real. That is the problem with falling asleep after work; it's hard to shut the mind off! Tomorrow is another show, and then I'll get a weekend break and get to be home with daughter/dogs and life.

JOEL PLOTCH
Film Editor

Photo credit: David Thomas, www.davethomasstudio.com

Ask Joel Plotch what it takes to be a good editor and he'll tell you first and foremost, you must be a good storyteller. Editing is so much more than stringing scenes together, and when it's done well, it's like a symphony. When it's not, well, it lacks all meaning.

If these last two sentences reveal anything, it's that Joel is an artist at heart. Growing up in New York, he developed those artistic skills with the complete support of his parents, even if they were not thrilled with the fact that a traditional artist often makes no money. But Joel is anything but a starving artist. He earned a bachelor of fine arts degree and then put that degree to good use by becoming a sought-after film editor.

Joel's path was unconventional. He didn't start out as an apprentice or an assistant; he did a multitude of other jobs instead. Eventually, he landed his first feature film gig, and *unconventional* describes that experience as well. Let's just say it involved a then-obscure director and a series of midnight phone calls. So at the risk of rambling on and getting edited by the editor himself, let's get started.

INDEPENDENT: A film that's produced, for the most part, without the backing of a major motion picture studio. These are also referred to as "art house films" or "indies." Budgets are usually smaller for these films than they are for major motion pictures.

INDUSTRIALS: A film, short, or spot that's produced solely for the internal use of a company or organization. Some may be instructional in nature.

ROUGH CUT: The early version of a film that will undergo many edits and revisions before it becomes the finished product.

SPEC SPOT: This can be a scene, a short, or an entire film that an editor creates in order to showcase his or her work. He or she is not paid for this.

STORY BOARD: A series of illustrations laid out panel by panel to give the director and producers a pre-visual of the film.

SUNDANCE: The Sundance Film Festival is an annual event celebrating the best in independent filmmaking. It was established by Robert Redford in 1981.

Describe what you do as a film editor.

I take the film that's shot on a movie and sculpt it together to create the final product, in collaboration with the director or producers.

Good, concise answer. Just how we like them. Did you study film in school?

Yes. I went to Washington University in St. Louis, where I got a BFA (bachelor of fine arts). The BFA was in multimedia, which was theater, film, and the conventional arts. I also took a significant number of courses at the Chicago Art Institute.

As a kid, did you want to work in this industry?

Yeah, absolutely. I started shooting short movies in ninth grade. There was an English course where we had the opportunity to write a story and then film it. Then, in junior and senior high we had a school radio station that played music, but there were also interviews and talk shows, and some radio theater. I was co-head of the station. Also, at my hometown library they opened a place called Levels, which was a multimedia space, and we put on productions there. All original productions, original music, original everything.

What did you think you'd do with all this education and experience?

After college I thought I'd get involved in the traditional art scene. But at that time the kind of art that was shown was abstract and that was not my bag at all. So I started working for a commercial film production house and worked my way up from PA to production managing and then to producing. Then I moved on to a company called Media Works. They did mostly children's films, *industrials*, and some commercials. And I came on as the creative director. So I learned every avenue in the film industry and in the commercial arts.

What were your responsibilities as the creative director?

We did a lot of product releases. A company would bring their sales force down to, let's say, the Breakers in West Palm Beach, and we would put on a multimedia show. There'd be a lot of slides and some films, all introducing a new product. One of the big product releases we did was Zantac. So I did a lot. I art directed, I designed graphics, I did slide shows. Also, during that time I directed an entire PBS children's learning series.

You were obviously getting an education in every facet of production, which maybe isn't typical for a lot of editors. Has that made you a better editor?

It's made me better because I understand story structure in a lot of different environments. And it gave me a lot of challenges that I had to overcome. By doing so many projects in so many different media, I'd go from the scripting stage to visualizing that script to actually producing the material. There were times when I literally wrote the script, *story boarded* it, and designed the slides to support that script. Then I would edit the film.

At that point in your career you were at the head of the food chain as a creative director. Where did you go from there?

I started getting my own clients. It created friction with the owner of Media Works, so I started my own company called JP Studio. We were a production and editorial company. We got to the point where we had three edit bays, five directors on staff, and an animation division.

At what point, then, did you become an editor?

I got into editing because I wasn't very happy with the editors I had hired. I had edited my own projects all throughout high school and college, and I started to sit down and do it myself and found that I was really good at it. So my career path started to invert in a way. At first I really wanted to direct, and I was already creative directing all these projects anyway, so I began to edit as well. And that turned into a lot of people coming to me strictly for editorial. Then I hooked up with a group of people who were in feature development. I had done a lot of music videos, a lot of commercials, and I said to myself, "You know, I'd really like to start getting back into features." So in 1994 I started making a foray into the *independent* scene.

Meaning?

I'd go to all the festivals, all the independent meet and greets, trying to find people who had a screenplay or a *rough cut* and seeing if I could get in there and actually edit a picture.

How did that work out for you?

I was having a really hard time finding something. I was prepared to take the dive, but that meant doing it for the art and for little money, so my standards were extremely high. Then, a friend of a friend of mine called and said, "Listen I have this film. It's called *In the Company of Men* and it's completely crazy." It was Neil LaBute's first film, and he was one of the producers. I watched it and was blown away. It was three hours long but it was incredible. So we made a deal, and I edited for about four weeks and cut it down to fighting weight, which was probably two hours. They got it into the *Sundance Film Festival.*

Did you know who Neil LaBute was?

No. And neither did anyone else.

What happened next?

I worked on the movie another two and a half weeks, we resubmitted it, and then did another six weeks of editing, all never even meeting Neil. I was pretty much working on my own.

Wait. You never met the director?

No. Steven, the producer, would come down and we'd have these midnight calls with Neil. Neil was working the graveyard shift at his job in Indiana, and twelve o'clock was his break. We'd discuss as many scenes as we could. The rest is history. It was a strong movie, it won the Filmmakers Trophy at Sundance.

Did this seal your working relationship with Neil?

He began to trust me. At first we just talked over the phone and had some pretty charged intellectual, theatrical-type arguments and conversations. I think we gained respect for each other right off the bat. And going back to your earlier question about experience, I don't think I would've been able to relate to someone like Neil, who had a serious theater background, without my varied background. He needed somebody who could talk his language. He also needed someone to dig in their heels when they thought it was right for the movie, and then be able to acquiesce when they realized the director had a strong opinion.

Talk in general about the relationship between the editor and the director.

A lot of directors don't want to be in the editing room all the time. Neil and I have developed a level of trust where he comes in after

I feel I'm ready to show him something and we discuss it. I would venture to say nine out of the ten great editors have the same kind of relationships with the directors they work with. I think once you have some sort of simpatico with a particular director, there's a level of trust whereby the editor's able to create the rhythm and style of the film as long as it's within the parameters of what the director's looking for.

What happened after *In the Company of Men*?

Neil and I kept in touch. I went back to New York and kept on doing the stuff I was doing at JP studio and worked on Neil's next movie, *Your Friends and Neighbors*. I went back to L.A. for six months and was running JP studio, getting up at four o'clock in the morning. Then the next film we were thinking of doing was *Nurse Betty*. When I decided to go on to *Nurse Betty* I closed down JP studio. I came back out to L.A., rented a place and did *Nurse Betty*, and then continued to work.

Allow us to rattle off some of your other credits. You did *Lakeview Terrace* with Samuel L. Jackson, *The Wicker Man* with Nicolas Cage, *The Shape of Things* with Paul Rudd, and lots more. Someone with these amazing credits probably has some tips for breaking in.

I think it all depends on how aggressive you are. There are people who come in at the apprentice level, move to assistant editor, then start being the second editor or additional editor. I've known assistant editors who've done it for ten years and who now are editing features. Then I know some people who got into assistant editing, thought they were going to edit, and felt, "You know what? I really like assistant editing. The kind of pressure that's on the editor is just not for me."

What do you look for in an assistant editor?

I'd love to know if someone would like to cut or has the juice to do it, but primarily that person has to be up on all the technology. Before, the workflow was much less complicated, and I could say to an assistant editor who I knew had the chops, "Do you like to cut, because I can hand you some scenes to see what you can do." Now I'm almost entirely basing my hiring decision on how well they know the different workflows and the different ways of doing things.

So for you, it's the technical . . .

That supersedes the artistic.

Are there courses on film editing that are useful?

Yes. There are editing programs at schools like USC, UCLA, and NYU. I think they're useful just to give you a basic understanding because like everyone says, once you know the rules, then you can break them. But there's really no substitute for doing it. I would recommend you find a director you like, somebody who's young and hungry, and do some *spec spots*. Cut as much as possible. Doing it is the best teacher. Just be sure to have someone critique your work before presenting it.

Where does someone go to learn the editing systems like Avid or Final Cut?

You can learn that from a book, but there are courses in it.

What's the salary range for an editor?

I would say the general range is anywhere from $4,000 a week on a $20 million movie, to $15,000 a week on a $100 million movie.

What are the skills necessary for this type of work?

I started out initially being someone who loved to draw. When I was in college, I would literally draw eight hours a day. I loved the solitary process of being able to sketch something out and fill it in and come out with a finished thing. And I think that kind of mentality translates to editing. It's a solitary venture. You have to have the mettle for it.

Anything else you'd like to add?

I think people mistake the editing craft for being much more technical than artistic. There is a craft element to it, but there's a lack of meaning going on right now where people put a lot of images together, and they're fancy looking, but ultimately they're just images strung together.

So how does one become a good artist?

I think as an artist in general, you have to be well rounded. If you're not well rounded and you don't have an education in music, in theater, in playwriting, in all the different aspects of trying to express yourself, then you're doing yourself a disservice. It's not that hard to learn an editing program, but you need to be able to draw on life experiences. That's important.

Last question. Do you find you take longer to edit a sex scene than say, a car chase scene?

I would say the chase scene is probably harder to edit, but you savor the sex scene.

Well said.

A DAY IN THE LIFE OF JOEL PLOTCH

5:30 A.M.: Wake up. Eat a banana, drink some Kangen water, get ready for online trading.

6:30 A.M.: Make breakfast for a sleeping son and wife and monitor investments on e-Trade at opening of the trading day, while reading newspaper.

7:00 A.M.: My son wakes up, and breakfast and getting ready for the day ensues.

7:50 A.M.: Drive my son to school every other day, shower, exercise, and head out to the editing room. Every other day, play nine holes of golf.

9:00 A.M.: Get into editing room and debrief on the major battles of the day. Look at the dailies from the previous day's shoot, report to set about quality of the footage and what needs to be reshot, or things that need to be addressed with the studio, the producers, and the director.

10:30 A.M.: Start cutting the previous day's dailies, looking at all the footage and coordinating first-cut scenes with the card layout on the "big board" so that I keep up with camera on editorial.

3:00 P.M.: Go out to set and show first-cut scenes of the previous day to the director and director of photography and discuss.

5:00 P.M.: Back at editing room to continue cutting and revising previous scenes from the days before. Getting assistants started on cleaning up dialogue in the previously cut scenes and going over any effects requirements, sound requirements, sound EFX.

7:00 P.M.: Phone calls to set to see if film is making it to the lab so that dailies are on schedule for the next day.

8:00 P.M.: Meeting with my crew concerning the upcoming day/ week events so that everyone is ready for workload.

9:00 P.M.: Answer all e-mails for the day. Make "to do" list for the next couple of days.

10:00 P.M.: Drive home.

10:30 P.M.: Arrive home. Sit outside and meditate. Cuddle with my sleeping son for half an hour.

11:00 P.M.: Sleep.

MIKE ALEXANDER
Lead Animal Trainer

If you want a job working with animals, but you don't aspire to work at your local Petco, you may want to consider working in Hollywood as an animal trainer. Mike Alexander did, and check him out, he's in a book.

Mike made a decision to train animals years ago. He went from being a volunteer at an exotic animal rescue, to performing on stage in Universal Studios Live Animal Show to becoming the lead animal trainer in *Harry Potter and the Chamber of Secrets*.

Mike can literally train anything—well, anything with a brain and the slightest cognitive capacity. So he can train an owl, a pigeon, a rat, or a moth, believe it or not. Can he make a Great Dane break dance? Come on, be reasonable (but that doesn't mean he wasn't asked).

Mike's a busy man. He works nonstop, so chances are you have seen his work and not even realized it. He has huge blockbusters to his credit like *Night at the Museum, Beverly Hills Chihuahua, Planet of the Apes, Eight Below, Charlie and the Chocolate Factory,* and *Marmaduke.* How he got Marmaduke to talk, we will never know.

Mike has a bag of treats and forty chihuahuas seated around him. Seeing this many chihuahuas up close is both cute and frightening. Let's begin the interview so we can get out of here before the treats run out.

> **DIRECTOR OF PHOTOGRAPHY (DP):** This person works behind the camera and takes the director's vision and brings it to life in the visual sense. Also known as a cinematographer (see Shane Hurlbut's chapter).
>
> **SCRIPT BREAKDOWNS:** When a particular department head reads a movie or television script to see the extent of their involvement in each scene. This is also the opportunity to flag any demands in the script that may not be possible to execute.

Can you explain what you do as a lead animal trainer and an animal coordinator?

I train animals to perform for a movie and then get them to perform on the set. The coordinating part of my job involves casting, crew hires, budgeting, scheduling, and *script breakdowns.* For instance on *Beverly Hills Chihuahua,* in addition to actually training the dogs, I hired almost 100 trainers to work for me. We were the biggest on-set department on the movie.

Got it. Let's shelve the chihuahua chat for now and learn about you. Talk about your childhood and your influences as a kid.

I grew up in Chatsworth, California. As a kid, I always had dogs in the family and I would go out and catch snakes in the hills, but I didn't grow up in an animal environment or a movie environment. After high school I worked as a volunteer for a lady named Martine Colette, she runs the Wildlife Waystation. It's an animal shelter for wild animals where they have lions, tigers, leopards, wolves, chimps, and bears.

Is that when you decided you were going to work with animals for a living?

I knew I enjoyed it, but I still wasn't sure it would be my profession. I liked it enough to leave the Waystation to attend Moorpark College, where I graduated with an associate degree in animal science. It was a lot of work. I was either taking care of the animals, in class, or performing live shows with the animals for the public on the weekends.

That must've left very little time for keg parties and toga wearing. So how did you make the degree apply to a career upon graduating?

Actually, I was scouted, while I was still in college, by Gary Gero, who owns Birds and Animals Unlimited. It's the leading Hollywood animal training company that trains animals for movies. A couple of months before graduation, Gary visited the school, observed us, and asked if I would be interested in working for him.

Something like that won't happen to everyone. Are there other ways to break in?

My advice would be to find a trainer or a company who places trainers, and work as an apprentice. As an apprentice, you'll be required to clean the animal's kennels, bathe the animals, and feed them. An apprenticeship could last as long as two years. It's not like a person needs to be a good poop picker-upper to be a good animal trainer, it is just the chain of events in my business.

So once you break in as an apprentice, how do you work your way up?

The next rung on the ladder would be to go to the set with the animal trainer as an assistant. There you learn about the set, but you don't have pressure on you to perform.

Next, you'll become a full-fledged trainer. You will be the person on the set with the animal and you'll be expected to make that animal perform on command.

When I started with Gary Gero he would say to us, "Train something." He encouraged us to go to the shelter, adopt a dog, and train it. If the dog that you trained gets called for a movie or a TV show, then you can work with it on set. It was good advice and I followed it.

Talk about the pressure on set for you to make the animal perform. It must be intense.

The pressure is enormous sometimes. I won't lie. In the beginning the pressure is intense. The better you get, and the longer you do it, the less that pressure is a factor. With experience comes faith in yourself and in your abilities. There are times when people will change their mind on set and ask for ridiculous things. Like, "Can you make the dog break dance?"

Break dancing, really? When did that come up?

I was asked that on the set of *Marmaduke*. There's a scene where Marmaduke is dancing on that arcade machine called Dance, Dance Revolution. They wanted to know if the dog could actually do break dance moves. We did a bunch of tests, and we did pretty good with him. We were able to teach him to bounce up and down. The *DP* shot closeups, and when the scene was cut together it looked pretty believable. Was he break dancing? No, but it worked out.

Are the majority of people in your business freelancers?

Most people in this business are freelancers. When I do a movie, the movie pays me. So I'm not really employed by anybody, but I work through Birds and Animals Unlimited. It's really difficult for people, including myself, to buy a variety of animals and make those animals movie ready. You really have to go and work for someone who has an entire stable of animals.

So Birds and Animals Unlimited has the animals at their facility and you have the access to them? You don't need to actually buy and raise llamas?

Right, no llama rearing.

Can you talk about your experience working on *Night at the Museum* with that little devious monkey, Dexter?

Dexter's real name is Crystal, and Crystal was just *acting* devious. In real life she's charming. We had to have Crystal bite Ben Stiller's nose through the bars of the cage. That was difficult. The challenge, obviously, was to figure out how we would get the shot and make sure Crystal wasn't going to take a chunk out of Ben's nose.

Yeah, he's a pretty big star. There aren't many roles for nose-less actors.

Exactly, and were that to have happened, my career would've come to a screeching halt.

So how did you train her?

First we went to the costume store and we bought one of those Groucho Marx noses and taught her to bite that gently. Then we taught her to bite our noses. She'd put her mouth on us, but not squeeze. Then when we got very comfortable with the stunt, we talked to Ben to find out how he felt about it. He was a little apprehensive, but he tried it a couple of times on camera and Crystal did really well. Ultimately when we shot it, we put a big prosthetic nose on him and the visual effects cleaned it up so it looked real.

You also worked on that little wizard movie called *Harry Potter and the Chamber of Secrets*.

That was a monster. I had to move to England for thirteen months to work on it. I worked heavily with owls. I taught an owl to fly with something in its mouth, which is a very hard and unusual trick to train a bird of prey to do. They are not the smartest creatures on earth.

How many hours went into training the owl for that stunt?

I spent hundreds and hundreds of hours. There was a scene where the owl had to fly while carrying Christmas crackers, which are like little party poppers. The owl had to carry them, and then drop them. I spent six months just to get the owl to hold this thing in his mouth. When we were finally on set ready to shoot the scene, the director, Christopher Columbus, decided he didn't want an owl in the scene at all and that was it. All my work went down the drain.

Oh, that is just painful. What about a situation where you not only had to train the animal, but you had to train the actor as well?

Making animals perform is one thing, but making animals and actors work together seamlessly is difficult. Matter of fact, that is probably the hardest part to my job. I have done it a lot, and have been successful with it, but it's not easy.

Do actors always do their own death-defying stunts?

No, actually, a lot of the time I do the stunts with the animals on camera. I'm in *SAG*, so if there is a scene with an animal attack, I will double the actor and be the one who's attacked.

Do you get paid a stunt rate for doing that?

Oh, yeah, absolutely.

Mark is available if you need someone to get attacked by a bear or a gator. (At this point in the interview, we notice a moth is flying around the room.) Can you train that?

You know what, anything can be trained. I am serious. You can train anything that has the ability to be trained. I could train that moth, but there are limits to what it can do.

Can you train it to rob a bank?

No. You would need a chimp for that.

Noted, and filed away for possible later use. Talk about a standout moment in your career.

One of the best moments, and the most difficult, was working on *Charlie and the Chocolate Factory*.

Wasn't Gene Wilder amazing?

I did the one with Tim Burton and Johnny Depp, which was also amazing, I assure you. I had previously done *Planet of the Apes* with Tim, and he was remaking *Charlie*, and wanted to do it word-for-word from the book. In the book there wasn't a goose that laid the golden egg, there was the squirrel room. The scene was insane, and I had no idea how I was going to pull it off. The producers were ready to use visual effects, and create fake squirrels, but Tim was insistent about using real squirrels. I didn't want to let Tim Burton down, so I moved to England for six months to find the squirrels, train them, and work on set on the movie.

Can you explain the scene for us?

Walnuts came down a chute onto a conveyer belt. The squirrels grabbed the nut, they tapped it, they listened to it, shook it, bit it and broke it open. Then they put the meat of the nut back onto the conveyer belt. The squirrels also had to attack a little girl and carry her away. Tim would come by my workshop all the time. He was very involved in the process. We created special nuts that were plastic and held together by dental adhesive and a dab of Super Glue. I taught the squirrels to bite the Super Glue off, which would allow them to easily open the shell take the nut out and set it down.

In the scene where the squirrels ran all over the girl, I came up with a method that I thought would work. The squirrels would be in boxes and I had another trainer lying down. Behind him was another set of boxes with food in them. I would let them out, and they would run over the trainer and into the individual boxes. A door would come down behind them and close them in. I trained twenty-five squirrels for this stunt. We shot some test footage and when Tim and Johnny saw it, they went nuts.

Eh, squirrel pun.

When I look back, that was probably one of the stunts I am most proud of.

What advice do you have for someone looking to do what you do?
You have to love animals. You have to have patience. You have to have a real passion for it, because it's a huge commitment. If you are expecting it to be a glamorous Hollywood business, find something else to do. There's a book called *The Lassie Method*, written by the legendary trainer, Rudd Weatherwax, who trained Lassie. Pick up his book before you make a decision to go this route. It's an enlightening read.

What can someone, who does what you do, make?
We are union teamsters, so there are set rates for animal trainers. Our rate is $40 per hour, on an eight-hour minimum. You can make more by doubling an actor, like we discussed, or working overtime.

Do you work steadily throughout the year?
I work almost constantly. I've had to turn down work to be at home. And through the company we bill out constantly. It seems like more and more jobs are shooting out of town. I'm not in Los Angeles as much as I used to be, and being on the road can be exhausting.

We should go so you can walk all these chihuahuas, but before we do, translate this sentence we read in an animal trainer book: "I am going to bridge the dog and use the clicker to pay him when he hits his last mark, and then I need him to run home."
You want the dog to walk and stop. You will use sound cues made by a hand clicker to give him commands, as opposed to speaking. Then you will pay him with a treat and have him walk into his cage.

Impressive!

A DAY IN THE LIFE OF MIKE ALEXANDER

No two days are ever the same. Every day seems to bring a new challenge and or adventure, but here's my typical day right now.

5:00 A.M.: Wake up and put the dogs out in the yard to do their business. (The movie I'm working on right now stars a beagle dog.)

5:30 A.M.: Breakfast and coffee (Cheerios with fruit). Then take a shower.

6:30 A.M.: Load the dogs in the truck and drive to the set location in Thousand Oaks to rehearse with the actors (mostly kids on this show), and the director.

8:00 A.M.: Arrive at set, and let the dogs out to exercise.

8:00 A.M.–10:00 A.M.: Drink coffee and b/s with Matilde (the other trainer working with me on this show) and *wait* for the actors to arrive.

10:00 A.M.: The actors and director arrive, and the next few hours are spent training the dogs to work with them. And training *them* to work with the dogs.

1:00 P.M.: We eat lunch on the set.

1:30 P.M.: Spend a couple more hours training beagles on location.

3:30 P.M.: Load the dogs in the truck and head home.

5:00 P.M.: Arrive home. Jasmine (my daughter) is waiting for us, gives me a quick hug and "Hi Daddy," then spends the next hour playing with the dogs.

6:00 P.M.: Feed and put dogs to bed.

6:30 P.M.: Dinner, then a bath for Jasmine (she's a mess after an hour of wrestling around with the four beagles!).

7:30 P.M.: Read Jasmine *Green Eggs and Ham* (her favorite book right now).

8:00 P.M.: She's asleep, so a quick shower, half hour of TV, then to bed, ready to do the whole thing again tomorrow.

JACKIE BURCH
Casting Director

Photo credit: Laurence Maultsby, www.accidentalphotography.com

"Don't mess with the bull, young man, you'll get the horns" (*Breakfast Club*); "Yippee-ki-yay, motherfucker" (*Die Hard*); and "No more yankie my wankie. The Donger need food" (*Sixteen Candles*). The actors who uttered those lines might not have if it wasn't for casting director extraordinaire Jackie Burch. The writer puts it on paper, the director puts it on screen, the casting director puts it in perspective by finding the perfect person to play each part. Jackie has found that person more times than we can count. She is humbled by her success and very much still enamored of Hollywood, despite it.

In a career that has spanned thirty-one years and over seventy-five movies, Jackie's worked with some of the biggest actors and directors in Hollywood, like the legendary John Hughes. Not to mention, she's put new blood like Anthony Michael Hall on the map and taken chances on others like Alan Rickman in *Die Hard*.

Jackie has a God-given talent for reading a script and knowing who should play the part. You either have it or you don't. She can't take all the credit for her success, though. In fact, some of the toughest decisions in her life she refuses to make, so some of her success is thanks to her longtime advisor, her psychic. Here's hoping that psychic thinks this interview is a good idea.

BREAKDOWN SERVICE: This service connects the casting professional with talent and talent agents, and is used when casting a project. The actual breakdowns are complete synopses of the characters contained within scripts.

INDEPENDENT: This is another word for "freelance." When a person is not employed full-time, but rather works on a contract basis and is hired for a specific amount of time and then released when the job has ended. In some instances people who are independent or freelance work more than one job at a time.

SELECTS: Another word for "finalists." These are the actors who have auditioned for a casting director and are deemed fit for the part. Their headshots and audition tape are screened by the director and producer. Usually a casting director will make three to five selects per part.

THE SIDES: A section within an actual script that has been selected and given to actors for them to prepare for an audition with the casting director.

STAGE DIRECTION: As pertains to a script: The details that inform the reader about the setting and the other character descriptions and explanations of what those characters are doing. The stage direction is exposition designed to help the reader envision the scene.

Jackie, please rattle off just some of the movies you've cast over the years.

Okay, there's *The Breakfast Club*, *Sixteen Candles*, *Die Hard*, *Predator*, *Coming to America*, *Three Amigos!*, *Mask*, *Vegas Vacation*, *Dick Tracy*, and about sixty others.

It may be obvious to most people, but tell us what a casting director does.

My job is to read a script, understand the characters, and then go out and find the best person for the role. I find actors, and agents submit actors to me as well. I start reading people for the parts, which means I give them a section of the script to study and then they come in front of me and I tape them performing the character. Then I bring my *selects* to the director and the producer.

Where did you grow up, and was the entertainment industry in your sights from an early age?

I grew up in Newburgh, New York. And, no, my plan was to be a teacher. I never had any dreams or aspirations of being in the movie business. I went to college and I got a degree in special education. When I graduated, I moved out to California to teach and got a job working with autistic kids. Then I went for my masters. I always liked Helen Keller, so I specialized in deaf education.

How did casting come about?

It was 1980, I was teaching and I ran into a friend named Michael Chinich. Michael was a big casting director who was on staff at Universal. He had cast *Coal Miner's Daughter* and *Animal House*. He asked if I wanted to come work for him, because his assistant was going on vacation.

How did you become friendly with him?

My brother, who was in the entertainment business as a producer and director, hired him, and we became friendly. Too bad my brother never hired me, but that's for another book. I told him if his assistant ever quit I wanted the job assisting him as a casting coordinator. As fate would have it, she ended up quitting and I got her job.

How long were you with Michael?

I was with him for a year, and when he wasn't able to promote me, I decided to leave and go *independent*. That was a bold move, but it forced me to meet more people and expand my contacts. For a short time, I worked as a casting coordinator for Bob Edmiston, who cast *Star Wars: The Empire Strikes Back*, and Ellen Chenoweth, who cast *Diner*. I was hired by Roger Corman, and I actually cast a movie on my own that was my first independent I ever did, called *Forbidden World*.

Then later Michael pulled me back to Universal and put me on staff, and the first movie I did was *Psycho II*. That was very exciting, because I was working with Anthony Perkins and I brought Meg Tilly in. The movie did really well.

So how did your relationship begin with John Hughes?

When I was working for Ellen Chenoweth I was on a movie called *The Joy of Sex* that he had written. I was very involved and did a lot of work on that project. John and I became friendly instantly. When I went back to Universal, John set up *Sixteen Candles* with them and said, "I want Jackie to cast the movie." That was probably the biggest break of my career. I was running the show on that movie and getting all the credit. That was a wonderful movie to work on, and he and I were like simpatico. He was just so easy to work with in the beginning (of our working relationship). And then after the success of *Sixteen Candles*, he asked me to do *The Breakfast Club*.

Give us some *Breakfast Club* and *Sixteen Candles* behind-the-scenes scoops.

When John and I screened *Sixteen Candles* we knew we had to get Anthony Michael Hall for *The Breakfast Club*, he was hands-down our first choice. Then we hired Ally Sheedy. We originally wanted her for *Sixteen Candles*, but she wasn't available.

Emilio Estevez's role was originally written for a football player. When I brought Emilio in, I thought, "this kid works, but he's too small for a football player." I asked John if he would consider changing the part to a wrestler. And John was all for it.

Then there is Gedde Watanabe, who I cast as Long Duk Dong in *Sixteen Candles*. He read for me and pretended he didn't speak any English. So finally he told me that he could speak English just fine and I loved that. He totally got me. Then Gedde and I played the same joke on the producers. I told them that Gedde couldn't speak any English and when he came in to read for them he played it perfectly. The producers were trying to communicate with him by talking louder hoping he would understand them. It was hilarious. Finally, when he was done with the read, he started to speak perfect English. I love to have fun like that.

Can you give an example of a time you had to fight for an actor?

I wanted Alan Rickman for the lead terrorist, Hans, in *Die Hard*. I knew he could play an intellectual heavy and I knew he was perfect for the part. I said to Joel (Silver), "I want to see all the terrorists be foreign and really good-looking." He trusted me. When you have a producer who trusts you, it makes all the difference. McTiernan (the director) didn't trust me, for whatever reason. He would reject actors based on their eyebrows. Literally, he and his wife would sit in a room and look at the head shots. I would walk out of the room and tell Joel, "I can't work with this guy. He doesn't understand talent."

You can tell a lot from eyebrows. Explain the process of casting from the moment you get a script.

I always approach each job with an open mind. When I read scripts I never read the *stage direction*. For instance, if it said the character was a white guy, I don't want to know that, because maybe it shouldn't be a white guy. I might read it and think this role should be filled by a black guy or an Indian guy. I'll even bring a woman in for a part that was originally intended for a man. I don't think you always have to lock into what the writer, director, or producer thinks it should be. I read it and I get a sense of what I think it should be, and then I try different avenues. And that is how I've always done it.

What are some things you look for when you hire a coordinator?

In today's market, you really have to have excellent computer skills. You cannot do this job without understanding cameras, uploading and downloading video. You need to be organized. You have to be familiar with the *breakdown service*; it is an incredible service, and a mandatory tool of the trade. It takes the scripts and gets *the sides* to all the agents. If you really want to move up, you really have to go out and do your homework. What I mean by that is you've got to see a lot of theater. You have to be open to meeting new actors and keeping your eyes open constantly. I see everything, movies, TV, and theater. You need a passion for it. And you have to have integrity. That's very important.

Does your process stop once a show is cast, or will you actually go to the set?

I usually go to the set once just to make sure there is no bad behavior and everyone is happy. I get one free lunch, I always say, and then I move on to the next show.

I was summoned to the set once on the movie *The Breakfast Club*, because they were really worried about Judd Nelson. What happened was he was staying in character off set, which is called method acting, and they were ready to fire him because he was being such an ass to everyone. Judd is a great guy and a good actor, but it was risky for him to do that, because he was still sort of young and unknown at the time. As a young actor you don't want to build a bad reputation for yourself. So when I got that call, I got on him and he straightened right up.

After years at Universal you broke out on your own. What was the impetus for that?

I was tired of being part of the big studio system, and John Hughes wanted me to cast *Weird Science* for him, so I took the job on the condition that I would be hired as an independent contractor. That movie allowed me to break out on my own. I was ready to start making some real money and have the freedom to do projects that I wanted to do. So I took the risk, and it paid off because I've never stopped working.

So in your world you can be at a studio, or work as an independent contractor?

Right, those are your options, be in a studio and cast what they tell you to, or be independent and work freelance on whatever you like. It depends on the personality and the person really. Unless you are running the department, you won't make huge money in the studio system, whereas independents can make much more, but there is no job stability. There's always a catch.

You took a lot of risks and made a lot of bold moves.
Well, I go to psychics, and I definitely listen to them. And my psychic said, "Go out on your own." She also saw that there were awards surrounding the movie I was working on, which was *Mask* at the time, and as you know, it was nominated.

We have heard of managers, agents, and even shrinks in Hollywood giving advice, but psychics?
Every major decision in my life is made by a psychic. I got into psychics and mediums when my father died. A woman I had never met read jewelry, and I asked her to read his watch that I was wearing. She put it up to her forehead and said, "Irwin." That was my father's name. Then she says, "He loves you very dearly." And my father used to always say to us, "I love you very dearly." Not "I love you very much," those words exactly. I was hooked ever since.

Did you ask your psychic if it would be a wise career move to be interviewed for this book?
I did, and that's why I'm here.

That's a relief. Take us through an average day of a casting session.
Okay, if you're doing a movie you get total submissions, which are resumes and headshots. Once I pick the people I want using headshots and online profiles, my assistant will begin to set up the readings. We tape all the readings. It's interesting because sometimes you

see one thing live when the camera picks up something completely different. So shooting video really helps.

So then you make selects?

Yes, I end up seeing hundreds and hundreds of actors, make my selects and submit them to the producer and director. I may see hundreds of actors for even a one-line part. I like to see everybody. Then, of course, I will chisel it down.

What kind of money can you make in your business?

Casting directors on big-budget movies are making $120,000 for a ten-week job.

Do they also have to pay their staff from that?

No, and they get overages as well. Now I hear that the purse strings are tightening a little bit, and even the big-budget films aren't as generous as that. It really ranges now because of the economic climate. As an independent, you are looking at more like $50,000.

What is a home run audition for you and stands out in your career?

I met with Dakota Fanning when she was very young, before she did the movie *I Am Sam*. She came in so overly polite, I thought she was putting me on. But I realized she was from the South, and that's how people are in the South. She picked up the material and you saw a De Niro style of acting in this little child. It was amazing. I never saw someone pick up material and be so different than what she was like in real life. That was an education for me. In general, when someone can come in, pick up material, and make it work, that is so exciting for me. And when someone brings something different to what you think the material is or should be, that is equally exciting. That is what I live for.

Can you give an aspiring casting director a bit of advice?
Intern for a good casting director. Go to a lot of plays. Watch a lot of TV. See a lot of movies. And, maybe most importantly, care about actors.

Is there a director or actor working today who you want to work with?
Jack Nicholson. Really anyone young and talented. I'm easy.

The last, and arguably most important question. Casting couch, myth or fact?
Hmmmm, I might have used it once.

A DAY IN THE LIFE OF JACKIE BURCH

7:00 A.M.: Wake up.

7:30 A.M.–8:30 A.M.: Walk my dog Fanny.

8:30 A.M.–9:00 A.M.: Feed Fanny.

9:00 A.M.–9:30 A.M.: Shower and get ready.

9:30 A.M.: Go to my office, which is an extension of my house.

10:00 A.M.: Open gates for actors.

10:00 A.M.–1:30 P.M.: I audition thirty actors.

1:30 P.M.: Lunch at the house.

2:00 P.M.–5:00 P.M.: Audition another thirty-five actors.

5:00 P.M.–7:00 P.M.: Screen tapes and narrow down my selects.

7:00 P.M.: Dinner.

7:30 P.M.: Check DVDs of actors that have been mailed in because they live too far away to audition in person.

8:00 P.M.: Skype actors in other cities so I can direct their reads.

9:00 P.M.: Walk Fanny.

10:30 P.M.: Sleep.

MARK STEINES
Cohost Entertainment Tonight

Photo credit: John Russo

Let's get this out of the way right now. There is a resemblance between Mark Steines and Tom Cruise. Poor Cruise has been living in Mark's shadow for *years* now.

Mark Steines is seen by millions of people nightly as the cohost of the highest-rated and most-watched entertainment news show in America, *Entertainment Tonight*. He travels around the world to cover the biggest entertainment stories of our time and has interviewed all the A-listers from Halle Berry to George Clooney and everyone in between, including one of his favorites, Cher.

If you think his job is easy, think again. He deals with huge personalities who have even huger egos, and he walks a tightrope between not offending his interview subject and mining juicy details for the viewers to lap up. The man literally has a carry-on bag packed by the door at all times and, like any good journalist, is ready to drop everything at a moment's notice to race to the front lines of entertainment for our viewing pleasure.

We've turned the tables on Mr. Steines and put him in the hot seat. We've tied him to the chair, and we aren't letting him go until he shares every Hollywood secret he's got.

> **AFFILIATE APPEARANCE:** Affiliates are local network stations in various markets around the country that air a particular show. Often the show hosts will visit the different markets and appear at events in order to stay in the good graces of each market.
>
> **SET VISIT:** A TV crew's access to the set of a movie or TV show while the show is shooting. The majority of the stories that come out of a set visit are referred to as "behind-the-scenes."

Mark, we're going to get you in the mood . . . (clearing throat) Dada, dada, da, da, da, da, da-da-da . . .

Hello everybody and welcome to *Entertainment Tonight*, I'm Mark Steines.

Wow, you are on automatic pilot.

What, sorry, where am I? Oh, interview, right. Hi, I'm Mark Steines.

Well, Mark Steines, thanks for joining us. Please tell us what you do for a living.

I go to someone else's wedding every single day. That is how I would describe my job. I'm there for their day of celebration, their big moment. That's kind of how it feels, you know? I don't mean that in a bad way, I mean it is great to be able to be around that sort of celebration every day. Whether it's the Academy Awards, or the Grammys, or the Emmys. I am constantly in the center of the eye of the entertainment news storm.

How many years have you been in that storm?

I'm in my sixteenth season.

Wow, and in Hollywood years that's like 122.

(Laughs) It is, but you know what, my dad worked at John Deere for thirty years, and I wear makeup and have my hair done every day, so I can't complain.

Talk about where you grew up and what you were into as a kid.

I was born in Dubuque, Iowa. My parents, Betty and Leroy, have been together fifty-six years. They raised both my brother and me. I was really into sports when I was a kid. I actually wanted to play professional football and ended up going to college and played football, but injured myself to the point that I couldn't play anymore. I was well behaved; I didn't get into trouble very much and never served any jail time, so I'm proud of that. . . .

There is plenty of time for you to become a Hollywood scandal. Talk about college and your path to becoming a journalist.
I went to the University of Northern Iowa. I went there not because of its journalism program, but because I had a full athletic scholarship to play football. Once I started to study journalism, things started to click and make sense for me. I began gravitating toward the video department, and my grades really excelled and I ended up getting an academic scholarship as well. The academic scholarship opened doors for me to the local TV station's internship program, and I started to work there as a camera operator. I was immediately over my head, but I just knew that I had a passion for this, and I could work with all the equipment and learn how everything worked.

That's an amazing opportunity you made for yourself.
Well, that's just it, we are all dealt a hand of cards and the question is how we play that hand. I learned early on to chase opportunity and not money, because you may never catch the money, but opportunity exists. I was making $11,000 a year. I knew that was nothing, but I realized that I could learn from everyone I was working with, and there was value in that.

That's some good advice. What sparked your move from Waterloo, Iowa, to Los Angeles?
If you were going to ask me about my big break this would be it.

We're asking . . .
I struggled and struggled to find a job on TV, but people would tell me that they couldn't hire me because I didn't have enough experience. So I'd say, "How can I get experience if you don't give me a

job?" It was a real catch-22. Then, in 1988, I was assigned to go to the Republican National Convention with my mentor, Ron Steele, who was one of the main anchors at the station.

Is that his real name? He was meant to be an anchor from the womb with a name like that. Sorry to interrupt, but that is an awesome name.

It is. I'm good friends with Ron Steele to this day. So we went to New Orleans and when we were there I was mistaken for Tom Cruise. This was right after *Top Gun* and *Cocktail* came out. One thing led to another and *Entertainment Tonight* got wind that Tom Cruise was in New Orleans making a movie. They sent a crew out to locate him and, lo and behold, they found out that I wasn't him. So they decided they just wanted to go along and do a behind-the-scenes story on me. The story aired, and by the end of the week I had three job offers. And that's how I got my first break on camera.

Wow, press is a powerful thing, huh?

It really is. I ended up taking a job in Springfield, Missouri. I worked there for a while, and one day I got a call from IMG (an agency), which I subsequently signed with, and they got me a lot of interest and I flew to San Diego and Los Angeles for interviews.

When I got to L.A. I stayed with my best friend from high school. I had to borrow his beat-up Honda and I broke down twice on the way to the interview. I was so flustered that when I got there I actually talked them out of hiring me because all they wanted was a reporter, and I said that I wanted to be an anchor. I didn't want to take myself out of that seat. And she thanked me and I was on my way. I got home and I guess they liked what they saw because they offered me the job as their Saturday night anchor. I took it.

So overnight, you jumped from market eighty-two to market two. That's the fast track, my friend.

Yeah, but you know what, to be honest with you I was scared to death. When I came out to Los Angeles I knew there were far more talented people with more experience. But I just knew I could work harder, show up earlier, and stay later.

How did *ET* come about?

Linda Bell, who is my boss at *ET*, was the executive producer of *Hard Copy* at the time, and she saw me one Saturday night. She tried to hire me from KCAL to work at *Hard Copy*, but I was in a contract and they wouldn't let me out. Eventually she made it to *ET*, and when I freed up from my deal she got me to come over.

Can you describe a typical day?

As far as a regular tape day in the studio here in Los Angeles, I will get up early and do a little cardio. I always try to take my good energy in the morning and put it on myself rather than give it away to someone else. Then I am out the door by 7:45. I fight the L.A. traffic and get to work by 8:30 and go right into hair and makeup.

So far sounds just like our day.

By 8:45 I'm in the voice-over booth and do whatever copy is ready for me. Then I get on the set and we roll from 9:45 until 11:30. Then I'll get called to go back in the studio for any voice-over changes they may want to make. Then if I have nothing going on after that, I can technically leave by 2 P.M.

If that was a typical day, go all atypical on us.

Over a ten-day period I did the following: I flew to Hawaii to do the *Hawaii Five-O set visit*. I was there for three days, which was a long, long time. I came back to Los Angeles for the Emmy Awards and worked the event all day on a Sunday. Monday I did voice-overs from home. Monday night, went out and shot until three in the morning on *Pirates of the Caribbean: On Stranger Tides*. I taped the show in the studio on Tuesday. Wednesday I did the show then raced off the set and flew to Las Vegas to do an *affiliate appearance* for the sales people there and got back to L.A. at ten at night. Thursday and Friday were normal shows. On Sunday I flew out to London to interview Halle Berry for the movie *Dark Tide*. With the time difference, I literally landed and showered at the hotel which was at Heathrow Airport, drove to the set, worked about eight hours, had a meal, fell asleep, woke up, and flew back to L.A. Once in L.A., I had a three-hour layover. Enough time to go home, shower, repack, reintroduce myself to my kids, head back to the airport, and fly to Hawaii to do a set visit on the USS *Missouri* with Rihanna. Then I came back to L.A. and continued work on our daily show.

We need a nap just hearing that. So you are always packed.

Yeah, I keep a bag packed by the front door.

Do you have some top-line characteristics and traits that you think would work well for someone looking to get into your business?

I can tell you what works for me. I'm very aware of time-management skills, and I am very good at organizing my life. Multitasking is a big skill to have. I am in a newsroom and constantly having to deal with three or four different things at once, but also have to remain focused.

People can get really distracted in this business. There are so many things coming in, wire news, producer notes, script changes, a massive amount of information exchanged. So being focused and being able to multitask are two very important characteristics. At the end of the day, you have to remember to be human. In the position that I am in, you really have to know how to connect with people.

So for people who might want to become a journalist, in your opinion what makes a good interview?

Being a good listener. Being a good celebrity interviewer is different than being a good interviewer. There is a big balancing act that is going on. You can interview a politician all day long and you can throw the hard-hitting questions. But you have to remember when you're sitting down with a celebrity, there's usually a sales pitch: "I am going to sit down and talk with you about my new movie." But I want to talk to them about the baby they are pregnant with. So there are all these little things that you need to do to get to the point where you can ask those questions. There's a line where our audience wants to know all of the gossip and dirt, then there's a line where I personally stand, and a line where my producer wants me to go. I need to tread lightly at times and be more aggressive at other times; it's a balancing act.

Who have been your favorites?

I love Cher. Love her! She can handle just about anything you throw at her. She is so grounded and connected. I thought Lisa Marie Presley was a really good interview as well. A few years back Lisa Marie did an album and she had to sit in front of the press to promote it. She's known for not talking about anything private or personal. Not Michael Jackson or her dad, Nic Cage, no one. Right around this time there was a story circulating about her and Nic, where he supposedly threw her $60,000 wedding ring into the ocean. She shows up for the interview and she had a cowboy hat on that had the words "Fuck off" on it. I knew this was going to be interesting.

I got to a point where I said, "Lisa, let me ask you something. You know I've been married before and it didn't work out. We went our separate ways, but it wasn't until I learned my involvement in that relationship and why it went wrong that I grew as a person. You've been married and divorced three times. How have you gotten better by that?" She looked at me and she curled her lip like her dad and she said, "Man I like your questions." And it just turned into something positive to talk about.

Anybody left who you haven't interviewed that you would like to?

I think I would like to sit down with Sean Penn. I think he would be a really good interview. It's fun to see who is up and coming though. . . . But I've pretty much talked to everybody.

We've saved the most important career question for last. On your resume under "awards," does *People* magazine's Sexiest Man Alive come before or after multiple Emmy Award–winner?

It comes before, and in boldface!

A DAY (AND A HALF) IN THE LIFE OF MARK STEINES
Labor Day Holiday, September 6, 2010

2:00 P.M.: Car arrives to take me to LAX.

4:00 P.M.: Depart for London.

10:00 A.M.: Land in London (local time). I have fifteen minutes to run to the hotel and shower.

11:00 A.M.–5:00 P.M.: On the set of *Dark Tide* at Pinewood Studios. Interview Halle Berry, Olivier Martinez, and director John Stockwell.

7:00 P.M.: Back to hotel. Ate my first meal of the day with my *ET* producer and director.

10:00 P.M.: Restless night's sleep.

6:00 A.M.: Up.

10:55 A.M.: Depart London Heathrow for Los Angeles.

2:15 P.M.: Arrive at LAX (local time). Three-hour layover. Race home to see my kids and wife, swap out luggage, and quick wardrobe fitting.

5:55 P.M.: Back at LAX. Fly to Hawaii.

8:35 P.M.: Land in Honolulu (local time).

10:00 P.M.: Restless night's sleep.

** ** **

9:30 A.M.–5:00 P.M.: *Battleship* set visit. Sit-down interview with Taylor Kitsch, Alexander Skarsgard, Rihanna, Brooklyn Decker, and director Peter Berg. Helicopter tour of the battleship USS *Missouri* in Pearl Harbor.

9:15 P.M.: Fly back to L.A.

5:30 A.M.: Arrive back in L.A. (local time).

DAVID THOMAS
Creative Director

Photo credit: www.davethomasstudio.com

If there's a shortcut to becoming a creative director, then no one ever told David Thomas. But that wouldn't have made any difference anyway because David isn't one to take shortcuts. On the contrary, he's someone who relishes the journey and has a thick resume to prove it. Along with that resume he's racked up life experiences that have made him a success and earned him an Emmy nod to boot.

Whether you're a TV addict or just a mild-mannered channel surfer, chances are you've seen David's work. He's had a hand in creating main titles for popular shows like *The Amazing Race* and has been a creative force behind huge promotional campaigns for shows like *Nip/Tuck*. He's also rebranded entire networks, like the Food Network, for example. In Hollywood terms, that's a facelift.

David's got a few words of wisdom for those seeking a job as a creative director, or CD, as it's known in the biz. See, you've already learned something and we're still in the introduction. Read on and you'll learn lots more. For instance, how dinner out with his sister one night altered the entire course of his life.

LAUNCH CAMPAIGN: A campaign that kicks off a brand-new TV series or a new season of an existing series.

MAIN TITLE: The opening sequence of a movie or TV show where the soundtrack is heard while the show's logo and opening credits roll.

ORIGINAL SPOT: An A-to-Z execution of a commercial, a series promo, or network identity piece that's conceptualized, shot, and finished by the creative agency.

POST HOUSE: A facility where a film or a TV show goes after it's been shot. Postproduction involves things like editing, recording, adding visual effects and sound effects, recording, and sound mixing.

PRINT CAMPAIGN: A creative initiative executed in print that can appear in places like billboards, bus shelters, and magazines.

Can you tell us what a creative director does?

As the creative director, you serve as the creative visionary for clients and their projects. You lead a team made up of designers, writers, editors, photographers, and animators. In short, everything creative is ultimately your responsibility.

You used the word *creative* three times in that description. We're guessing that's a big part of the job. Were you always creative?

Well, yes. As a kid I always wanted to make something, do something, paint something, or put on a show. And I got a lot of encouragement from my parents. My dad is an accomplished vocalist, and my mother is very creative herself, and she decided that if her youngest son showed creativity, she would do whatever she could to support it. In fact, one of my favorite gifts, which I would get almost every Christmas, was something I would refer to as "The Junk Box." My parents would go to an art store and buy everything you can imagine: pens, pencils, scissors, tape, glue, construction paper, feathers, clay, wire, you name it, and they'd put it all in a big box and wrap it up. It was the greatest gift ever. Nothing but hours and hours of imagination.

Cleanup must have accounted for half of your childhood! So did you think you'd do something artistic when you grew up?

I remember my fourth-grade teacher, Mrs. Wells, went around the class asking everyone what they wanted to be when they were older. There were lots of firemen, hairdressers, and a few hunters—I grew up in Arkansas. Everyone gave one-word answers. When it was my turn I said, "I think I'd like to be the guy who creates shows, or events, or weddings, or maybe holiday specials, things like that." She kind of looked at me and said, "Interesting," then moved on. So my head was definitely in entertainment.

Where did you go to college?

I originally went to Central Baptist College on a vocal scholarship and later transferred to the University of Central Arkansas.

Majoring in music?

No. Although every weekend I was traveling somewhere and singing or designing and painting concert backdrops. I was very busy, always doing something.

So what *did* you major in?

As funny as it sounds now, I majored in pre-pharmacy.

Huh? What about all those shows and holiday specials? What about Mrs. Wells? What about the Junk Box?

(Laughs) I know. Although I was very creative as a kid, I never really thought that would lead to a career. You were supposed to be a dentist or doctor, or some other "respectable" profession. Then, a few semesters in, my sister Julie took me to dinner and said, "Why would you possibly want to be a pharmacist? You're so creative. It's your entire life." And I said, "But art is just stuff I do for fun, you can't really be successful as an artist." To which she replied, "You're crazy. If anyone can do it, you can." She pushed me in the right direction, and I became a design major the next day. That dinner became known in my family as the "What are you thinking?" dinner.

Way to go, Julie! So what was your first job out of college?

I was a conductor, as in music, not in train. I had toured with a company for young musicians during summer sessions my last two years of college, and during my senior year they offered me a job conducting and emceeing tours around the world. After my last class, I packed my car and headed to Los Angeles, where I'd be based.

What was that experience like?

It was a dream job to travel the world, entertain, and play music. As a creative person, it was a gold mine. So many countries, so many cultures. It was amazing.

I mean, here I was a young kid from Arkansas standing in places like Mumbai, India, or the north coast of Ireland. The colors, the textures, the languages, it was a creative feast every day. Those experiences still feed my artistic appetite! Plus, it gave me an insatiable appetite for travel.

Then let's continue to travel along your career path. What happened after you stopped conducting?

The first thing I did was sleep! As much fun as it was doing music tours around the world, we kept up a grueling schedule. For a couple of years after that I continued as creative director for the music company. I would oversee all the creative aspects of the company's concert tours. This was also lots of fun, but I was increasingly becoming interested in film and television, and I decided if I was going to do that, I needed to move on.

And so?

After my job as creative director for the music company, I did a little freelance design and photography. I was looking for ways to break into the entertainment industry, but I wasn't having much luck. Then I got an offer to work at the Pacific Design Center in Los Angeles and thought, "Why not? I've always been interested in interior design; let's see where this goes." The best thing about the job was getting to work alongside a successful, longtime interior designer. I was getting an education and getting paid for it at the same time.

It seems you had a very open approach to trying new things, which is probably a good philosophy for finding work. Where did this new venture lead you?

Sometimes it's so interesting if you just go with the flow of life. Out of the blue, I got an offer to do window design for Macy's. I accepted, and spent the next few years designing for Macy's and then got recruited by Gap, where I headed up visual merchandising for a group of L.A. stores. It was creative, it was fun, and it was very successful. But I wasn't any closer to working in film or television. I had to make some hard decisions. I knew making the transition was going to be difficult.

How did you make that happen?

I thought about going back to school, but in the words of a successful creative I had always admired, "I had the education, I had the talent, I just needed to do it." So I decided, with my visual and music skills, my path to CD would be as an editor. The hard decision was: Do I quit my real job, start at the bottom, and have no money? Or do I work two jobs and have money, but no life and very little sleep? I chose the latter. And dug in.

Proof that anything worthwhile in life often takes sacrifice.

Exactly. So I worked hard all day as a visual merchandising manager of Gap stores in L.A. and eventually got the opportunity to help out the assistant editor on *The Nanny*, starring Fran Drescher. After a season on that show, I landed a night job at a specialty *post house*.

How does a guy in the visuals department of a major retailer end up at a post house, or helping out on *The Nanny* for that matter?

Like I said, I had decided my way in was going to be editing, so I was determined to find someone who was doing it, to ask for advice and maybe get a job. I was also buying books to understand the process. A friend of mine had worked with a guy who was an assistant editor on *The Nanny*, and he hooked me up with him. The funny thing was I realized about halfway through the season that this assistant editor had sort of suckered me into doing his job. The more he taught me, the more he could sit back and watch me do it. Then, also through a connection, I was introduced to the owner of a post house called Autonomy. We had an initial meeting, but no job offer. A few weeks later, I was on my way to an interview at another editorial house, but I was early so I stopped by Autonomy to say hi to the owner, and he basically hired me on the spot. Later he told me he liked my initiative. Or, maybe he said "chutzpah" and I looked it up.

What did you start out doing?

I was a part-time assistant editor. That's when things got really intense. I was still working all day for Gap and my part-time job had me working at night until one in the morning. Then I'd be back at Gap by 8 A.M. It was killing me. But I was loving it.

How long did you keep up this pace?

About four months, then I got to a point where I was just too physically exhausted to do it anymore. I had to make yet another choice. So I quit my Gap management job, and two days later I got a full-time editing offer from Autonomy. I stayed with that company for eight years and moved up the ladder. After a few years I was promoted to creative director and later VP of creative.

What were some notable projects you worked on while you were there?

We had a relationship with John Wells Productions and shepherded a lot of his *main title* sequences for shows like *The West Wing* and *Third Watch*. We did other main titles like *Monday Night Football* and *Fear Factor*.

One of my best experiences was getting to work with John Ritter and the cast and crew of *8 Simple Rules*. We created the title sequences for the show. John was so much fun to work with. The first season the titles all happened at the front door of his character's house, and we decided every title sequence would have a different ending. It was a big success. Season two was going to be a whole new set of scenarios. But, sadly, John died on what was going to be the day we would shoot the new titles.

That was such a huge loss.

I know.

And so sudden, too. Where did you go after Autonomy?

I went to a theatrical and broadcast advertising agency called mOcean, where I've been for over five years as a creative director.

Aside from main titles, what are some other things you do in your job?

I do TV show *launch campaigns* and *print campaigns*. I also shoot and direct *original spots*. But mostly I do a lot of branding.

Which is?

I'm asked this question a lot, so I'll give you the prepared answer. Brand really is story. That's the best way to describe it. It's what you see, what you hear, ultimately it's what you feel about a company or a product or person. Branding is telling that story, and telling it any way you can. Logo, color, font, voice, attitude. What does your advertising look like? Where do you advertise? Every touch-point with the public tells a part of the story, and the part you, as the consumer, remember, that's the brand.

What are some examples of your work in this area?
I think the most recognizable branding impression I've ever created is the Sony Pictures Television logo. It's the logo animation at the end of every one of their shows. That's every episode of *Seinfeld, Damages, Breaking Bad, Jeopardy!, Wheel of Fortune,* and many more. It must be seen by millions of people every day of the year. It's still very cool to see that on TV. I also worked on the rebrand of Food Network and TLC.

In your opinion, what makes a good creative director?
Rock-solid vision that appears to be totally flexible. Oh, and a winning smile.

He says that with a big smile on his face. What do you like most about the job?
I love the process of taking on a challenge and coming up with creative solutions to solve it. There's nothing more exciting than a great idea.

What are some of the pitfalls?
It can be easy to cross the line into what *you* want to do and lose track of what's best for the client.

Can you talk salary range for this job?
I'd say anywhere from $125,000 to $250,000 and beyond.

Talk about the other jobs in your department that someone might want to pursue.
There's the account executive, that's the person who manages the account and keeps the client happy, then there's the art director, who's my right-hand person. You've got designers, those are the people who really articulate the graphic look and style. Then there are animators, editors, and writers.

What's a good entry-level position?
Junior designer or assistant editor. Or gofer.

Where else might someone look for a job as a creative director?
Almost any type of large creative business has need for a CD or a creative lead.

You've had a wide range of jobs and life experiences. How has that helped you in your career?
Well, I have to say it's really worked for me. I remember thinking I had too many interests. I wanted to take so many classes, I wanted to do so many things, it was hard to get my schedule to work. People would say, "You really need to focus." But I think all of those varied interests have really paid off. Music, photography, art, conducting, interior design, travel . . . having all of those experiences to draw on makes me good at my job.

You also got an Emmy nomination for your main title work on
***The Young and the Restless*. Is it true that it's an honor just to**
be nominated?

For the record, I wouldn't have been any happier if I had actually
taken home the statue. Was that believable?

Not really, but it sounded good. So what other advice do you
have for someone who'd like to do what you do?

See the world and have lots of experiences. Get out there. Listen to
music. Be open. You don't have to be an expert in everything; you
just need to be passionate about the possibilities.

Sounds like some great advice. On a lighter note, tell us . . .
how many Dave Thomas Wendy's jokes have you heard over
your lifetime?

Actually you're the first ones to ask me that . . . today.

A DAY IN THE LIFE OF DAVID THOMAS

7:30 A.M.: Hit the snooze on the iPhone.

8:00 A.M.: Coffee. *Today Show* on DVR. Quick e-mail check. Shower.
Sketch Sony Movie Channel logo ideas on the steamed-up shower
door.

8:45 A.M.: Twenty-seven-minute drive to West L.A. for work. Listen
to podcast of "Design Matters with Debbie Millman." Call to director of photography, Jim Belkin, to discuss lighting for upcoming
Dish Network commercial shoot.

9:15 A.M.: Arrive at office, coffee in hand. Meet with Jen Holstein,
producing partner, about today's "hot" projects. Give notes to

designers and animators on projects in progress. Review Sony Movie Channel logo designs with my art director, Craig Oelrich.

11:00 A.M.: Direct *Housewives of New York* voice-over session for Bravo.

11:30 A.M.: Call my mom for her birthday—before I forget.

12:00 noon: Wardrobe preview with stylist Karen Mann for upcoming shoot.

12:15 P.M.: Pre-preproduction meeting for Food Network rebrand shoot with DP Jim Matloz.

1:30 P.M.: Give notes, via e-mail, to freelance writer for *Millionaire Matchmaker* scripts for Bravo.

2:15 P.M.: Lunch—Cobb salad. Call contractor about our NYC apartment renovation.

3:00 P.M.: Last looks—SMC logos.

4:00 P.M.: Sony Movie Channel logo presentation on the Sony lot in Culver City.

5:30 P.M.: Back to the office.

6:20 P.M.: Final review and notes with designers and animators on current projects.

7:30 P.M.: Drive home. Sync the iPod for classic rock playlist. Starbucks stop—iced Americano.

8:30 P.M.: Dinner: tofu stir-fry courtesy of my partner, Mark (he's a great cook). *NBC Evening News* and *Jeopardy!* on the DVR.

9:00 P.M.: Off to Crunch for workout.

11:30 P.M.: Back home. TCM on demand—*The Great Escape.* Eat a bowl of cereal. Last e-mail check of the day. Additional notes to free-lance designers. Pull reference images for Food Network presentation tomorrow.

1:15 A.M.: Off to bed—never earlier than 1 A.M.

SARA HOLDEN
Stunt Woman

Photo credit: Adrian Carr

When you think stunts you think big burly guys who are built like Mack trucks and are as fearless as they are crazy. Sara Holden blows that stereotype wide open, at least where gender and size are concerned, because she is definitely fearless and maybe a touch nuts. Standing five-two and weighing 107 pounds, this blonde is up for anything. Drag her behind a Jet Ski, fine. Throw her off a balcony, do it. Set her on fire, she'll hold a marshmallow and use the flames to make s'mores.

Sara has made a career pulling off amazing stunts, be it on TV for shows like *House*, *All My Children*, *How I Met Your Mother*, *Hannah Montana*, and *True Blood* or in movies like *Due Date*, *Piranha 3D*, and *Iron Man 2*.

Sara's a risk taker, so her method for getting her "foot in the door" should come as no surprise to anyone. She did what any self-respecting risk taker would do, she crashed a holiday party for stunt people and walked around introducing herself, determined to get her first big break or get kicked out trying. Thankfully, the former happened. But that's nothing compared to the time she grabbed Joel McHale's junk in the middle of a stunt on the show *Community*. Don't worry, we'll explain.

MARK: A location on the stage or on a set, usually marked with tape, that an actor must stand on to be framed correctly by the cameras. An actor will often hear, "Make sure you hit your mark."

STUNT COORDINATOR: A current or former stunt person who hires other stunt people for film or TV jobs. He or she also choreographs the stunt sequence and maintains a safe working environment.

STUNTMEN'S ASSOCIATION: An invitation-only organization, founded in 1961, dedicated to the professionalization of stuntmen. The exclusive organization is tailored toward stunt coordinators, stuntmen, and second-unit directors only.

Describe what you do for a living.
I'm a stuntwoman, I fall down a lot. I make the actor look good by taking the fall.

Talk about your background. Where'd you grow up? Where'd you go to school?

I grew up in Michigan in a suburb of Detroit. I got into theater in the seventh grade and knew then that I wanted to pursue a job in the entertainment industry one day. I was in every school play. I was also a total tomboy. You know, ripping Barbie doll heads off and all that stuff. I always liked extreme sports; I was also a gymnast and a cheerleader. I was what they called a flyer, that's the person who gets launched into the air and does flips and twists. I was, and still am, a total adrenaline junkie.

What about college?

I graduated with honors from Western Michigan, majoring in advertising with a theater minor. My parents are my biggest fans, but they suggested I study something other than acting because I don't think they wanted to pay for me to become a struggling actor. I also joined the women's rugby team and played all four years.

So you graduate school and realize you can't play pro rugby, what next?

I still wanted to pursue acting. So I moved to Chicago and studied with Second City. I studied for three years and loved it. That was just such an amazing stepping-stone for me. Even now when I show people my resume, Second City is what stands out. I knew I had to move to Los Angeles if I was serious about my career. So I did what any respectable girl would do, I lied to my parents and told them I had a job offer in Los Angeles. In reality, I drove out in my Dodge Neon. I had no job and I didn't know a single person.

Bold.

I know. It was one of those things where if I didn't do it I was going to regret it forever. So there I was, a Midwest girl with a thick accent. Trying to do the acting thing and realizing, wow, there's a million of me out here. Just not as cool, ha.

What was one of the first jobs you booked?

I was an extra in the movie *Beerfest*, do you remember that movie?

Classic. Right up there with *Deuce Bigalow: Male Gigolo* and *Dude, Where's My Car?*

I played a beer wench and worked eighteen-hour days. There was so much down time, just sitting around. I started a conversation with this guy on set who happened to be the *stunt coordinator*. I didn't know he was a stunt coordinator at first. I told him about playing rugby and being active and he said, "Have you ever thought about stunt work?" And, bam, a light bulb went off. It just hit me.

What did you do next?

I was desperate to find out how I could get into the stunt business. I figured it was all about knowing the right person and networking. I learned from talking to people that the way in is through the stunt coordinators. So, I wondered, how could I meet stunt coordinators? It was Christmas time in 2006 and I researched stunt groups on the Internet, and that's where I came across the *Stuntmen's Association* holiday party announcement, and I crashed it.

As I moved through the party, I ended up meeting Bob Yerkes. He's a legendary stuntman from back in the John Wayne days. He took a liking to me. He asked what I was doing there, and I said, "Oh, I just want to get into the business." He asked if I knew anyone there and I said, "Yeah, now I know you." Crashing that party got me an invite to his facility, which we call Bob's backyard. It's a training ground for stunt people in Los Angeles, literally in the backyard of his house. He's got a sixty-foot-high fall ladder, huge airbags for high falls, a trapeze, you name it. I started training there twice a week, for a good two years. I'd show up ten minutes early and work out hard. I was a sponge. I was just wanting to learn and learn and learn.

Did you have to pay?

No, that's the cool thing. Bob worked in the business for fifty years, and he just gives back to the stunt community. Someone has a hat and passes it around so we can donate.

What was the first stunt job you booked?

My very first stunt job was doubling Pamela Anderson.

Wow, those are some big, ahem, *shoes* to fill. What was the show?

It was called *Blonde and Blonder*. I got thrown into a speedboat and rode around the lake at ninety-five miles per hour. Not a bad way to make a buck. I was so green at the time, I didn't know anything. They just put these big boobs on me and I thought, this is un-freaking believable, I'm Pamela Anderson.

After you took the boobs off, did your career take off?

Well, let's just say I would book a job every couple of months, and I was very thankful for that. What helped me book jobs was putting myself in the Stunt Player's Directory, which is thought of as the bible in our industry. The directory has your photo, sizes, and contact information. It's the resource that all the stunt coordinators use when they are looking to hire stunt people.

So the stunt coordinator hires stunt people? Not the casting director or producer?
You got it.

Do you have to audition, or are you just picked out of the directory?
It depends on the scenario. There are times when you have to match the actor, where you need to really look similar to her. In those instances I audition because the producer and director want to see you in person and make sure you fit the profile. I'll also audition when they are looking for stunt acting roles that require you to deliver lines or act in some capacity; those are by far my favorite because of my acting background. Then there are times when you don't need to audition, when you are just doubling someone for a fall or something like that. That's when they just hire you from the directory and look at your body type, height, and weight.

Tell us about some of your other stunts.
I had a killer car stunt on the show *House*. I played a girl who wasn't paying attention while driving and I had to skid to a stop before hitting a guy in a wheelchair. I was nervous because at best I hit my *mark* and all is good, at worst, I hit the guy and the quarter-million-dollar camera and never work again. I am happy to report that one worked out just fine!

Your work seems super nerve-racking.

It is. Most times you get one chance and you have to do it right. You don't want to get hurt, you don't want to hurt someone else, and you have to be convincing; it's a lot. Once the cameras are rolling my adrenaline kicks in and I just go for it, but leading up to the stunt, when you have time to think about it, it can play with your head. I've never been seriously injured, but there have been stunts where I couldn't move the next day, big welts, contusions, but that's all part of the job.

Keith avoids injury by wearing a helmet when he plays chess. Are there a lot of safety precautions taken on set?

Yes, there are. The stunt coordinator plans the stunt and makes it as safe as possible. When there's a fire stunt there are people off camera with fire extinguishers to put you out. They also hire stunt people just to be safety people to assist the stunt both on camera and off camera. On the show *Castle*, I was locked in a coffin with a legendary stuntman, Gene Lebell. What an honor that was! He trained Chuck Norris and Bruce Lee, just to name a few. One of the pallbearers carrying the casket was the safety stunt person, and it was his job to make sure the coffin lid was lifted up high enough so I would clear it when we rolled out of the coffin. Because that was such an involved stunt and there were multiple people involved, we were given a full day prior to the shoot to rehearse it.

What are some of the other tent-pole movies and TV shows you've done?

My biggest job, stunt-wise, and my career turning point was on a movie called *Piranha 3D*.

Oh, the one with all the cute fishies . . .

Fishies with flesh-eating razor-sharp teeth. I was in a huge massacre scene on the lake. I had prosthetic blood and hundreds of bite marks on me because I was getting eaten alive by the piranha. In one scene I had to hang on to a Jet Ski, get dragged, and tumble off it. I did a lot of stunts in that movie. After that, I felt like more people took me seriously, and since then, I've been working pretty regularly.

Do most people in your profession try to saddle up to an A-list actor and double them? Like Zoe Bell did with Uma Thurman and Lucy Lawless?

That is a popular way to go, but it's also difficult. You try to be written into an actress's contract so you are guaranteed to be the double whenever she works. A few friends of mine double the same actor over and over. Is that a goal for me? I don't know, because I want to continue stunt-acting roles, so if I'm in the actress's contract, then I'm just a stunt girl. But is that so bad? I don't know. I like doing both.

Have you had any surreal moments?

All the time. Working on *Iron Man 2* was surreal. It was a party scene with Robert Downey Jr. and Don Cheadle, just before they broke out into a fight. There was an explosion and a waterfall of glass, and there were about thirty extras in the scene, but you couldn't put them anywhere near the glass because they could get hurt. So they placed me and ten other stunt people around it. It was a fun gig. When Robert Downey Jr. walked onto the set in his suit everyone clapped. He was a super-cool guy.

Wow, big scene.

I also did a stunt on the show *Community*. I was in a huge food fight scene with the stars of the show and a bunch of extras. We only had one take, because the place got trashed. The stunt was to do a flip over a table while throwing food. I did the table move and then decided to stand on top of it. Food was everywhere and I slipped, for real, and fell to the floor. On the way down, the star of the show, Joel McHale, was standing next to me wearing just boxer shorts and I brushed his . . . you know.

Let's just say, while I was falling down, he was getting felt up. It was totally by accident.

Sure, it was an accident. Real professional, Sara.

I couldn't even look at him after. I was so embarrassed. Now, every time I see him on *The Soup*, I'm like, "Yeah, I felt him up."

Let's get down to the basics. What are some key qualities you need as a stunt person?

Good timing and athleticism. You can't be scared of heights. You can't be scared of speed. You can't be scared of getting hit or falling down. You definitely have to have a thick skin.

So what schooling or training would you recommend for someone starting out?

There aren't really schools per se, but if you can get yourself into Bob Yerkes's backyard, do it. Stunt and precision driving is really great to learn, and there are classes for that. There's a place called Gymnastics Olympica in Van Nuys, California. There are a lot of well-known stunt people who train there. Also there's a facility called XMA in North Hollywood, which is run by stunt people. Keep in mind the key to success is commitment. You need to commit to the training 100 percent and really hone your skills.

Give a range of what a stunt person can make.

We're all in SAG/AFTRA. SAG/AFTRA scale is $838 for one day's work. That's good pay, but remember, many of us don't work every day. You also get a stunt adjustment, depending on the severity of the stunt. The adjustment is money on top of the flat day rate.

What else does an aspiring stunt person need to know?

I haven't talked about hustling, but that's a really big part of the job. Hustling, for lack of a better word, is kind of crashing a set and walking up to the stunt coordinator with a headshot in your hand and introducing yourself.

Sounds ballsy.

That's how you meet people and get jobs. Everyone does it. During those two years while I was training I was really hustling. I was getting out there and getting my picture into everybody's hands. It's expected of you. I clawed my way into the stunt world.

How hard is it for someone to break into this field and what are some parting words of advice?

It's very hard, because it's a small community. It's very political. But once you get in, you're in. I think the first thing you have to do is network with other stunt people. That's where I learned the most. I made a couple of friends at Bob's and I'd learn one thing from one person and one thing from another. So network, train, and hone your skills. Also, go to the events. Stunt people like to drink, so put your drinking cap on and go out and be friendly with them. Because if you become friendly with a stunt coordinator, and you have the talent, they're probably going to hire you.

How much would it cost for you to be our bodyguard at our book signing?

You want me to be your bodyguard? I would probably take SAG scale, plus a big adjustment. Because I'm sure I'd have to deal with some unruly, out-of-control fans!

A DAY IN THE LIFE OF SARA HOLDEN

6:30 A.M.: Wake up, grab an apple, and head to boot camp. I go there three times a week. We do sprints, push-ups, pull-ups, rings, and a bunch of different exercises with the yoga ball.

8:00 A.M.: Visit and play with my niece and baby nephew in Michigan via Skype. Call my mom. This will only be the first of several calls today.

9:00 A.M.: Quick surf session in Malibu. Hopefully spot a couple of dolphins nearby and catch some nice waves.

11:00 A.M.: Get ready for work! I'm doubling Emily Procter from *CSI Miami*. Her regular double wasn't available, so I was called as a backup. I'll be getting beat up and abducted by an intruder. I'll have a plastic bag over my head and then get knocked to the ground. Yes! Oh, and all this in four-inch heels.

12:00 noon: Hair and makeup. The special effects guy is giving me a black eye and bruises on the back of my neck and arms. I have to match Emily exactly.

1:00 P.M.: Onto set. I watch Emily's movements so I can match her the best I can.

2:00 P.M.: My turn! Get manhandled, pushed, tackled, and held at gunpoint. Good times!

5:00 P.M.: Wrapped! I call my mom to tell her about my day. I let her know I hung out with David Caruso and what we talked about (moms love that stuff).

6:00 P.M.: Going to meet some friends at the original Farmers Market in L.A. A few glasses of wine always makes me feel better after a day of beating my body up.

8:00 P.M.: Check e-mails, write in my journal, and race to LAX to catch the red-eye flight to Detroit. Going to visit my family for a few days!

VIN DI BONA
Executive Producer of America's Funniest Home Videos and Chairman of FishBowl Worldwide Media and Vin Di Bona Productions

Photo credit: Alan Weissman

We've met a lot of people in our lives and we've never met anyone who didn't like to laugh. Whether it's a giggle or a guttural knee-slapper, laughter is the universal language for people of all ages and from all walks of life. So imagine being the person who, for the past twenty-five years, has been "Oz behind the curtain," providing that laughter to millions around the world. Vin Di Bona is that person, and as the creator of the hugely successful *America's Funniest Home Videos*, it's something he doesn't take for granted or laugh off.

Vin has been at it for a while, and in his time he's seen the TV business model shift. He's seen legends peak and retire. Through it all he has continued to reinvent both himself and his company to stay current and ahead of the curve. Simply put, Vin doesn't need to work; he has made enough scratch to live a very comfortable life. Like anyone who is passionate about their craft, Vin is not in it for the money; he's in it because he loves it.

Get ready to read about a guy who blames the Beatles for ruining his professional singing career, pitched the same TV show 136 times, claims the Fonz as a frat brother, and got rejected by Dick Clark.

Vin has so many amazing stories, we just turned the tape recorder on and hit record. He did the rest.

CLIP SHOW: In the case of *America's Funniest Home Videos*, a TV show made up of short clips, such as videos. In scripted TV, it's an episode made up of excerpts from previous shows, sometimes presented in flashback.

DEVELOPMENT PEOPLE: Every studio, network, and production company has a development department that "develops" material with the goal of getting it on the air. There are often separate drama, comedy, and reality development departments under the same roof.

PRESENTATION TAPE: A sales tool made by a producer or show creator. The footage represents the tone, pacing, and characters that would be portrayed in a show.

RIGHTS: Legal permission to air, distribute, and/or remake a specific piece of content for television.

SLOT: A specific time that a show airs within a TV network's schedule. The schedule is broken up into time slots that represent morning, afternoon, primetime, and late night.

Talk a bit about your childhood and your exposure to entertainment growing up.

It started with my mom, who was a big fan of the industry. I was in sixth or seventh grade and it was about 6:30 at night; we just finished dinner and my mom asked if I finished my homework. I said, "No, not really," and she said, "It's okay. Let's go to the movies." And from that point on, that is really the way my childhood ran. I was in dramatic shows from the time I was eight or nine years old. I had a professional singing career. I recorded three or four records, one of which was a minor hit on the East Coast. Then I came out west to record a second and third song, and the Beatles broke onto the scene, and I was singing ballads, so I was pretty much shit out of luck.

So where did you go to college?

I ended up going to Emerson College for radio, and in my second year I took a TV course and I really became enthralled with television. While I was at school, I co-created a dance party show called "Help" that was sort of reminiscent of the Beatles. I decided when I went to grad school that I should do something other than TV, so I went to UCLA and got my MFA in documentary film.

So you're the one who earned all those diplomas on your wall. Other than wall art, explain what you did with them.

When I finished my master's degree I went back to Boston and got a job at WBZ, which was a powerhouse station in New England. Westinghouse was very smart; they hired all young guys and paid us peanuts and they were kind enough to let us work ninety-hour weeks. We learned a hell of a craft.

At a certain point, I came out to L.A. where I got my first lesson in rejection. A friend of mine from Boston set up an interview for me with Dick Clark. Dick took the time to watch my reel. He said, "Vin, your reel looks very good, but let me tell you what the problem is. Say I'm going to do a special for CBS and I could hire Vin Di Bona or hire Marty Pasetta." At the time Marty was the biggest director in town; he directed all the Academy Award shows and *Elvis in Hawaii* (a very famous TV special). So Dick says, "So say I hire you to direct the show for me and for some unforeseen reason the show is a disaster, CBS comes to me and tells me I ruined their show and I catch all the crap. They asked what happened and I tell them that I hired this young new director and I thought he was great, but it just sort of fell apart. Now what if I had hired Marty Pasetta and the same thing happens and the show is a disaster and CBS comes to me and asks me what happened? I tell them I don't know, but I hired the best director in town." Lesson learned. Dick Clark put it to me just that way and it wasn't what I wanted to hear, but it made sense. I needed more experience.

So what did you do with that resounding vote of confidence?
I got rejected again. I went to Paulist Productions, which was the television arm of the Catholic Church. Father Kaiser, a very famous television priest, ran everything. He was one of the pastors at my church, so I brought him my reel. And he thought I was a very good producer and director, but he didn't think I had the right experience. He made dramas and I had only done documentaries. So I walked out of that meeting realizing I had just offered my services for free and I still couldn't get hired. I just broke down and cried. I really balled my eyes out. About a month later he gave a sermon in church. He said, "The problem that I see in many people is that we don't give back. If you are a doctor and somebody comes in and there is something you can do for them, but they can't afford to pay for it, why not help them out? If you're a lawyer and somebody is in need, do something; if you are a producer, writer, director, give back." I wrote him a letter the next day. I said, "Dear Father Kaiser, why don't you practice what you preach?"

Two days later I got a phone call. In this deep voice I heard, "Is this Vin Di Bona?" I knew who it was immediately. I was crapping in my pants. I said, "Yes it is." He says, "Well, Vin, you're going to regret writing that letter for the rest of your life. I'm about to do a documentary on gangs in East Los Angeles, and I think you'd be the perfect guy to do it." So I did the documentary, won an Emmy, and became ensconced with him. I ended up working on a lot of his dramatic shows, and now I'm chairman of his board. He has since passed, but that was my route. I mean you never know. You just never know.

So now you have the experience *and* an Emmy. What happened next?

I got an interview at *Entertainment Tonight*. I observed the show for a week and then I went in to meet the executive producer. I told the person I was meeting with that I had seen his wife the night before at a Father Kaiser dinner. He said, "Oh, yeah, we're getting a divorce." I thought to myself, "Oh, shit, not a good opener." So I moved on and said, "I observed the show." He asked what I thought of it. I said, "Well, I think you don't really have reporters who give a point of view and you don't have reporters who sign off and say this is *Entertainment Tonight*, and I'm not crazy about your cohost." He pauses and says, "I'm dating her."

Ohhhh, you are two for two.

Thankfully he agreed with me about her hosting abilities. After another three-hour interview with two of the top guys at Paramount, I was offered the job. I was at *ET* for about two years. Then I went on to work as a supervising senior producer for a show called *On Stage America*, great fun. Then, Henry Winkler, who was a dear friend and fraternity brother, got in touch with me about working on a show he sold called *MacGyver*. I ended up working on that show as a supervising producer for the first season.

We imagine you have amazing TV bomb-making abilities. So how did *America's Funniest Home Videos* (*AFV*) come about?
It all started when I got *the rights* to a Japanese show called *Waku, Waku Animal Land*. I put a twelve-minute sales *presentation tape* together, and tried to sell it here in the states.

So you took a personal financial risk by buying the rights to the show?
Nope, I got the show for free. Nobody had ever brought a Japanese show to America before, so there was no precedent set. I pitched the show 136 times. On the 136th pitch, I was talking to Squire Rushnell, who had hired me back in the day at Westinghouse. I told him I had a show that was like *Wild Kingdom* meets *Hollywood Squares*. He said, "Really? Well, *American Bandstand* with Dick Clark is going off the air, and I need something to replace it." He thought my show might work. So I FedEx'ed him the presentation tape, and the next day he called and told me he wanted to buy two pilots. I made the two pilots, and before they aired he bought the series.

The show was on the air for three years and ensconced me with the Japanese. Three years later, in 1989, we were having dinner in Hollywood and these producers from Japan told me they had a variety show for me. The show had a musical number, a comedy sketch, a talk segment, and then they showed three home videos that viewers had sent in.

Three *home videos*. A-ha!

That is right, a-ha! Again I made a pitch presentation tape, but this time things were different. I sold *America's Funniest Home Videos* on the very first pitch, to ABC, in four minutes.

How was the show received when it premiered?

There are four things necessary for a show to do well: preparation, premise, execution, and luck. The first episode aired Thanksgiving weekend on Sunday night at seven o'clock. This was known as a death *slot* for ABC for twelve years. Shows that aired on that day and at that time did horribly in the ratings. As luck would have it, there were tremendous blizzards from New York through Chicago and deep into the Midwest. There were torrential rainstorms from the Rockies to California. Everybody was at home watching TV at seven o'clock on Sunday night. The show rated through the roof. Eventually, we got bombarded by people sending us their funny videos.

How did you handle the influx?

It was amazing. We had three shifts of people, five people in each shift, watching clips twenty-four hours a day. The Hollywood post office had to staff three extra people just to handle all of our mailbags.

And the rest, of course, is history. So can you give advice to someone who is looking to get started in your business?

Sure. Never go to somebody and tell him or her you are looking for a job. Instead, get creative. Come in with an idea, because an idea can translate into money for the other person. And, to be crass about it, that's kind of what it's all about. It's all about how you can "do well," for them. If you are going for a job interview, do your homework. Find out who the person is you are meeting with and what shows they have worked on. Know about the company and any recent news they may have generated. If you're interviewing with a network, know the shows on the network. Watch the network the night before the interview so you can have a conversation about the programming. Say, "I love that show *X*." This is Hollywood; everybody loves to be complimented.

Your suit looks very nice.
Thank you. See, I love that.

The industry has changed a lot since you first came on the scene. What is your take on reinvention and staying current?
This industry changes every day. It changes every minute. Here's a perfect example, I just launched a new company. I have become known in Hollywood as "the guy who does great *clip shows*." Well, I wanted to do more. I want to do scripted shows and animation. What I theorized was that in order to do that, I had to start a whole new company. I hired an amazing man, Bruce Gersh, to run it with me. We hired the best *development people* we could. It's like a stand-up comic, the last joke is the one that people remember. You know, I am sixty-six years old, and I'm still having great fun and I am taking a gamble. I like making entertainment for the public. That's what my life is all about.

Vin, we're sure you get this question a lot. Say you are on the edge of a very steep cliff, and in one hand you have your friend and former host of *AFV*, Bob Saget. In the other hand you have your entire *AFV* library. You can only save one, which do you save and why?
(Laughs) I would give Saget the shirt off my back, tell him to make a parachute out of it, and wish him well. (More laughs)

A great man once told us, the last joke is the one people remember.

A DAY IN THE LIFE OF VIN DI BONA

6:30 A.M.: Wake up, look at late-night e-mails, check nationals (ratings).

7:45 A.M.: Walk one and a half miles.

8:15 A.M.: Cup of Hawaiian Hazelnut coffee and a serving of Greek yogurt. Watch CNN and *GMA* (flip between).

8:30 A.M.: I've produced over 2,500 network or syndicated programs, specials, or documentaries over the past forty-two years. So for the next ninety minutes I take a leisurely shower and shave, choose my clothes carefully, and drive to work . . . at this point in my life I see no need to *rush* into the office.

10:30 A.M.: First meeting and return calls.

11:15 A.M.: Screen clip reel for upcoming show with writing and producing staff. Give notes and select three finalists for that day's *AFV* proposed future show.

12:00 noon: Senior creative management meeting.

1:00 P.M.: Lunch with producers of current project.

2:30 P.M.: Arrive at stage (Raleigh Studios, Manhattan Beach) for camera meeting with crew. Rehearse special segments with Tom Bergeron, set for show.

4:00 P.M.: Direct first show.

5:30 P.M.: Break for meal.

7:15 P.M.: Direct second show.

9:00 P.M.: Head straight home. Watch a little bit of TV and return some e-mails. Off to bed.

SAM MAHONY
First Assistant Director

When Sam Mahony landed his first job in the entertainment industry, he thought he'd won the lottery. He was working as a production assistant on a movie directed by the legendary William Friedkin,
making thirty-five bucks a day, eating as many free donuts as he
could. Sam was happy, but it was more than the donuts. He'd found
his calling in life. It was on the set of this movie that he watched the
first assistant director closely and said, "That's what I want to do." So
he set out to make *that* happen.

Sam's journey took him from his native Massachusetts to the "Great
White North"—that's Canada for the geographically impaired—and
finally to Los Angeles. He crossed paths with Quentin Tarantino
along the way and eventually became his go-to guy on classic movies
like *Reservoir Dogs* and *Pulp Fiction*.

Sam opens up about the job of first AD, and as you'll discover, it's not for the faint of heart. He's experienced his fair share of challenges. Like the time, for instance, he literally had to pull an enraged B-list actor off a terrified director whose head was getting pounded into the ground. Or the time his entire crew dropped like flies from heat exhaustion while filming in the Nevada desert during the summer. If you think you've got what it takes to be a first AD, you should know it's a demanding, high-stress job. But it's also one that pays well. Like two-hundred-grand-a-year well. That's a lot of donuts.

CANNES: Cannes Film Festival. A prestigious festival held annually in this resort town in the south of France.

DGA TRAINEE PROGRAM: A two-year program designed to give a very limited number of people the opportunity to become assistant directors. As part of the application process there's an exam and an in-depth interview.

DIRECTORS GUILD OF AMERICA (DGA): The union representing directors in the film and television industry. It also represents other crewmembers like assistant directors and unit production managers.

DIRECTORS GUILD OF CANADA: According to their website, the DGC represents directors and other creative and logistical personnel in the film, television, and new media industries.

LOCATION MANAGER: He or she is responsible for finding locations to be used in filming a TV show or movie. That person also works out logistics like crew parking and is responsible for dealing with any issues that might arise within the neighborhood where production occurs.

LOCK OFF: When shooting outside on location, the production team must secure the area so that there are no bystanders in any given shot.

MAIN UNIT: Also known as first unit. This is the team involved in shooting scenes with the actors. The second unit shoots footage that includes scenery, inserts, or close-ups of objects and other less crucial shots.

PRODUCTION DESIGNER: The person responsible for designing the look of a film as it relates to locations, sets, colors, and texture (see Carlos Barbosa's chapter).

SECOND AD: The second assistant director is a more administrative position. He or she generates call sheets that list, among other things, the time when all crew need to show up on set. This person also generates production reports that detail what happened during the day. The second also coordinates with the production manager in terms of delivery of equipment as well as dealing with the on-set caterer.

Can you explain the job of first assistant director (first AD)?

You're going to start with the really hard questions, huh? Okay, the first AD is at the pivot point between the director and the producer. In preproduction, he or she takes a script, breaks it down into its separate elements, scene by scene. What actors are in the scene, what background you need, what effects are involved. You coordinate with the *location manager*, the DP, and the *production designer*. Then you consult with the director as to whether he can actually shoot with the time and the money budgeted.

What does your job entail when you are actually in production?

I'm required to *lock off* our perimeter before we start shooting, making sure everything's safe. I'm responsible for actors. My team runs them through makeup, hair, and wardrobe. We make sure they're all set with the script and whatever else they need. And then I get them to set so they can rehearse the scene. Then I call, "Roll camera," the director calls, "Action" and the actors do their thing. Then we do it again. And again, and again, and again.

You pretty much keep order on the set and keep things moving?
Yes. I'm also the head yeller.

You've got the perfect voice for it. You would've made a great drill sergeant.
I have a shtick. Mine kind of evolved into this pirate thing. And it's kind of like this: (in pirate voice) "'Ere we go. R-r-r roll sound. Backgr-r-r-ound."

Well, that explains the eye patch you're wearing. (He's actually not wearing one.) So what was your first gig in the industry?
It was a William Friedkin movie called *The Brinks Job*. I was in college in Boston and I had a classmate who had been in *Jaws*. He said, "Hey there's this movie coming to town and they're looking for production assistants and they're paying thirty-five bucks a day." This was a little while ago, it was good money at the time for a college student.

Not to mention all that free food.
Exactly. Free donuts and coffee at the craft service table. Can't beat that.

What were some of your tasks on that film?
I was given a list of fifty names, background actors, and I had to get them all through costumes, makeup, and hair. Once I got them on set, the *second AD* had me set them in place. I was totally green, but it was really cool. That was thirty-four years ago. I can remember what the

shot was, and I can tell you what actors were in it. It was an epiphany because before that day, I didn't know what I wanted to do with my life.

So you had found your calling?

Yes. From my first big day on set with all my extras and all the madness, I saw the first AD and what he was doing and went, "Wow. I really want that job." So my goal was to become a first [AD]. I had a mentor in Canada who showed me the ropes. My ultimate big break was working on *Reservoir Dogs* and *Pulp Fiction*.

We'll get to Tarantino in a minute. First, talk about some of the key moments toward reaching that goal.

After *The Brinks Job* I continued working as a PA, but the work was intermittent. In the mid-eighties, the first wave of American productions went to Canada and used Toronto as a fake New York backdrop. So I moved there and started from scratch as a driver on some low-budget movie. I made a good impression on the first AD, and he got me a job on a TV series. I started as a PA and got promoted into a position called unit manager. It got me into the *Directors Guild of Canada*, and after a while I landed on a show called *Friday the 13th: The Series*. And it was the beginning of my long association with the *Friday the 13th* franchise.

What was your position on that series?

I was second AD.

So you're in Canada, getting lots of work, and moving up the production ladder. What next?

I decided I should probably get to Los Angeles. I was fortunate enough to leave with a producer who was on the *Friday the 13th* series. So he took me with him, and I worked as a second AD on *Friday the 13th Part Seven: The New Blood*.

Okay, let's talk about the movie that put Quentin Tarantino on the map, *Reservoir Dogs*.

I was a second AD on that film and there were some issues with the first. They decided to make a change, so about ten days into the shoot they hired me. Which was an ideal position to be in, because you're the new guy coming in and everybody will give you the benefit of the doubt. So I came on board and the show went off without a hitch.

What was it like to work with Tarantino?

I really enjoyed working with him. He's an enthusiastic guy. We moved very fast. He talked a lot, but he was very specific. He had the picture in his head when he wrote the script, so there weren't a lot of left turns and weird changes. I just had to make sure I could keep up with him and give him all the elements he needed, as he needed them.

For someone reading this chapter thinking they'd like to have your job, talk a bit about what it takes to be a first AD.

I think first and foremost you've got to be a people person. To be successful, you need to understand what motivates your crew and what motivates your actors. And be somewhat sensitive to the undercurrents. You also need to be extremely well organized. If you're the type of person who can't find your car keys every morning, you're probably not going to be a good first AD. In the preproduction phase, you're going to get a lot of notes from people. A good memory and a habit of writing stuff down really helps.

What about the ability to think on your feet?

That's really important. Also, being flexible is a really good quality in a first AD, as is the ability to think in a nonlinear way. So people who play chess, Parcheesi, or backgammon would make a good first. You have to think outside the box, especially during prep when you've set up a perfect schedule, then casting calls and says, "By the way, we forgot to tell you that your main guest star is not available for these four days," and your schedule gets blown out of the water. You then have to be flexible, try not to scream at anybody and go back to square one. One of the challenges of filmmaking is always teetering on the edge of something going wrong.

Give us an example of something that went wrong.

On *Beastmaster 3* we were shooting in the desert and the first day out it was 126 degrees and I had eleven crewmembers and a director pass out from heat exhaustion.

Hollywood types, so weak! What else?

On one movie where I was the first, the lead actor and the director got into a fistfight. We were at the Hoover Dam and the actor, who'll remain nameless, kept fouling up the scene. It was a drive-up, which means the car drives up, a guy goes to a kid in the car, "Wait here, I'll be right back," and he gets out. But he kept missing his mark. So it was like take fifteen, and the director came to me and said, "This guy's killing me. He's killing me. What am I going to do?" So I said, "Go talk to him." He walked over to the car where the actor was sitting, banged on the window and said, "Now look here!" The actor just looked at him and knocked him to the ground with the front door. It came down to five of us pulling the guy off the director as he was banging his head into the ground.

All this on *The Shaggy D.A.*?

(Laughter)

So how'd you end up on the movie *Pulp Fiction*?

Reservoir Dogs had done well at *Cannes*. Quentin had another movie, and we'd enjoyed our experience together, so he called me up and said, "Hey, I've got a show, do you want to do it?" I said, "Sure." So they sent me a script, I read it and went, "Wow, this is really good." We prepped it and shot it, it was another great Quentin movie. And we had a great cast.

More recently you worked on the hit TV show *Heroes*. What was that experience like?

Heroes was the largest, and most complex project I've ever worked on. I did two years and it was wicked neat, but I'm really glad it's over.

Difficult?

Extremely difficult. Network television is usually an eight-day shoot for an hour of material. On *Heroes* we always did nine or ten days. Once in a while we'd go twelve days. We always had two companies shooting at the same time. Especially the first season. We'd shoot eight days with the *main unit*, or first company, and then depending on how many days over that eight we'd go to another company, fully staffed, all the trucks, the whole nine yards. I'd have a completely different staff.

How many jobs in general can someone in your position work in a year?

In television, two. If you're on a series you work the series and that's usually around a ten-month commitment. After ten months of working on a show you want to go hide someplace and chill out. In feature films, the low-budget world has a lot of opportunity for people, and you can crank out four or five low-budget features a year. There's a whole niche of low-budget production right now, which is a great place for people to come into the business and get started.

What are some other ways for people to become a first AD?

There are a couple of ways to become an AD and to get into the guild. The first is through the *DGA Trainee Program*, taking a test and competing with 3,000 other people for ten slots or so. The other way is to come in as a PA and to get a certain number of days to qualify. It could take a PA anywhere from three to four years to accrue the number of hours needed.

As a first AD, what do you look for in a PA?

For our key guys we're going to be working with every day, we're looking for someone who's got a good head on their shoulders and has the capacity to think ahead. In production, the people who succeed are the people who can anticipate potential problems and solve them before they become actual problems. Anticipate what's coming down the road. That's a quality we're looking for. Usually, the way you discover that is through references.

What advice would you have for somebody who's looking to get into your line of work?

Stay with it. Don't be afraid to work as a cashier at a gas station at nights until you get going. I think persistence is a key quality in most of the disciplines. Everybody I talk to, when we reflect on our careers, jokes and says, "I was just too dumb to quit." It's just staying power. Keep trying. You get turned down, but you've got to keep pushing.

Knock on the door again or make the call again. There are a lot of people who I started out with who aren't in the business anymore. They didn't have a burning desire to do it.

Assuming all that hard work and persistence pays off, how much can a first AD hope to make?

If you're a working AD in television, the *DGA* rate for a first is around $4,500 a week for a five-day week. Then there's a production fee, which you get paid when you're shooting, and that's another $700 or $800. If you're a good working first in television, you can do around $200,000 a year.

Final question. I'm an A-list star refusing to come out of my trailer. What do you do?

Break down and cry at your door.

A DAY IN THE LIFE OF SAM MAHONY

This is a timeline of my day on Love Bites, *a one-hour, single-camera comedy.*

6:00 A.M.: I arrive at our location for the day, an elementary school in the San Fernando Valley, one hour before the 7 A.M. crew call. Today we're shooting our first two scenes in front of the school, and we are bringing in 120 nine-year-old kids to populate the scenes. Each child has a parent or guardian with them, so my team has to wrangle 240 people at the top of our day. All told, between cast, crew, and background we have over 400 people working at our location today.

6:10 A.M.: The second and second-second ADs and I walk around the location, talk about the day's work and go over our plan on how we will coordinate the logistics.

6:30 A.M.: I meet with our location manager, driver captain, and our lead LAPD officer to discuss the exterior work in front of the school. Six police officers will assist in traffic control and shut the street down each time we roll.

6:45 A.M.: Carts full of lighting, grip, and video equipment begin converging onto the set. The crewmembers pushing the carts want to know where to stage the gear. Props guys want to know where to set up chairs for the actors. Camera wants to know where to set up the "village" (the bank of monitors the director, producer, writer, and so on watch when we're rolling). Everyone has questions.

7:00 A.M.: We're in. The actors arrive on set and huddle with the director to read the words of today's first scene and then block it. In the scene, a dad meets his nine-year-old daughter as school lets out for the day.

7:10 A.M.: The actors perform the scene for the crew as camera assistants lay down chalk marks at the actor's positions. Stand-ins for the actors will stand at the marks when we light the scene. The cast is sent to prepare, and the director of photography, the director, and I huddle to discuss the setups required to cover the scene. Our day will proceed with the same routine for each scene. Read, block, rehearse, and mark. Then light. Then rehearse one last time and shoot. The core of the filmmaking process is this repetitive drill.

7:30 A.M.: One of my guys brings me my first double-pumper heart stopper of the day. Three shots of espresso topped off with black drip coffee and six sugars stirred in.

7:45 A.M.: Here come the extras! One hundred and twenty nine-year-olds. Yikes . . . it's mayhem!

8:10 A.M.: First shot. The AD team have wrangled 120 kids onto the set, positioned and rehearsed their business. The actors come in, hit the marks, and we roll.

9:30 A.M.: Done with scene thirty-four, on to scene twenty-seven. Every day is a race against time, the weather, and sometimes the setting sun. Today we have another element in the mix, children. California labor laws prescribe the amount of time children can work on set, be schooled, break for lunch, rest, and relax.

11:50 A.M.: Fortunately, our director, John Scott, is well prepared; our DP, Ed Pei, is quick; and the crew is tip-top. We complete scene twenty-seven and our work with the children, with a little time to spare. The kids go off to their classrooms to get schooled. We move into an empty classroom to rehearse our next scene.

12:35 P.M.: Roll on the master of scene thirty-six.

1:00 P.M.: Lunch, one hour.

1:30 P.M.: My staff and I spend the second half hour of the lunch break scouting a nearby site where we will be staging a stunt driving sequence tomorrow.

2:00 P.M.: We're back from lunch and resume shooting scene thirty-six, a PTA-type meeting. Six actors are in the scene, which means lots of camera coverage.

3:30 P.M.: We rehearse our last scene of the day while we turn our lighting around in the classroom. Part of the AD's responsibility is staying ahead of the moment we are working in. Rehearsing an upcoming scene an hour or so ahead of our arrival on a new set allows our technicians to get a jump on prepping it in advance of the camera's arrival.

5:00 P.M.: Scene thirty-six is done. All involved were on their game, and we finish thirty minutes ahead of our planned time. Since scene twenty is already rehearsed, the set has been lit in advance of our arrival.

5:12 P.M.: Start shooting scene twenty.

6:36 P.M.: Wrap. Great day. Tomorrow's call time: 7:00 A.M.

6:45 P.M.: A quick meeting with my team to go over tomorrow's work and make sure everyone knows the plan.

7:00 P.M.: Heading home.

Note: The end of our season came quicker than we all thought it would. Five days later the network pulled the plug on our show. Welcome to Hollywood!

TRACY MOODY
Script Supervisor

Photo credit: David Thomas, www.davethomasstudio.com

Tracy Moody is one of only a few people who can claim she's seen *Mad Men*'s Jon Hamm dressed in nothing but a skimpy towel. Now before you start getting any ideas, you should probably know this viewing occurred while Tracy was executing her duties as script supervisor on his award-winning show. You should also know there were at least twenty other people around, and Jon was most definitely wearing a pair of shorts under that towel. Minor details, as far as she was concerned. For that day, Tracy was saying to herself, "God, I love my job."

Although not well known, script supervising is a critical part of any film or TV production. As a script supervisor, Tracy's the direct pipeline to the editor, who sits in a dark editing bay and has only her notes to make sense of all the footage that's been shot on any given day. It's a job Tracy has done for many years and one she knows very well. It's also a job she was literally thrown into at the start of her career.

Yes, there's more to the Jon Hamm story, but you'll have to read on. You'll discover other stories too, like how an elevator ride at college kick-started her career in entertainment. Ladies and gentleman, make some noise for . . . Tracy Moody.

ASSISTANT PRODUCTION COORDINATOR: A production office position in the TV and film business. He or she assists the production coordinator, who's the link between the production office and the set. Among other tasks, he or she makes sure everyone has copies of the latest script, puts out schedules, orders equipment, and coordinates travel and accommodations for actors.

GRIP AND ELECTRIC: These two departments work with the DP to shape the light of a scene. This can be done with flags, nets, and diffusion frames in front of or inside a lighting instrument to impact the light on set.

SECOND UNIT: A team that shoots footage that includes scenery, inserts, or close-ups of objects and other less crucial shots.

WIDE SHOT: A film shot where the actor or actress takes up the entire frame. It's also called a "long shot" or "full shot."

Before we begin, can you please tell those readers who are scratching their heads, what a script supervisor does?

I'm responsible for keeping track of every scene of a TV show or movie as it's being filmed. I basically make a blueprint for the editor to figure out how to put all the footage together. I take notes on every shot that the cameras capture. This includes what sound roll it's on, what film roll it's on, what date it was shot, the time it took to shoot it, and how many takes there were. Then I include a brief description of what it is so the editor can find the *wide shot* as opposed to the over-the-shoulder shot, or whatever he's looking for.

And you also do continuity right?

Yes.

Explanation, *por favor*.

Because we shoot out of sequence, I have to make sure that every shot matches. So if an actress is wearing a blue shirt in a scene one day, I need to make sure she's wearing it again a few days later when we shoot another part of the same scene. Or that her hair looks the same from shot to shot. In the film *The Untouchables*, for example, there's a relatively talked-about scene where Sean Connery's collar is buttoned in one shot, and then unbuttoned in the next. Then it's buttoned and unbuttoned every time they cut back to him. That would be an example of bad continuity.

Like maybe the script supervisor was thinking about what to have for lunch that day?

The truth is, it wasn't necessarily the script super's fault. Most of the time performance is chosen over continuity.

Got it. So how did you end up in the biz?

From the time I was small I wanted to be a veterinarian. I went to college in Colorado with the intent of getting into veterinary medicine. Then, my first year in college, I got in an elevator one night with my roommate. When the door closed I noticed a sign for auditions for a play. My roommate said, "I think you should try out. You'd be good at it." And I said, "No, that would require being in front of people. I don't do that." There was someone else in the elevator with us who was going to the audition, and by the time we got off, the two of them managed to drag me there.

How did you do?

I was bad. The director was sitting there with the book in his hand and I was talking so fast he couldn't understand what I said. He actually offered me the stage manager job instead. I went, "What's that?" He listed a bunch of duties, and the only one I heard was "You'll be in charge," so I said, "Okay." So I ended up in theater. I switched majors and became a technical theater major, with a minor in psychology. My mother was not happy. I think she was looking forward to saying, "My daughter the doctor."

Yeah, "My daughter the struggling artist" just doesn't have that same ring to it. So when did you make the move to L.A.?

I graduated and worked with a traveling dance company for a while. I had a boyfriend who decided to move to Los Angeles and work in the movie business, and he was not taking me. We broke up. Sometime later he came back to Colorado and he was regaling us with stories about working on low-budget horror movies, and I was fascinated. A year and a half had passed and I thought, "If this moron can do it, so can I."

Can we quote you on that?

Yeah. He's still in Los Angeles. I can give you his name.

Probably not a good idea. Lawsuits and all. So you went to Los Angeles. Did you have any contacts or connections?

No. I came out here and ended up finding low-paying jobs in theater and I went, "Okay, I can at least put gas in the car." I also did some freebies because I didn't know anything about the entertainment industry and I thought, "Well, I've got to dip my toe in somewhere." So I got on set. At first I worked in the art department. And as much fun as that was, it wasn't the right fit.

You were basically working for free to gain experience?

Yup. Really short-term jobs.

And you were still figuring out what you wanted to do?

Right. I thought, with my technical background either construction or *grip and electric*, realizing that would be an uphill battle because there are very few female construction people, or female grip and electrics. Basically, I took any job I could get because I didn't know enough. I needed information.

Would you say it's a good idea to try a few different disciplines, or is it better to have one job in mind and figure out the best way to get there?

I think if you have a passion for something, that'll guide you. If you're a designer or an artist, then art department is going to be a good fit. I didn't have anything that quantifiable. I don't think of myself as an artistic person. I'm much more of a technical person. So my skills lend themselves to many applications.

Those skills led you to . . .

I ended up getting hired as an on-set PA for *Tales from the Crypt*. And I also got hired for the second season, which is when I learned to script-supervise.

What did you know about script supervising when you first starting working as a PA?

I didn't know anything about script supervising. I would watch this chick on the set with a stopwatch thinking, "I have no idea what she does." I didn't think anything more of it until probably six months into a nine-month shoot when the *assistant production coordinator* said to me, "The script supervisor called in sick today. I need you to go to her house in Burbank, pick up the script, and get it to the set." So I got the script, walked on set, found the second AD, handed the book over to him and he said, "You're doing this." I was like, "Dude. Hold on. I can grip, I can electric, I can even do craft service if you put a gun to my head. This is the only job on the whole show I don't know how to do."

A great example of opportunity mixed with a little on-the-job training, topped off with a dash of terror.

Right. So he said, "Everybody knows you don't know what you're doing, and everybody will help you." And here's a funny for you. Brad Pitt, before he was a huge star, was in the scene. So I'm standing there, and I'm looking at the script supervisor's notes, and there are a lot of abbreviations and I'm going, "Hmmm. Obviously I need to write this down, but I don't know what all this is or where to get the information."

Then the sound guy walked up to me and said, "I have a number for you," and I said, "Fantastic." He told me the number, and I asked, "What's that? He told me it was the sound roll. "Great. Where does it go?" So the sound guy and I were standing there kind of looking at her notes and I said, "SR. Do you think that's sound roll?" And he said, "Could be." I said, "So *CR* might be camera roll," and he replied, "That makes sense."

Little by little you were putting the pieces together.
Yes. I figured out a little bit. And a little bit of knowledge is a dangerous thing. But I was really fascinated.

Given what you now know, what's the best way to learn the job?
Take a class. And if you get a job as a production assistant on set, pay attention to what's happening. I talked with both of the script supervisors on the show, and I sat with them and would ask questions. And they had two completely different note-taking systems.

Where can people find classes?
Film schools offer them. UCLA has one. Also talk to the union if you're interested. They can give you a list of people who teach. But ply your way onto the set and pay attention to everything. Because everything is useful. Every bit of information that you take in is going to help you, in one way or another. Maybe not right away, but it will.

Do most script supervisors start off life as a PA, like you?
A lot of us do. Our job is a really hard one to walk into if you don't have any set experience at all. It's a really hard job to get into, period. Not that I necessarily experienced that, but I've watched other people have a hard time with it.

So after your break that day, how did you transition into the job full-time?

After *Tales from the Crypt*, the first script-supervising gig I had was on a low-budget feature. And once I'd decided I was interested in pursuing this as a career, I took it upon myself to take a class. So over the weekends, I did this feature, for no pay. But I figured it was worth doing for the contacts and experience. I got good reviews from that, and I ended up script-supervising four *Tales from the Crypt* episodes, for *second unit*, late-night stuff.

My first job where I got paid to do an entire movie was a feature called *Stepfather III*. From that job, I ended up getting a lot of other little features. Then I started getting some TV credits. Since then, I've worked on shows like *Community, Castle, Bones, Mad Men*, and a lot of others.

Any good stories from the set?

I have a story from *Mad Men*. You want to hear it?

No, that's okay, save it for another book. Yes!

It's my first day. I walk on the set, and there's Jon Hamm showing up to do a rehearsal, wearing only a towel. I'm like, "Thank you." (Laughs)

So he's sitting there and we do this great shot of him talking to his little daughter, and she unintentionally brings up something that points out the fact that he cheats a lot. He then shoos her out of the bathroom. He's contemplating his life and he sits down on the toilet with his legs really far apart and I went, "Hmmm." I turned to the director after he cuts and I said, "Boss, I'm not really sure how to say this, but Jon's legs are far apart, which I wouldn't normally comment on, except for the fact that he's wearing a towel." The director sits there and says, "Do we see anything we . . . shouldn't?" I said, "Oh, no, if we did, I probably wouldn't have said anything at all. It's just that if it drew my eye, I think it'll draw others." The director looks at me and smirks and says, "I should make you talk to him." To which I replied, "I would feign a migraine or something. I don't want that to be my first conversation with him." He laughed. He ended up letting me off the hook and walked over and talked to him, and I saw Jon look at me and I'm like, "Hey."

Did you give him a thumbs up and turn a bright shade of red?
I don't turn red. I probably ducked and smiled or something like that.

So what advice do you have for an aspiring script supervisor, other than make sure your lead actor keeps his legs together while wearing nothing but a towel?
Two biggest things I would say to anybody who's getting into the business is first, rein in your ego, especially when you're very low on the food chain. Second, go out and buy a suit of rhino skin, because you are going to get yelled at and how you respond to that will determine whether or not you'll be back after lunch. Very often that's true in my job position, because you're going to make mistakes when you're new. I've made mistakes, I made one last week. Very minor, I immediately caught it and we fixed it, but it happens.

What's the salary range for a script supervisor?
Last year I was doing second unit on three different shows. All of them had different rates. One was for cable; that was $29.50 an hour. Then I was doing a Paramount comedy that was kind of like *Arrested Development*, that was $31.64 an hour, and then I was also doing a prime-time one-hour show, and that was $32.78 an hour. It has to

do with the length of the project and how many seasons it's been on and for what network.

Final question. Your professional life is all about being meticulous and detail oriented. Would you say that's carried over into your personal life?
(Laughs) What personal life? I'm always working.

A DAY IN THE LIFE OF TRACY MOODY
On the set of CSI: NY – Second Unit.

5:00 A.M.: Wake up. Take a shower, check e-mail for script revisions/changes. Drive to set.

6:55 A.M.: Introduce myself to the first assistant director, and the director. Ask second assistant director for any notes from the first unit script supervisor.

7:10 A.M.: Begin running through the first unit script super notes for today's work. Set up my paperwork, find the film and sound roll numbers, check to see if there are any continuity issues I need to watch for and inform others of.

7:30 A.M.: Introduce myself to the camera and sound departments. Give them the film and/or sound roll numbers we'll be starting with. Let them know how we'll be slating the shots.

8:00 A.M.: We watch as the grip, electrics, camera, and stunt people set up equipment underwater, and cover the pool with black plastic to simulate night shooting. I use the time to check script totals and set up my script for shooting.

9:30 A.M.: Head into the warehouse, where they've set up craft service, to grab a bottle of water. Come around the corner to find it's a special effects studio. There are dead bodies in various levels of decomp hanging on the walls, an alien lizard thing crouched in the rafters of the ceiling and a giant killer robot, covered with a flowered quilt. And no one on the crew notices as they grab their donuts and coffee. I love Hollywood people.

10:30 A.M.: Actors and extras arrive and the director runs them through the action they will be doing today. Stunt coordinator explains the safety procedures and equipment that will be used. Actors and extras are sent to hair, makeup, and wardrobe to get ready for shooting.

11:35 A.M.: Actors are shuttled back to set, one more dry run-through is explained, questions are asked and answered, actors get into the water, and rehearsals begin.

11:45 A.M.: Tweaks occur as we find out one of the actors can't swim very well and is afraid of the water, and another is nervous about using the scuba gear.

11:55 A.M.: Adjustments are made. Actors are relatively comfortable and more rehearsals are run.

12:28 P.M.: The director yells "Action," and I hit my stopwatch and note first shot.

1:56 P.M.: The first big shot of the day is complete. "Lunch" is called for a half hour.

2:48 P.M.: We are called back from lunch. Actors are put back into "the works" for touch-ups.

3:45 P.M.: Actors are back, and we have a quick dry run-through. Safety procedures are gone over again, and questions are answered. "Picture's up."

3:50 P.M.: Everybody back in the pool. Cameras are put on shoulders, sound mics are checked, and we are "rolling."

3:54 P.M.: The director yells "Action," I hit my stopwatch and note first shot after lunch.

4:10 P.M.: We spend the next several hours filming several actors struggling to get out of the cab of the truck, having a fight underwater, and swimming to the surface in a panic.

6:55 P.M.: The sun has set, lighting cranes and platforms are in place, crew members, extras, and actors are in the water and we begin shooting the night surface stuff.

8:45 P.M.: We're done with the actors, and extras; they are pulled out, dried off, and sent home. Sound is also wrapped. We start rigging for dropping the cab of the truck into the water for the look of the "first impact."

9:40 P.M.: We're ready. The truck cab is pulled back and in place. Lighting and cameras are in place.

9:45 P.M.: The cameras are rolled, the cue is given, and the truck cab is released.

9:50 P.M.: It takes three minutes to lower the cab into the water. *Very* anticlimactic. We'll speed it up in postproduction. We're done.

10:39 P.M.: It's a wrap.

10:42 P.M.: I turn in my notes to the second AD, send another set to the first unit script super, the production office, and postproduction and the editors via e-mail.

11:25 P.M.: Arrive home, reset alarm for an 8:30 A.M. wake-up, for a 10:30 A.M. call time, and fall into bed.

STEVEN J. SCOTT
Vice President, Creative Director, Supervising Digital Colorist (EFILM)

Once a feature film is shot and edited and the sound mix is done, it makes one crucial stop before heading out to theaters. That stop is called the Digital Intermediate (DI), where people like the HPA and Emmy Award–winner Steve Scott add their artistic touch. Steve's job title is vice president, creative director, supervising digital colorist, but we prefer to think of him as a visual magician. It's a pretty accurate description of what he does, plus it's a lot easier to remember. In that role, he creates every look imaginable, from relighting a scene to making colors more vibrant, to helping your favorite movie star look his or her best.

Steve's artistry is on full display in movies such as *Thor, Cowboys & Aliens, Iron Man 1* and *2, Children of Men, Hairspray,* and *Apollo 13.* He's gone from art school student to master of visual effects in a little over two decades. He's revealing all in this interview, like how a letter to a UCLA instructor got his career off the ground, and how that same career almost came crashing down to earth when he accidentally deleted thirty-six hours of work on a movie. Are we the only ones breaking out into a cold sweat?

> **CGI:** Computer-generated imagery is the use of computer graphics to create special effects in film and television.
> **TEAR SHEET:** A promotional sheet that's handed out to prospective clients with photo examples of an artist's work.
> **THE HOLLYWOOD REPORTER:** A trade publication founded in 1930 that covers entertainment news.

Of all the different jobs that exist in the movie business, digital colorist isn't one that automatically pops to mind.

That's true, but the practice of coloring movies has been around for a long time. It just wasn't a digital process until recently. Back then there were much more limited options. You'd play the movie for the director of photography and he'd say, "Let's go back and make that more green," or more red or darker, lighter, whatever. Then he'd hope and pray that by the next day some of what he'd asked for was in there. Today, the technology is much more advanced, but the practice of coloring a movie continues to be an art.

So would that make you an artist?

Yes. My background's in painting and illustration. That's what I did for a majority of my career, and that artistic foundation comes in handy every day. I approach my work as I would a painting, by breaking it down and putting it back together layer by layer; background to foreground.

When did you realize you had artistic talent?

My mom was a painter, and her paintings were the first artistic inspiration in my life. As a kid I used to think, "How can she make something so beautiful just by painting it?" I couldn't imagine ever having that level of talent, but I was very interested in art, and she cultivated that interest. My dad was always very artistic as well, so I had double inspiration. Then I started getting into musical comedy and theater in college, and made a good living singing, dancing, and acting for about five years.

Did you study art while you sang and danced?

Yes, I studied art at Golden West College in Huntington Beach, California. But at a certain point in my performing career I thought, "I don't want to be an aging chorus boy," so I left the performing behind and focused on becoming a painter and illustrator. I was successful at it, but being an illustrator can be a lonely life. You sit in your studio, you get everything by fax, deal with people on the phone, and then send your art off via Federal Express. You don't really interact with people that much. So I really just thought, "How can I combine my love of the entertainment world and my love of painting?"

That's a fair question. How did you answer it?

I started reading *The Hollywood Reporter* to better understand the entertainment industry. I read about something called the Quantel Paintbox, which is a computer painting and graphics system used for television. I didn't have much money at that time, but Bob, my spouse of thirty-two years, scraped up enough money to send me to New York for a Paintbox class. That was the very beginning of my new showbiz career. Learning the Paintbox was very intimidating, because I was an artist and this was the world of computers. So I started investigating what resources I could use to be successful in my new hoped-for career, and ended up taking a class with Rich Thorne at UCLA.

Rich was legendary in the field of television visual effects at the Post Group in Hollywood. Before the class started, I wrote him a letter saying what I hoped to gain from his class, along with a *tear sheet* of my illustration work. Meanwhile, a man by the name of Maury Rosenfeld, who owned the digital effects house Planet Blue, gave me the opportunity to work on the Paintbox system. He saw my classic painting portfolio, liked it, and gave me my first break. The only slot available was from late evening until early morning. I thought, "I've got to take this opportunity. I'm sure there are people banging on his door." This was about 1990. It only dawned on me years later that there was nobody banging down his door to get in there at such a late hour. I knew that I needed to learn as much as possible as quickly as possible to give me the competitive advantage.

So you had created an opportunity to apply what you'd been learning in class to the real world.

Yes. And then one day, right in the middle of class, Rich Thorne said he wanted to hire me. He was starting a new company called Digital Magic in Santa Monica (California). He had the account for *Star Trek: The Next Generation*. I asked, "What made you decide to hire me: a student with no experience?" He said, "I decided to hire you when I got your letter, before the class started. I never had anyone show me that kind of interest, or have the artistic skill to back it up." That floored me. I had no idea.

That's a great lesson in doing the unexpected in order to land a job.

Absolutely.

What did you learn at Digital Magic that might be helpful to someone considering this field?

If you want to quickly develop your visual effects skills, work in television first. They have little money and incredibly tight deadlines, so you have to be very creative and very fast.

Can you give us a specific example of that creativity?

On *Star Trek: The Next Generation*, an effects supervisor came to me on a Friday evening and said, "We didn't have time to shoot anything for this episode, but we need some sort of evil entity. See what you can come up with by Monday." I worked all weekend, drawing on my artistic skills to paint and animate it, and they ended up using what I'd done.

Always good to put yourself in a challenging situation. Sometimes you learn twice as much in half the time.

That's true. Eventually, I left the company for Digital Domain, which is a visual effects studio cofounded by James Cameron. A very talented compositor/VFX editor there named Fred Ramondi told me, "You know what advantage you have? You've been in the trenches with TV effects, so you'll have forty times the experience solving various iterations of various problems." In television, you go through twenty shots in a three-day period and then you move on. In film you can have one shot that may take you a month or longer to complete.

Talk about your experience at Digital Domain. What were some pivotal moments?

Well, the pivotal moment for me was when we were working on the movie *True Lies*. They were trying to make these Harrier jump jets suspended from cables look like they were actually taking off. The real jump jets have what is called a heat signature, which is the thrust that comes down and lifts the plane. Well, they had this huge *CGI* department to figure out how it would look as it took off and hovered just above the ground. James Cameron would come in time and again and would be very upset that they couldn't get this seemingly simple thing to look natural and believable. Since I was the new guy, they kind of threw me to the wolves and had me work on it using only a 2D compositing system.

What did you do that they weren't already doing?

As any artist would do when trying to copy something, I asked if there was any actual reference footage of the jet and its heat signature. Amazingly, I found out that nobody was looking at how the heat signature actually looked in real life. I asked for and I got footage, broke it down visually as I would a painting, and started hand-animating shapes of airflows thrusting down from the bottom of the jet. I was playing back a few of my more successful experiments on my monitor, when I heard this big ruckus going on behind me. All of a sudden I heard this, "That's it!" I turned around and it was James Cameron standing behind me. "That's the heat signature! That's what I've been asking you guys for." He told his CGI entourage, "Sit down and talk to this guy and find out what he's doing. That's what I want." It was such a fluke that he happened to walk by at that particular time.

Not a bad guy to impress. So where did your career go from there?

I was promoted to lead compositor at Digital Domain, then I went to the Post Group where I stayed for four years. After that, I went to 525 Studios, which was a very hip, happening studio. I did a great deal of high-end commercial projects there, as well as a number of music videos.

Were you lead compositor there as well?

Yes, and effects supervisor. Then I left for a company called EFILM, which is where I am today.

Is this where you made a career change and got into digital intermediate?

Yes. It was when I walked into the digital intermediate color-grading suites at EFILM to finish the "Climb" Marines TV spot, and saw those big, gorgeous images projected in one of their impressive theaters that I decided I wanted to pursue a career as a digital intermediate colorist. I embarked on a major career change from compositor to colorist at that point.

You mentioned getting some television experience. What other advice do you have for someone who'd like to get into visual effects?

Go to a good art school and do not touch a computer for the first two years of your education. Go out, look around. Observe the world you live in and experience it firsthand. Don't look at a movie and wonder how they did it. Look at the real world and learn how to recreate what you observe on a blank piece of paper or canvas. You burn what you've learned into your brain when you try to translate your observations into art.

Would you say this is a good field for a traditional artist?

I'd say a certain kind of artist, one who can suppress their ego and be in service to a client. I was also a waiter for a few years, and I tell the people

I'm currently mentoring that if they want to get the right perspective on what we do, then they should think of themselves as visual waiters, humbly serving up images to the client. You have to humble yourself, you have to understand what your client wants, and you have to give it to them in the most patient, agreeable way possible, even if it seems like an unreasonable request at the last minute of a very long day.

Secondly, I would say, be a well-rounded, well-versed, well-educated person in addition to your artistic skills. You want to fulfill your client's requests, but when they get stuck creatively, you want to be able to provide a well-informed opinion based on your knowledge of the world as well as your knowledge of your craft. All of that comes into play. You also have to get past the daunting barrier of mastering the technology.

How does someone master the technology?
You just have to learn it. Realize you're going to have times when it's two in the morning and you're pounding your head on the desk because mastering all you need to know can be overwhelming, and takes time you don't often have. In the beginning of my career as a compositor, I worked on a job for thirty-six hours straight. The last thing I did before I showed the client my work was to save it. Or so I thought. I had accidentally pressed delete instead of save! I had to walk into the next room and tell the client what I had just done. Fortunately for me the client (Debra Ross) was amazing and didn't insist on having my head on a platter. She could have had me fired, but didn't.

What *did* happen?
I went back to the drawing board. And what I ended up with was this main title that I'm still proud of today. It was for *Three Wishes*, a movie with Patrick Swayze. The whole main title is like an abstract

impressionist painting that resolves into the opening scene on a tree-lined street. Nobody had done anything like that before.

Can you talk about your work on other projects?

Sure. On one movie, they had the challenge of shooting scenes all around the world and matching them to greenscreen imagery shot elsewhere. For instance they had a Monte Carlo sequence, which was partly shot in Monte Carlo on a beautiful sunny day and partly shot on a backlot in Downey (California) on a cloudy, overcast day. So I had to match those shots to one another. I got in there and I started playing with color, light, and shadow to balance and even out the disparate shots. I ended up loving the resulting sequence.

On another film, the director came in with a book of auto-chromes, which were early twentieth century experiments in color photography. He wanted the movie to look like a moving auto-chrome. The source cinematography was beautiful, but it was a real artistic challenge to get that look. I pored over this book and did my own research online, and just started breaking down the images as I would a painting. What are the layers? What's my background? And how would I layer this to achieve the desired effect? The director just kind of let me go, and to have that sort of artistic freedom was very gratifying.

How long does your job take with a movie like that?

You have the time you're given. They have a budget, so it can go any-where from forty hours, which is a bare minimum, to other projects, which can take a couple of months.

Can you talk about some of the other jobs that exist in this field?

One is compositing. I still think that's the most creative and the most difficult job in the visual effects world. If something can't be fixed in the DI, or be done using CGI, it goes to the compositor, who has to fix it. They take various images and digitally layer them together like you would do in a painting. It takes great artistic skill and an artist's eye to create convincing images as a compositor.

Then there are the CGI artists: the ones who basically build the models and build the architecture and animate it all together. The *Toy Story* series is an obvious example of that. There are shaders, the people who light and put the texture and surfaces on those models. There are the indispensible VFX and DI producers and coordinators who manage the various components of any job. There are also jobs managing data for all that and there are jobs working in the media vault and jobs making the clients feel at home. Any job that gets your foot in the door can be great in the long run.

Can you give the reader an idea of salary ranges?

Well, I can't talk about mine, but a compositor can make anywhere between minimum wage and the mid six-figures, depending on what they're doing and responsible for. Usually, if you want to be a highly paid compositor, you'll often go and start your own facility. In my profession, the range can be from minimum wage to the high six figures. Again, it all depends on your artistic skills, your people skills, your management skills, and what range of responsibilities you are willing to take on.

Lastly, the process of doing this book is going to age us by about ten years. Would you be willing to correct our photos so we look young and fresh?

You guys don't need any help, and if you did, I'd never discuss it publicly. It would be our secret.

A DAY IN THE LIFE OF STEVEN J. SCOTT
Any day, 2011

7:00 A.M.: Wake up. Walk and feed my two Italian greyhounds; Sonny and Boots. Check around the house to see what needs to be tended to (a 1929 Spanish Colonial needs lots of loving care). Shower and dress, light breakfast, and, depending whether I will need my car that day, or how late I'll have to work, drive, or walk for twenty-five minutes to get to work.

8:30 A.M.: Arrive at work. Check in with my DI producer. Check to see what the schedule is for the two colorists I supervise. Make sure the room is up and in proper working order. Check the footage to be worked on for that day.

8:45 A.M.: Review material worked on by various departments from the night before that will be reviewed in today's session. Make tweaks as needed.

9:00 A.M.: DI session starts. This is usually a supervised session with either the cinematographer or the director, or both. Sometimes we have lots of fun and have the cinematographer, director, VFX supervisor, editor, studio executives, and lab timer in the room all at once.

12:30 P.M.: Break for lunch. Review film reels from the lab to make sure that the color matches the digital. However, I am incredibly picky about the film matching digital, so I will sometimes send reels back multiple times to make sure the match is as identical as possible.

1:30 P.M.: Continue project session supervised by the client or unsupervised.

6:00 P.M.: We often go longer than 6:00 P.M. The schedule for any job is highly volatile. There are so many variables for any particular job that are hard to control or anticipate. That often results in long hours toward the end of any project.

Sometime later: Go home to my family.

DAVE CASSARO
President of NBCUniversal Cable, Entertainment and Digital Sales

Photo credit: Doug Goodman

Mr. Cassaro is to Hollywood what the Federal Reserve is to America (well sort of). He controls huge sums of money; only in this case it's advertising dollars. (He's arguably more efficient, too.) You've probably heard the term, "Where Hollywood meets Madison Avenue." What you may not know is that meeting place is in Dave Cassaro's office.

Throughout his career, Dave has literally been responsible for putting networks like Fox, E!, and the Style Network on the proverbial map by securing advertising dollars selling commercial time. The buck literally starts and stops with him.

Currently Dave holds the title of president of NBCUniversal Cable Entertainment and Digital Sales. Throughout his career he and his teams have literally raised billions of dollars. Not bad for a guy who started as an NBC page.

Dave is a lot like Don Corleone in the movie *The Godfather*, minus the "swimming with the fishes" part. He lives by many of the same mantras and quotes the film regularly to his staff. But, where Don Corleone demanded respect *or else*, Don Cassaro has done something much more honorable. He's earned it.

APPRENTICE FILM EDITOR: A position in the post-production arena of TV or film. The job is entry level and in some cases unpaid. Duties usually involve assisting the editing staff as well as the post supervisor.

Don Cassaro, can you start by taking the cotton out of your mouth and giving us your job title?

I am president of NBCUniversal Cable Entertainment and Digital Sales and essentially I am responsible for the sale of all of our networks' entertainment, plus all of the company's digital products.

You weren't always president; tell us about yourself pre–suit and tie.

I was born in Brooklyn, New York. My father was a doctor at the time at Brooklyn Jewish Hospital, so that's where I was born. Shortly after, we moved to Massapequa, Long Island. I went to Saint William the Abbot Grammar School in Seaford. Then I went to Archbishop Molloy High School in Jamaica Queens and Marist College. Catholic all the way.

Get hit by a ruler much?

More times than I care to admit. Corporal punishment was part of education back then.

Was there a positive takeaway from your strict scholarly upbringing?

Yeah, you know part of the thing with my earlier years, my career, my personal life, my family, my finances, it was about goals. I sat down with a financial planner early on when I first started, and we wrote down my personal and financial goals and a target date for me to achieve them. I think it's really, really important to set goals. Lots of times people graduate and flounder when they enter a world of no structure; they have no plan, no path and they don't know where they want to go or what they want to do with their lives. I encourage young people who work for me to set goals. It starts not with what am I going to do today, but where do I want to be twenty-five years from now?

So what were your goals early on?

Actually, when I graduated college I wanted to direct movies. Lofty or not, that is what I wanted to do. Breaking into the film industry when I got out of college was difficult. I didn't really know anybody, but I did manage to get a job as an *apprentice film editor*. All I essentially did was rewind film, and the job didn't pay very much at all. What I discovered was the film industry was very segmented in terms of job task and discipline, and it was highly unionized. The nail in the coffin for my directing dreams was the fact that it was all happening in Los Angeles, and I lived in New York and didn't want to move.

That would have been a hell of a commute. So you had to make a hard decision.

Exactly. I took my large goal of being a director of motion pictures and tailored it more toward television production, which led me to the NBC Page Program. The Page Program is still in existence today, somewhat maligned on the TV show *30 Rock*. But that is a great way for folks to get into the business, where you can go in and sort of get a sense of what is going on at every level across all disciplines.

Some very successful people started their careers in the Page Program, like Ted Koppel, Regis Philbin, and Michael Eisner.

Right, there's a wide range of people who have gone through the program. It's a chance to get in on the ground floor and infiltrate that company. In my case, I happened upon people in the affiliate relations side of the company, people who dealt with the television stations all over the country. It's an interesting job that can make you a jack-of-all-trades. You have to know a little about programming, news, marketing, sales, and ratings, a little bit of everything.

Let us point out that you began as a page at NBC and now, thirty-odd years later, you're the president of a division within the very place where your career began.

Technically you're right; it's been a full-circle journey for me. One I would have never been able to predict, but I couldn't be happier how things have turned out.

When you were in the Page Program you had a wide-open field, but you leaned toward affiliate relations. Why?

Back in the day you had something like fifteen months in the program and after that, if you hadn't landed a job within the company, your tenure was up and it was time to leave. I was in the program only a few months, and what happened was my networking led me to people who were working in affiliate relations. It was that simple.

So your goals changed a bit from what you had planned.

Well, it's fine to switch gears, so long as you are progressing toward something. So when you create goals, you create a path from where you are today to the long-term goal you seek to achieve. In my mind, becoming an apprentice film editor was the first step on that path, but I wasn't quite sure what the path would look like and where it would take me. Going into TV production, my first step on that path was to become a page, which I did, and hoped it would lead to a production job. When I hit a wall on both of those endeavors I bounced back and selected another path, but at the same time was looking at the same long-term goal.

So let's talk about your career path. Can you give us the run-down? Thirty years in fifty words or less please.

I'll try. I interviewed for a job at NBC, but didn't get hired. So, thanks to my networking, I was able to land an entry-level job in affiliate relations at ABC.

While I was at ABC, I noticed that the guys who worked on the sales floor wore better suits than people who worked on the other floors. So I took that as a tip to the fact that they must have been making more money, which again lined up with my goals. So I managed to get a job at an outside sales rep firm for local stations called TeleRep. I didn't work in sales, because you don't just go right into sales, but I worked in the research department. I was in research for a couple of years, then I was able to get promoted into sales. How many words is that?

Oh, you're way over, but this is fascinating, please go on.
Next stop was CBS, which was the number-one network. They hired me as a district manager. I parlayed that job into a job in network sales and that was my first big-time national sales job. I was selling sports, but I quickly learned if you really want to advance in sales you have to sell prime time. I told my boss at the time that I wanted a shot at prime time, and he gave it to me.

It seems that you were achieving everything you set out to do.
I was, but one of my goals that hadn't been met yet was to obtain ownership. I wanted to have some equity where I worked. I didn't just want to be a wage slave. This leads me to my next opportunity, launching a new start-up network called Fox Broadcasting. I sold the very first commercial slot that ever aired on Fox. It was a Bristol Myers spot that aired during Joan Rivers's late-night talk show. My desire to go over to Fox was multifaceted. It was a little entrepreneurial; I was offered a better title, more money, and I was offered some, not a lot, but some, equity in that company. I helped take that company from literally zero to hundreds and hundreds of millions of dollars in ad revenue. It was a thrilling time.

How long were you there?
I stayed at Fox for five-and-a-half years, before my next move. I got an offer of some real ownership opportunity at a little start-up company nobody heard of called Movietime. I was hired by the network president, Lee Masters, and soon Movietime changed its name to

E! Entertainment Television. Then, in success, we launched another network called the Style Network.

And now you're with a little mom-and-pop start-up. We kid, of course. You're with the media giant Comcast.
Comcast is a terrific company to work for. Their corporate culture and values mirror mine. How you deal with people as people first, as opposed to just employees. I oversee about 250 people, and I have an amazing team. I'm very happy.

What are some pointers on being a good salesperson?
Don't be scared off by the word "no." Part of my thinking is that the sale sort of starts when someone says "no." You want a "yes," but how do you get there? You also need to have a thick skin to be able to take the rejection. You need common sense, and you need the ability to deal with people and to understand math and numbers to review spreadsheets and be able to project and know how numbers play on different numbers. Finally, you need to have integrity. That is key.

We thought you were going to say slicked-back hair and the ability to memorize the "A, B, C speech" from *Glengarry, Glen Ross.*
(Laughs) The ability to read body language is helpful too. If you go into someone's office and they are tapping their foot and looking at their watch, they're probably stressed out and don't have a lot of time. You don't want to go in there and shoot the breeze with these people.

We notice you've been tapping your leg and looking at your watch the entire time we've been here.

Yeah, can't you guys take a hint? My leg is getting tired. Another helpful hint is to look around the person's office to pick up some clues of where you could make a connection with them.

So that poster hanging here in your office, what's that about?

Very good. Actually, it's my favorite movie, *The Godfather*, but more than that, I believe that every business and many personal situations have a line from that movie that is applicable. There is a book I read about *The Godfather* that was about the management style of Don Corleone. For example, never let anyone outside the family know what you are thinking. I'm thinking, what does that really mean and how does that apply to business? There are literally dozens of them.

Talk about the networks under the Comcast banner and the new merger with NBC.

We have E!, Style, Exercise TV, G4, the Golf Channel, Versus, and SPROUT, a new children's network through a partnership with PBS, Hit Entertainment, and *Sesame Street*. Then with our merger with NBCUniversal we acquired Universal Studios, the theme parks, NBC Television, USA Network, Bravo, SyFy, Oxygen, CNBC, MSNBC, and IVillage.

Can you offer advice to someone who wants to do what you do?

Use your professional network, to the extent that you have it, to open doors. A lot of companies just get blind resumes; you want to send a resume to somebody with a personalized letter. When you go into an interview make sure you do your homework; ask good questions.

You have to know what you want as far as a career path. As a sales-person, you have to ask for the order, so at the end of the conversation if you determine it's a job you might like, it is always a good practice to say, "I really want to work here and I really want the job, may I have this job?" Most people will say, "We'll get back to you," but it is still a good thing to say.

So have you achieved all your goals?

Originally I had a list of personal and professional goals that I wanted to accomplish by the time I was fifty-five. On my fiftieth birthday, my financial planner sent me a framed copy of the goals we had set twenty years prior. And he said, "You've accomplished all your goals; time for some new ones." That was pretty gratifying.

If we had a dollar for every dollar you were responsible for bringing into a network over the years, how much money would we have?

Over a twenty-five-year career of impacting sales it would be in the multiple billions of dollars. This year alone we are near a billion dollars—and that's just this year.

A DAY IN THE LIFE OF DAVE CASSARO

5:30 A.M.: Wake up. Feed and walk the dogs.

5:45 A.M.: Meditate for twenty minutes, followed by thirty-four minutes of exercise on bike or elliptical machine.

6:45 A.M.: Breakfast at home while reading local newspaper and watching the first ten minutes of *The Today Show*.

7:15 A.M.: Shower, shave, dress for success.

8:09 A.M.: Long Island Railroad into Manhattan . . . read *NY Times* and a few e-mails.

9:00 A.M.: Returning phone calls and answering e-mails, scope out the schedule for the day.

9:30 A.M.: Internal meetings with my management team.

10:30 A.M.: Sales management staff and revenue meeting.

11:30 A.M.: E-mails and more phone calls.

12:30 P.M.: Client lunch.

2:00 P.M.: Out-of-office client meeting.

3:30 P.M.: Meet with corporate finance team to discuss forecasts.

4:30 P.M.: Meet with network programming executives on upcoming acquisitions or new development.

5:00 P.M.: Call West Coast research on projected audience projections followed by e-mail clean-up and next-day schedule review.

6:00 P.M.: Meet client for a drink.

7:00 P.M.: Head out for train home.

7:30 P.M.: Dinner with my wife.

8:00 P.M.: Check e-mail one last time for the day.

8:30 P.M.: See who's playing what game or check out my favorite programs on the DVR.

10:00 P.M.: Watch the TV news in bed . . . sleep.

GAIL BECKER
President, Western Region, Chair,
Canada and Latin America, Edelman PR

Photo credit: Mikel Healey

Gail Becker works for the largest independent PR firm in the world, though she started out as a TV reporter in Beaumont, Texas, covering chili cook-offs and dead bodies for the six o'clock news. She even put a naked man on TV once, but that's a whole other story.

Eventually, Gail traded the bright lights of Beaumont for Washington, D.C., where she found herself working on the 1992 Clinton/Gore presidential campaign and, later, in that administration. It wasn't until later, however, when her biggest political battle was waged. This one took place where many do: not in the nation's capital, but in the nation's capital of entertainment—Hollywood, where Gail landed in search of new challenges. In this instance, the opponents were Sony and Time Warner and what was at stake was the very future of home entertainment.

The outcome firmly established Gail's reputation as a winning campaigner and her work captured the attention of Richard Edelman, who offered her a job within his public relations firm. We've got her for the next ten pages or so, and she's got a few words to say about getting into the field of entertainment, particularly PR. We also get the lowdown on that "naked man on TV" story. Come on, you know you're curious.

THE MOTION PICTURE ASSOCIATION: According to their website, the Motion Picture Association of America and the Motion Picture Association serve as the voice and advocate of the American motion picture, home video, and television industry in the United States and around the world. They champion, among other things, intellectual property rights and freedom of expression.

VARIETY: An entertainment trade publication established in 1905.

Here we are sitting with Gail Becker, president of the western region and chair for Canada and Latin America for Edelman. You got our attention with that title. Can you tell us what it all means?

I oversee the six offices that make up our western region as well as serve as chairman for Canada and Latin America. We work with clients, helping companies engage with their various publics and, in turn, helping people engage with brands through information and content.

You work with clients in many different sectors and industries correct?

Yes. Everything from cars to technology companies to big Hollywood studios.

Since this book is about entertainment, we'll focus on that. Talk about some of the work you've done in this field.

Our work includes everything from developing launch plans for companies introducing a new entertainment technology to creating the most accessible content to tell a compelling story. We listen closely both to our clients and their key audiences to ensure we understand the issues that impact them and develop communications strategies accordingly. We develop crisis plans for when the unexpected happens and determine which opportunities are going to make the most sense for the business. In short, we help companies tell their stories to the audiences and stakeholders who matter to them most. We're in the business of communications and engagement.

Which companies do you work with?

We've worked with a number of different clients, including several major studios, such as Warner Bros. and Fox; various leaders in the digital entertainment space; and several industry associations such as the *Motion Picture Association of America* and the Recording Academy on supporting the entertainment industry in their efforts to combat piracy of their content and property. For the Recording Academy, which is the organization that produces the Grammy Awards, we created a campaign that helped communicate the value of paying for music. We've also worked on the global launches of a number of groundbreaking and innovative entertainment technologies from Xbox to Hulu to the latest in 3D.

You mentioned communications a bit earlier. Did you go to school for that?

I went to UCLA and started off as a communications major, then I switched to political science. I graduated with a BA in political science, and then received a master's degree in journalism from Northwestern.

Where did that degree take you?

To Beaumont, Texas, market number 124 at the time. It was my first job as a TV reporter, and I covered everything from chili cook-offs to 100 ways to kill a man. I even put a naked man on television, but we won't get into that. Suffice it to say, it's better that you don't use my name should you visit Beaumont.

We'll come back to that naked guy story in a bit; we're not letting you off that easily. So your first job was in television. Was this something you dreamed of as a kid?

I remember being very interested in journalism after my parents, Holocaust survivors, talked me out of a career in acting and recommended that I choose a more stable path. Clearly not listening, I decided I wanted to be a journalist. I have always been infatuated with words and love a good story—then through reporting and now via helping clients tell their stories. Ultimately, I made the decision to go into broadcast news instead of print and strongly believe that if I had chosen print, I would probably still be a reporter today. The things I didn't like about the profession had more to do with the on-air nature of the business, than it had to do with being a reporter, and it didn't take long for me to realize that local news really wasn't for me.

Where did you go after that? I mean, once you make it in market 124, you can pretty much write your own ticket, right?
(Laughs) I went to Washington, D.C., where I covered national stories with a local angle for news stations across the country. I loved that job. Then, I came back to L.A. for personal reasons, did some freelancing, and interviewed Ron Brown, who was then chair of the Democratic National Committee. The day after the interview, he offered me a job at the Democratic Convention in New York that year and then for the Clinton/Gore 1992 presidential campaign.

Doing?
I produced many of Clinton and Gore's satellite media tours during the campaign. I'd be in the field, helping to produce their interviews for local stations across the country. In the administration, I received a political appointment as Director of Communications for the Department of Health and Human Services, where I worked with a large communications team to help get out the health-related messages of the administration. It was a wonderful experience. I was there almost two years.

That added some weight to your resume. What then?
I came back to L.A. and thought, "What am I going to do?" I didn't want to go back into local news but I found myself in a one-industry town with no entertainment industry experience. As I always tell people looking for career advice, one of the most important things you can do when considering a career path, is to take off the blinders and see all the opportunities you never knew were there.

So you took your blinders off, and . . .

There was a half-page, blind ad in *Daily Variety*. It said something about launching a breakthrough technology for a large entertainment company. Someone convinced me to send in my resume even though I had no experience in technology or entertainment. Two months later, I got a phone call from Warner Bros. for a job to launch the DVD format on behalf of Time Warner and Toshiba, the leaders in the development of the technology. I interviewed six times and was given the job. The reason, according to the architect of DVD: "We'd seen lots of people from the entertainment industry and lots of people from the technology industry. But there are so many political battles right now happening over the specs to this format that we wanted someone with political experience." So I ended up getting the job.

Explain those political battles, if you will.

There was MMCD (multimedia compact disc) on one side, which was led by Sony and Phillips, versus SD (super-density disc) on the other side, which was led by Time Warner and Toshiba. At the end of the day it's all about who owns the specs, right? Clearly, you want more of your specs on the technology than your competitor as it ultimately means more money. That was one of several format wars in which we ended up prevailing.

Your candidate won again.

My candidate won again.

What was your title?

Vice president of communications for what is now Warner Home Entertainment. I served as the primary spokesperson for Time Warner and Warner Bros. on the launch of the DVD format, starting about two years before the format was ever introduced to consumers.

So the DVD launches. How long did you stay with the job?

I was there about seven years and, again, faced the notion of taking my blinders off. I was so entrenched in what I was doing, I didn't really look outside despite wanting to try something else after the DVD format launched globally. I had hired Edelman as our PR firm to help with the launch and various format battles. One day, Richard Edelman offered me the job to run the Los Angeles office. I said no . . . and I said no about five more times.

In one meeting?

Over a several-week period. On the last occasion he asked me why I didn't want the job and I said, "Well, at my core, I'm a journalist. And I can't be nice to everybody. In PR you have to be nice to everybody. And you have to tell people exactly what they want to hear. I can't do that." He said to me, "Gail, people don't want you to tell them what they want to hear. They want you to tell them what you think." And I said, "You mean you're going to pay me to tell people what I think?" And he said, "Yeah." And I said, "I'm in."

What year was that?

I started here in December, '99. I came in as the GM of the L.A. office. When I started we had twenty-two people and we were doing good work, but not much for the entertainment industry, so it was helpful to be able to leverage my experience to pursue the industry. Thanks to the efforts of so many, the L.A. office is now number one.

How did you grow that part of the business?

I hired a lot of really good, smart people who I'd known throughout the years. What happened along the way was the explosion in the field of digital entertainment. All the stars were in alignment. We had the best people, with the best experience, at a time when the industry was growing rapidly.

You also brought a company named Matter into the Edelman fold. They specialize in sports and entertainment marketing. Can you talk about that?

We've always done entertainment marketing, but we wanted to do it in a bigger way. We were looking for a firm that specialized in it. We found Matter. And since we've brought them into the firm and integrated them into our clients, they've really done some ground-breaking work—everything from integrating Brita into the hit show *The Biggest Loser*, to creating a comedy web series for Experian entitled *The Funny Truth about Credit*. They've also created relevant partnerships like NASCAR and Tony Stewart on behalf of Armor All.

Communications, as a whole, is vast. What would be the overall recommendation for going the agency route versus the studio-network route?

It depends what you're interested in. If, for instance, you want to represent movies or celebrities, working for a studio or celebrity publicist makes perfect sense. For people unsure of an area in which they'd like to specialize, an agency is a wonderful place since it exposes you to a myriad of areas you wouldn't otherwise know. Sometimes I say to people, "Go get a job in-house somewhere. You may love it. If you don't, then you can come try this."

What was the best advice you were ever given?

This was a life moment for me. When I was in college, I interned for ABC News in Washington and as a thank you they put us all in a room with Ted Koppel for one hour and we could ask him anything we wanted. That was our gift and what a gift it was. When it was my turn I explained to him my problem. "I worked really hard to become a communications major at UCLA, and I'm in it now and . . . well . . . I hate it." He told me: "Then study something else. I want people who can bring something new to me. Learn English, history, political science. Study something that you're passionate about and bring that knowledge to me." It was life changing. I went back to school that fall and the first thing I did was change my major to political science.

So the advice is more along the lines of become a well-rounded person?

What I look for and what many people in Hollywood look for are people who can bring something to the table, who are smart, who aren't afraid to say what they think even if they might be wrong, who wouldn't be afraid to challenge their boss or client, who know business, or marketing, or technology. This city is not a place for the timid. People with opinions do well here. The entertainment industry is ever evolving and, as a result, so must be the individuals who work in it.

What are some of the traits needed to excel in PR?

Confidence, intellect, and curiosity. You go in every day and you never quite know what you're going to learn . . . so many issues for which you help find a solution. That's the greatest part of the job, so if you don't have that natural curiosity, if you don't want to learn something new every day, this is not the place for you.

Since you mentioned curiosity, now might be a good time for the naked man on TV story.

Okay. So I was covering a story on a controversial group that liked to hold nudist gatherings in the mountains of Texas. I went to their campsite several hours away and spent the day with them. On the ride back to the station, I wrote the script for what was to be the lead story. We had to do our own editing back then so I tracked and edited as fast as I could. Like a scene right out of *Broadcast News*, I ran to the control room and threw in the tape just as the anchor was introducing the story. At the end of the piece, when you could hear me saying "Gail Becker, Channel 4 News," there you had it: full-frontal male nudity! The best part was seeing our lovely Southern anchor's face when the camera cut back to her. The next day, I had to go on the air and apologize.

We can just hear it. "I promise never to put a naked man on TV ever again." So do you have any closing thoughts?

Yes. There's a significant misconception outside Hollywood that everything here is glitz and glamour, and it's only about making movies, when in actuality the industry is about so much more. Incredibly smart people come here from all over the world with a myriad of backgrounds and expertise. There's a corporate side to Hollywood, a tremendous and dynamic business that can be equally as enticing and as rewarding as working on the set of a movie. Remember the advice of Ted Koppel: Bring to Hollywood a perspective it doesn't already have.

And on that note, we'll end with one last question. Will you do marketing for our book and if so will you take gratitude as a form of payment?

(Laughs) I'd be happy to help. If you guys want some advice, just let me know.

You heard it here first, everyone.

A DAY IN THE LIFE OF GAIL BECKER

4:30 A.M.: Wake up, alarmless.

4:45 A.M.: Log on to e-mail, cup of coffee in hand.

5:15 A.M.: Head to gym.

5:30 A.M.: Work out at gym, Blackberry in hand. Read the news of the day from the *Wall Street Journal, Los Angeles Times,* and *New York Times* online and catch up on e-mail.

7:00 A.M.: Get myself and my two sons ready for school (*Today Show* on in background).

7:45 A.M.: Drive the boys to school.

8:15 A.M.: Conference call with colleagues in New York in car on way to the office (hands-free, of course).

8:45 A.M.: Finish call parked outside the building.

9:00 A.M.: In my office. Second (okay, third) cup of coffee. Check e-mail, read *Variety,* and review materials for the day's meetings.

9:30 A.M.: Preliminary call with new business prospect to get a sense of their needs.

10:00 A.M.: Conference call with Edelman leadership in Brazil to discuss integration of our new acquisition and recent client wins including Bureau of Sports ministry of Brazil; begin planning for clients' roles in World Cup and Olympics Rio-style.

11:00 A.M.: Call with Edelman's Western Region leadership team for update on new business prospects, current client work, and any staffing concerns. Consume half a Diet Coke.

12:00 noon: Client call with new digital entertainment client.

12:30 P.M.: Leave office for lunch meeting in Beverly Hills (more calls from the car).

1:00 P.M.: Client lunch at Barney Greengrass at Barney's in Beverly Hills (avert eyes from merchandise on sales floors and head back down toward car).

2:30 P.M.: Video conference call with Edelman teams from Los Angeles and New York to prepare for new business pitch. Finish Diet Coke.

3:30 P.M.: Deal with crisis of the day.

4:00 P.M.: Call with one of our studio clients. Venti, nonfat, extrahot, two-Splenda latte.

5:00 P.M.: Meeting with head of HR to discuss recruiting efforts and hiring decisions.

5:30 P.M.: Call with general manager of Edelman's Silicon Valley office to discuss new technology client.

5:45 P.M.: Deal with another crisis of the day. Return more calls.

6:15 P.M.: Return calls.

6:30 P.M.: Leave the office and drive home.

7:00 P.M.: Dinner with the family.

8:00 P.M.: Get kids ready for bed.

9:00 P.M.: Read newspaper; watch Bill Maher, CNN, or *Modern Family*.

10:30 P.M.: Read what is on nightstand; lights out.

CONCLUSION

While writing this book, it was our intention to give you the feeling that you were right there in the room with us, listening to the stories of these remarkable people. We hope that, through them, we were able to shed light on an industry that is as captivating as it is elusive. Every person in this book is living proof that there are a lot of ways to break into the industry, and no one single trajectory to success. While their stories are different, they each share a common characteristic: passion. It's the one word that was uttered over and over again. If you have an undying passion for what you do, the rest will come.

Some jobs require years of schooling, credentials, and certifications. Hollywood is a little different. All you need is will, talent, and passion . . . oh, and a little luck! We hope you've been inspired to forge your own path and create your own success story.

Please keep your eye out for our upcoming books in the *Hire Me* series. We'll be shedding light on other industries such as Broadway, Wall Street, fashion, sports, and a whole lot more. We'd love to hear what you thought of this book and would be happy to answer any questions you may have. Please feel free to visit our website at *www .hiremeguys.com.*

That's a wrap!

INDEX

ABOUT THE AUTHORS

Mark Scherzer has worked in the entertainment industry for more than twenty years. He grew up in Montreal, Canada, and moved to New York after college to become a buyer for Macy's. After a few years of toiling in retail, he decided it wasn't for him and he set a course for Hollywood. Mark landed in Los Angeles in 1991 where he pursued every lead to get that all-important first break. Eventually, he landed a job as a PA (Production Assistant) charged with the task of getting the director to the set every morning, and the film to the lab each night. Luckily, he never mixed the two up. Over the years, he climbed up the ranks and became a television writer on shows like *USA High*, *Hang Time*, and *Port Charles*, to name a few. In 2006, Mark was hired as an in-house Writer/Producer for ReelzChannel where he met and worked with Keith Fenimore. Mark is also the author of *Ironwill Kids*, an innovative wellness program used in schools across the country. Visit *www.ironwillkids.com*.

Keith Fenimore grew up with big ideas, but came from a small, one stop light town called New Hope, Pennsylvania. He's been a fixture, much like a cool lamp, in the entertainment industry since 1994. As in the spirit of this book, his career path has taken many unpredictable twists and turns. He put his degree in marketing to use working at an entertainment PR firm in Los Angeles out of college before making a move to a more executive position within the marketing department at E! Entertainment Television, where he helped launch many of their franchise series like *The E! True Hollywood Story* and *Wild On*. In 2000, Fenimore stepped out of his comfort zone of promoting other people's ideas and began to create, sell, and promote his own, in the form of TV shows. He sold original concepts to networks like A&E, E!, VH1, TV Guide Channel, PBS, and Ovation. Over the last decade, Fenimore has worked hard to evolve into an award-winning executive producer, director, and writer. In 2006, Fenimore was on the launch team for the new movie network ReelzChannel, where he served as an executive producer and development executive. Now in New York City, Fenimore is a senior producer, writer, and director for the "King of All Media," Howard Stern.